Integrating Curricula With Multiple Intelligences

Teams, Themes, and Threads

Robin Fogarty and Judy Stoehr

Foreword by Howard Gardner

IRI SkyLight
TRAINING AND PUBLISHING, INC.
Arlington Heights, Illinois

**Integrating Curricula with Multiple Intelligences:
Teams, Themes, and Threads**

Published by IRI/SkyLight Training and Publishing, Inc.
2626 S. Clearbrook Dr., Arlington Heights, IL 60005
800-348-4474 or 847-290-6600
FAX 847-290-6609
info@iriskylight.com
http://www.iriskylight.com

Creative Director: Robin Fogarty
Managing Editor: Julia E. Noblitt
Editor: Monica Phillips
Proofreader: Sabine Vorkoeper
Graphic Designer: Bruce Leckie
Cover and Illustration Designer: David Stockman
Cartoonist: Art Bouthillier
Type Compositor: Donna Ramirez
Production Coordinator: Maggie Trinkle

LCCCN 95-75388
ISBN 0-932935-81-8

1359V
Item number 1262
Z Y X W V U T S R Q P O N M L K J I H G F E
05 05 04 03 02 01 00 99   15 14 13 12 11 10 9 8 7 6 5

To the voices of our past, present, and future.

ACKNOWLEDGMENTS

Integrating curricula with multiple intelligences is an idea that we have been in the process of developing for several years, through workshops, classes, and writing. Now the ideas have come together in this book. It represents everything that we believe about education: differences are real and positive; teaching and learning must be relevant; and change is not only inevitable, it is desirable.

A book like this does not come together overnight, nor through the efforts of just its authors. With that in mind, we would like to thank Jim Bellanca for encouraging us to write as a team; David Stockman, Bruce Leckie, and Heidi Ray for their artwork and design; Donna Ramirez for typing and preparing the manuscript; Julie Noblitt, Monica Phillips, Amy Wolgemuth, and Sabine Vorkoeper for their editorial work on the manuscript; and Maggie Trinkle for shepherding the project through production.

Special thanks, also, to Jill Hendricks of Gallaudet University Press for her guidance in the use of sign language in this book.

And finally, without support from our husbands we couldn't have survived our crazy schedules, those meetings in Chicago, and writing throughout the night. Thanks Brian and Jeff!

CONTENTS

4 THREADS 135

Foreword

I have always insisted that there is no optimal way to introduce multiple intelligences (MI) theory into the school. Indeed, hundreds of educators have put forth their own ideas and approaches, and the growing field of "applied MI" has been enriched by this luxuriant, open-ended process.

Nonetheless, having looked at various applications, I have concluded that one frequent application of MI theory is not well founded. This is the approach that says, in effect: Kids have seven intelligences and we have to find as many opportunities to use the intelligences as we can. And so we will have youngsters sing, dance, draw, work with others, work alone, as much as possible, without special reference to the goals or the curriculum of the school.

Now, to be sure, I have nothing against the arts—indeed, I have devoted much of my scholarly life to understanding their particular genius. Nor do I have any objection to cooperative learning, or solitary learning, for that matter. However, I insist that any activity to which significant amounts of school time is devoted needs to fit into carefully articulated and well-defended educational goals.

And so, as a rough rule of thumb, I ask two questions of an MI school: (1) Are there standards of excellence for the development of particular intelligences? For example, if the development of musical intelligence is a goal, are there reliable standards for what constitutes an excellent musical performance or a sophisticated musical understanding? (2) Are the multiple intelligences mobilized so that students can effectively master basic literacies, develop skills of thinking and problem solving, and come to understand the important ideas that have occurred within and across the several disciplines?

Integrating Curricula with Multiple Intelligences takes seriously the task of putting multiple intelligences to use within the broader missions of schools for today and, equally important, the missions of schools for tomorrow. Rather than developing intelligences simply for their own sake, Robin Fogarty and Judy Stoehr give ample examples of how to approach authentic curricular goals and assessment needs within an MI framework. They are sensitive to the constraints that operate on teachers even as they are open to ways in which teachers can refashion their classes and curricula to reach more children, and to do so in more effective ways. This book should help teachers to enliven and enrich their classrooms; in addition, the book should stimulate teachers to forge new connections across concepts and curricula, as well as new links among students and colleagues.

Howard Gardner

Introduction

THE WHYS AND WHEREFORES

The rationale supporting the idea of a holistic, integrated, interdisciplinary curriculum is fueled by a number of significant forces that are referred to here as the *winds of change*. These winds of change come from four different directions. The winds from the north and south represent the ideas of the educational *theorists* and the challenges of the school *practitioners*, while the winds from the east and west represent the concerns of *parents* and the perspectives of the *children*. From the theorists come data on teaching and the human brain; from the practitioners comes frustration with an already overcrowded curriculum; from the parents comes concern for student preparation and readiness for issues outside the classroom; and from the children comes a feeling that learning is too fractured and fragmented to apply to real-life situations. A closer look at these cross winds reveals their effect on the current climate and curriculum of our nation's schools.

THE THEORISTS

The forceful winds of change have brought about curricula that are based on complex experiences in which students are immersed in multiple ways of learning and knowing (Kovalik, 1993; Gardner, 1983). The search for meaning is basic: the brain has memory systems for rote learning and spatial memory and performs many functions simultaneously (Caine & Caine, 1991). Each brain has a unique profile of multiple intelligences—verbal, musical, logical, spatial, bodily, interpersonal, and intrapersonal (Gardner, 1983). These many ways of receiving information and expressing ourselves lead naturally to integrated curricula, ongoing and authentic projects, student-produced newsletters, and thematic instruction (Willis, 1991).

THE PRACTITIONERS

Information doubles every year and a half (Burris, 1985). As one university professor told his premed students, "By the time you become acting physicians, 50 percent of what we've taught you will be obsolete . . . and we don't know which 50 percent" (Fogarty & Bellanca, 1989, p. 30). Curriculum overload is a reality that kindergarten to college teachers face every day. Drug education, health and safety, AIDS awareness, consumer issues, marriage and family living, computer technology, and tech prep—there is no end to it. Subject matter content and life skills—thinking, organizing, assessing, problem solving, decision making, cooperating, collaborating, and health and fitness—inundate the schedule.

The problem of trying to cover too much material in too short a time has been aptly described by Hunter. According to Hunter, covering the curriculum is like taking a passenger to the airport. You rush around and hurry up and get to the airport on time, but you leave the passenger at home. In the flurry of curriculum coverage, some students are left behind. Therefore, the winds of change indicate that it is important to seek ways to "selectively abandon" and "judiciously include" certain material (Costa in Fogarty, 1991) by integrating the curriculum both within a single discipline and across subject matter content (Fogarty, 1991).

THE PARENTS

A father of a thirteen-year-old commented on the fragmentation involved in a typical cellular model of schooling for the eighth grade:

> thirty examples to do for math homework, twenty minutes of trombone practice, an autobiography to complete, the verbs to learn for a test, and a chapter to read in the science text.
>
> There is a need to examine what students learn under these circumstances. Life can become a treadmill. For some students, "getting through" school becomes a matter of survival. . . . Surely, we must wonder: What do we want kids to know twenty-five years from now? And, we must create organizational structures that eliminate obstacles and enable students to grow and learn. (Carbol, 1990, p. 89)

This wind of change means schooling for a lifetime, not for a test (Bellanca & Fogarty, 1991). In terms of relevant learning, one student sums it up like this: "I have a million things on my mind, and not one of them showed up on the test."

IRI/Skylight Publishing, Inc.

THE CHILDREN

One young high school student likened the fragmented curriculum to a vaccination: "Math is not science, science is not English, English is not history. A subject is something you take once and need never take again. It's like getting a vaccination; I've had my shot of algebra. I'm done with that" (Fogarty, 1993, p. 5). While subject matter content falls neatly into discipline-based departments, students, unfortunately, do not compartmentalize themselves or their learning as readily. Learning is incidental, inductive (Kovalik, 1993); it's holistic and it's interactive (Bellanca & Fogarty, 1991). Kids learn the complex skill of speaking a language from authentic interactions with other individuals. So, what does this wind of change mean? It means a shift toward holistic, experiential learning that leads to lifelong skills and equal opportunities for all children to learn.

THE IMPLICATIONS

The winds of change are stronger than we think. The brain research, the unloading of an overloaded curriculum, the necessity for the life skills of thinking and cooperating, and the call for learner-centered schools are all forces that are moving educators toward integrated, holistic, and authentic learning. The logic of integrating curricula with multiple intelligences is embedded in the concepts of *curriculum* and *instruction*. While curriculum planning concerns itself with the big picture and the scope and sequence of the various disciplines, the instruction typically focuses on the teaching methodology or the delivery of the curricula.

School reform movements in several states and provinces across North America have targeted integrated, holistic, and natural approaches to curriculum and instruction. As a result, models, or frameworks, for integration have emerged. These models either build integrated curricula around certain *themes,* or "big ideas," or they develop the curricula by *threading* life skills, such as thinking and organizing, across subject matter content. Instruction, on the other hand, is frequently integrated by targeting various learning styles. By incorporating activities that tap into different modalities, the instruction and assessment are presented in connected and holistic ways.

Curricula that is integrated with themes and threads can be easily connected to instruction and assessment that are integrated with multiple intelligences. In fact, when the model for *integrating the curricula* is combined with the model for *multiple intelligences*, the result is *integrated learning*:

> **Integrated Curricula + Multiple Intelligences =**
> **Integrated Learning**

IRI/Skylight Publishing, Inc.

A LOOK AT THE BOOK

The framework of this book comprises four sections: theories, teams, themes, and threads. In chapter one, voices from both the tower (academia) and the field (the classroom) provide the underlying theories for the development of teams, themes, and threads. Several theories and theorists are included. Chapter two explores the concept of developing teacher teams to implement holistic, integrated, and interdisciplinary approaches to curriculum. Chapter three covers themes and presents a six-step process for developing thematic learning units that focuses on higher-order thinking, mindful decision making, and productive problem solving. The final chapter highlights integrating the curriculum by "threading" life skills within single disciplines and across subject matter. The authors' note, located at the end of the book, briefly describes the assessment issues surrounding integrated curricula and holistic instruction with multiple intelligences. It also includes a sample lesson that indicates the types of assessments used.

AN OVERVIEW OF THE CHAPTER LAYOUT

The **VISUAL/SPATIAL** intelligence, symbolized by a film projector, epitomizes the imagination of the mind's eye. Adhering to the "Show Me" cue statement, each chapter opens with a fishbone graphic depicting the key elements.

The **LOGICAL/MATHEMATICAL** intelligence, symbolized by a charted line graph, represents the full range of reasoning skills and signals the rationale for each of the major sections. It answers the question "Why Bother?"

The **VERBAL/LINGUISTIC** intelligence is represented by a megaphone. The power of the written and spoken word is at the heart of this intelligence. This section is cued by the heading "Who Says?" and focuses on the leading voices providing the research base for each major element.

The **MUSICAL/RHYTHMIC** intelligence, symbolized by a drum, represents the messages carried through the patterned rhythms of the human mind. Sections covering this intelligence are labeled with the heading "I Hear It!"

The **BODILY/KINESTHETIC** intelligence is symbolized by a clapboard. The heading "Just Do It!" labels the sections covering this intelligence. In chapters three and four, the headings "Take 1," "Take 2," and "Take 3" designate elementary, middle, and senior level activities, respectively.

The **INTERPERSONAL/SOCIAL INTELLIGENCE** is symbolized by conversation bubbles, which represent the give-and-take interactions between people. Sections covering this intelligence are labeled "Can We Talk?" and cue the processing portion of each chapter.

The **INTRAPERSONAL/INTROSPECTIVE INTELLIGENCE** is symbolized by a valentine, implying "Be Mine." This intelligence is signified by the heading "What's in It for Me?" This section suggests a reflective strategy for readers to help them internalize the key elements of each chapter.

IRI/Skylight Publishing, Inc.

UNDERSTANDING THE MULTIPLE INTELLIGENCES SYMBOLS

VISUAL/ SPATIAL

Show Me!

Give me the big picture.
Show me an overview.
Let me see the idea.

LOGICAL/ MATHEMATICAL

Why Bother?

What's the rationale?
Why does this make sense?
Why is this such a good idea?

VERBAL/ LINGUISTIC

Who Says?

Who are the leading voices?
What does the research say?
Who are the proponents of this idea?

MUSICAL/ RHYTHMIC

I Hear It!

I hear the input.
I am internalizing the music, rhythm, beat of this idea.
Its melody is in my head.

BODILY/ KINESTHETIC

Just Do It!

How do I use it?
How is it useful to me?
Let's dig in and do it.

INTERPERSONAL/ SOCIAL

Can We Talk?

Can we discuss the idea?
What are the pros and cons?
How can we evaluate this critically and fairly?

INTRAPERSONAL/ INTROSPECTIVE

What's in It for Me?

How does this affect me?
What is my connection to this idea?
What will I get from this?

IRI/Skylight Publishing, Inc.

ONE LAST NOTE

Although the main focus of this book is to combine multiple intelligences and curriculum integration models into powerful tools for holistic, interdisciplinary learning, assessment can hardly be left out of the instruction/curriculum cycle. Therefore, assessment strategies, clearly labeled with corresponding icons, are embedded within each lesson. The icons are matched to the tri-assessment model, which uses traditional, portfolio, and performance assessments.

Traditional Assessment

Portfolio Assessment

Performance Assessment

For further discussion of the tri-assessment model, see the authors' note at the back of the book.

IRI/Skylight Publishing, Inc.

CHAPTER 1

SHOW ME!

Theories

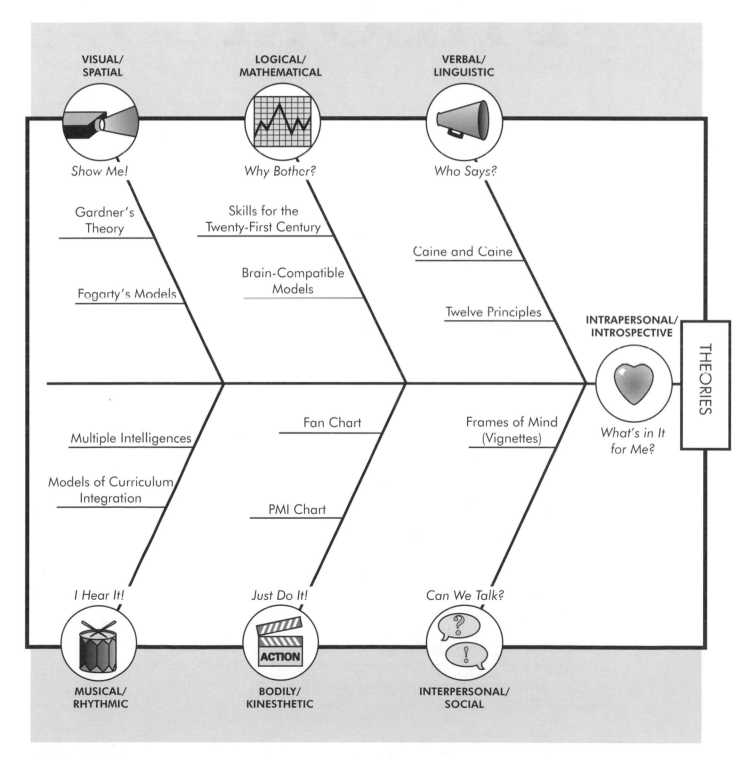

VISUAL/ SPATIAL

Show Me!

Gardner's Theory

Fogarty's Models

LOGICAL/ MATHEMATICAL

Why Bother?

Skills for the Twenty-First Century

Brain-Compatible Models

VERBAL/ LINGUISTIC

Who Says?

Caine and Caine

Twelve Principles

INTRAPERSONAL/ INTROSPECTIVE

What's in It for Me?

Multiple Intelligences

Models of Curriculum Integration

Fan Chart

PMI Chart

Frames of Mind (Vignettes)

THEORIES

I Hear It!

MUSICAL/ RHYTHMIC

Just Do It!

ACTION

BODILY/ KINESTHETIC

Can We Talk?

INTERPERSONAL/ SOCIAL

IRI/Skylight Publishing, Inc.

1 THEORIES

Change your thoughts and you change the world.
—*Norman Vincent Peale*

Why Bother?

WHY BOTHER?

What will students need to know and be able to do twenty-five years from now? What skills will they need for the twenty-first century? What big ideas will help them for the rest of their lives? Futurists believe that students in the twenty-first century will need greatly enhanced communication skills, including speaking, listening, and writing, and higher-order thinking skills that will allow them to be critical and creative. Other skills they will need are those of perpetual learning and accessing, researching, and organizing information. And, they will need strong, healthy self-concepts with self-management skills, self-initiating postures, and high levels of self-responsibility to ensure their health and wellness, which will help them work cooperatively with others to solve problems. Not only will students need to master all of these skills, they will also need to be able and willing to use new technologies in creative ways.

There is a distinctive link between how these skills are learned and certain brain-compatible models, such as Gardner's multiple intelligences theory (1983) and Fogarty's curriculum integration models (1991) based on Caine and Caine's (1991) findings on teaching and the human brain. This chapter elaborates on the extensive findings regarding brain research gathered by the Caines (1991). The rest of the chapter revolves around Gardner's seven intelligences and Fogarty's models of integration.

IRI/Skylight Publishing, Inc.

WHO SAYS?

Renate and Geoffrey Caine reviewed significant studies on the brain and how we learn, and compiled their findings in *Making Connections: Teaching and the Human Brain* (1991). These findings have provided the basis for the types of brain-compatible learning represented here. The twelve principles discussed in their work are paraphrased in this chapter (see also fig. 1.1).

BRAIN-COMPATIBLE LEARNING	
PRINCIPLE	**EDUCATIONAL IMPLICATION**
1. Parallel Processing	1. Orchestrate All Dimensions
2. Entire Physiology	2. Incorporate Health
3. Search for Meaning	3. Learning Environment
4. "Patterning"	4. Allow Brain to Pattern
5. Emotions	5. Affective Domain
6. Parts/Whole	6. Include Both
7. Focused/Peripheral	7. Organize Outside Focus
8. Conscious/Unconscious	8. "Active" Processing
9. Spatial/Rote Memory	9. Develop Both
10. Facts Embedded	10. "Real-Life" Learning
11. Challenge/Threat	11. "Relaxed Alertness"
12. Uniqueness	12. Multifaceted Technology

Figure 1.1

PRINCIPLE ONE

The Brain Is a Parallel Processor

The brain ceaselessly performs many functions simultaneously. The implication is that, like the brain, good teaching should "orchestrate" all the dimensions of parallel processing; simultaneous happenings are brain compatible.

PRINCIPLE TWO

Learning Engages the Entire Physiology

Since learning is as natural as breathing, teaching must fully incorporate stress management, nutrition, exercise, drug education, and other facets of health into the learning process. The implication is to infuse active strategies that permit physical movement and relief from long stretches of passive listening.

Who Says?

The Search for Meaning Is Innate

The search for meaning—the pursuit of making sense of our experiences—is survival oriented and basic to the human brain. To facilitate this principle, brain-based education must furnish a learning environment that provides stability and familiarity. Students need access to materials and supplies.

PRINCIPLE FOUR

The Search for Meaning Occurs through "Patterning"

In a way, the brain is both scientist and artist, attempting to discern and understand patterns as they occur and give expression to unique and creative patterns of its own. If learners are not attempting to impose patterns, information needs to be presented in a way that allows brains to extract patterns. For example, a teacher can foster the construction of knowledge and meaning by having students inductively learn about different types of poetry through the reading of several poems.

PRINCIPLE FIVE

Emotions Are Critical to Patterning

Emotions and cognition cannot be separated. Therefore, teachers must understand that students' feelings and attitudes are involved in learning and determine future learning. An illustration of the affective domain's connection to the cognitive domain is the positive effects on both student achievement and self-esteem from the teamness felt in cooperative learning.

PRINCIPLE SIX

Every Brain Simultaneously Perceives and Creates Parts and Wholes

The two hemispheres of the brain are inextricably interactive, irrespective of whether a person is dealing with words, mathematics, music, or art. The implication is that people have enormous difficulty learning when either parts or wholes are neglected. Therefore, when doing math calculations, students need to see how those same computations are applied to real-world problems. Learning must be contextual and purposeful so that discrete skills become tools for more holistic, problem-based learning.

PRINCIPLE SEVEN

Learning Involves Both Focused Attention and Peripheral Perception

The brain absorbs information that it is directly aware of; it also indirectly absorbs information and signals that lie beyond its immediate focus of atten-

4

tion. Therefore, the teacher can and should organize materials that will be outside the focus of the learner's attention. Teachers should engage the interests and enthusiasm of students through their own enthusiasm, coaching, and modeling. For example, as students are learning about coniferous and deciduous trees, they might learn about them by walking through a park in the fall, learning at the same time about various birds and animals in the forest.

Who Says?

PRINCIPLE EIGHT

Learning Always Involves Conscious and Unconscious Processes

We learn much more than we ever consciously understand. Most of the signals that we peripherally perceive enter our brain without our awareness and interact at unconscious levels. To promote this dual level of brain stimuli, "active processing" allows students to review how and what they learned so that they can begin to take charge of their learning and of the development of their own personal meanings. Using journals and learning logs often fosters this metacognitive reflection.

PRINCIPLE NINE

We Have Two Types of Memory: A Spatial Memory System and a Set of Systems for Rote Learning

The more information and skills are separated from prior knowledge and actual experience, the more we depend on rote memory and repetition. Educators are adept at focusing on memorization of facts. An overemphasis on such a procedure impoverishes the learner, hinders the transfer of learning, and possibly interferes with the development of understanding. Rather than having students "store and pour" information about a historic event such as the Civil War, why not let them experience it through simulations and role plays and by reading biographies? Then, let them generalize about their own experiences with conflict.

PRINCIPLE TEN

The Brain Understands and Remembers Best When Facts and Skills Are Embedded in Natural Spatial Memory

Our native language is learned through multiple interactive experiences involving vocabulary and grammar. It is shaped by internal processes and by social interaction. Teachers need to use a great deal of "real life" activity including classroom demonstrations, projects, field trips, visual imagery of certain experiences and best performances, stories, metaphors, drama, and interactions among different subjects for youngsters to fully internalize learning. Orchestrating a school store project or publishing a school newspaper are examples of purposeful learning activities.

IRI/Skylight Publishing, Inc.

Who Says?

PRINCIPLE ELEVEN

Learning Is Enhanced by Challenge and Inhibited by Threat

The brain learns optimally when appropriately challenged, but "downshifts" under perceived threat. Quizzes, tests, and exams are often seen as threats, whereas a student's understanding can be fully evidenced through a challenging, yet nonthreatening, portfolio development project. Teachers and administrators should strive to create a state of "relaxed alertness" in which students are intensely involved and meaningfully engaged in learning.

PRINCIPLE TWELVE

Each Brain Is Unique

Although we all have the same set of systems, they are integrated differently in every brain. Multifaceted teaching allows students to express visual, tactile, emotional, and auditory preferences. Incorporating multiple intelligences in teaching, learning, and assessment tools helps to foster this multidimensional approach.

Based on the Caines' findings, schools need to strive for meaningful learning through interactive elements, relaxed alertness, immersion, active processing, and high-challenge, low-threat activities. They need to orchestrate the immersion of their students in appropriate experiences and foster active processing through activities such as questioning and genuine reflection, which allow learners to take charge of consolidation and internalization.

I Hear It!

I HEAR IT!

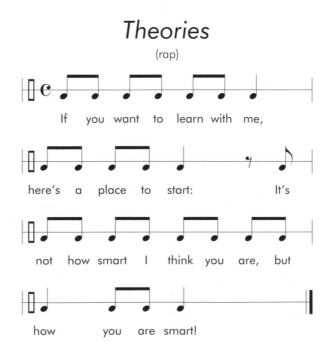

Theories
(rap)

If you want to learn with me,
here's a place to start: It's
not how smart I think you are, but
how you are smart!

IRI/Skylight Publishing, Inc.

▌FROM THE TOWER
GARDNER'S THEORY OF MULTIPLE INTELLIGENCES

It's not how smart you are, but how you are smart. This idea refers to Gardner's theory of multiple intelligences, which first appeared in his seminal piece, *Frames of Mind*, in 1983. Inspired by his work with brain-damaged veterans at Boston's Veteran Medical Center and with developing minds of children through his work at Project Zero at Harvard's Graduate School of Education, Gardner used what he had learned to formulate a theory advocating seven ways of viewing the world. Rounding out the accepted and established *verbal* and *mathematical* intelligences, Gardner hypothesized that human potential encompasses *spatial*, *musical*, and *kinesthetic*, as well as *interpersonal* and *intrapersonal* intelligences. His comprehensive view of intelligence further suggested that while the seven intelligences are independent of one another, they do work together.

Gardner postulated that his theory of seven intelligences would offer an alternative to the theory of intelligence as indicated by an intelligence quotient (IQ) score. Multiple intelligences theory allows one to assess the talents and skills of the whole individual rather than just his or her verbal and mathematical skills. Indeed, the theory of multiple intelligences does provide a more holistic, natural profile of human potential than an IQ test.

A closer look at the seven intelligences reveals the complexity Gardner's theory offers in terms of developing human potential. The human mind seems to receive and express ideas in myriad ways. These ways, or as Gardner terms them, intelligences, are listed in figure 1.2.

Visual/Spatial Intelligence

The symbol of the film projector epitomizes the imaginary movies of the mind. As the mind conceptualizes ideas about its surrounding environment, it often employs the visual/spatial intelligence of images, pictures, and graphical representations. This intelligence might be referred to as the mind's eye—the lens that sees through visual metaphors and memory imprints.

Looks and Sounds Like

The visual/spatial intelligence looks like a child locking in place the final piece to a puzzle, a toppling tower of blocks, or an architect's rendering of a contractor's blueprints. It looks like Rodin's sculpture, *The Thinker;* San Francisco's Golden Gate Bridge; the Leaning Tower of Pisa; and Old Faithful at Yellowstone National Park.

The visual/spatial intelligence embodies the talent of a designer/architect as well as the skill of a civil engineer. It manifests itself in CAD/CAM computer programs and software such as Aldus PageMaker. The visual/spatial intelligence provides mental pictures of road maps, faces, and places. Storyboard plans for film shoots, hopscotch grids on sidewalks, political cartoons, and Sunday comics are all products of the visual/spatial intelligence.

IRI/Skylight Publishing, Inc.

GARDNER'S SEVEN INTELLIGENCES

Visual/Spatial: **Show Me!**

Images, graphics, drawings, sketches, maps, charts, doodles, pictures, spatial orientation, puzzles, designs, looks, appeal, mind's eye, imagination, visualization, dreams, nightmares, films, and videos.

Logical/Mathematical: **Why Bother?**

Reasoning, deductive and inductive logic, facts, data, information, spreadsheets, databases, sequencing, ranking, organizing, analyzing, proofs, conclusions, judging, evaluations, and assessments.

Verbal/Linguistic: **Who Says?**

Words, wordsmiths, speaking, writing, listening, reading, papers, essays, poems, plays, narratives, lyrics, spelling, grammar, foreign languages, memos, bulletins, newsletters, newspapers, E-mail, FAXes, speeches, talks, dialogues, and debates.

Musical/Rhythmic: **I Hear It!**

Music, rhythm, beat, melody, tunes, allegro, pacing, timbre, tenor, soprano, opera, baritone, symphony, choir, chorus, madrigals, rap, rock, rhythm and blues, jazz, classical, folk, ads and jingles.

Bodily/Kinesthetic: **Just Do It!**

Art, activity, action, experiential, hands-on, experiments, try, do, perform, play, drama, sports, throw, toss, catch, jump, twist, twirl, assemble, disassemble, form, re-form, manipulate, touch, feel, immerse, and participate.

Interpersonal/Social: **Can We Talk?**

Interact, communicate, converse, share, understand, empathize, sympathize, reach out, care, talk, whisper, laugh, cry, shudder, socialize, meet, greet, lead, follow, gangs, clubs, charisma, crowds, gatherings, and twosomes.

Intrapersonal/Introspective: **What's in It for Me?**

Self, solitude, meditate, think, create, brood, reflect, envision, journal, self-assess, set goals, plot, plan, dream, write, fiction, nonfiction, poetry, affirmations, lyrics, songs, screenplays, commentaries, introspection, and inspection.

Figure 1.2

IRI/Skylight Publishing, Inc.

The sounds of the visual/spatial intelligence are heard in analogies, similes, and metaphors: "His teeth were as white as pearls"; "Transfer of learning is like a bridge that connects two things"; or Carl Sandburg's famous line, "The fog comes on little cat's feet." Visual/spatial intelligence sounds like an eyewitness' testimony given at a trial, a radio announcer's voice giving a play-by-play description of a baseball game, or lingo used by a tour guide to describe the Austrian Alps.

I Hear It!

Development

As with all of the other intelligences, the visual/spatial intelligence follows a progressive development. In fact, with early childhood programs, degrees of maturity are sometimes measured by the sophistication of a "draw-a-person" exercise. Drawings that go beyond a large oval head with eyes, nose, and mouth and include details such as five fingers on each hand, strands of hair, freckles, etc., receive a higher score because they indicate a greater developmental maturity.

The development of the visual/spatial intelligence is often evidenced in sketchbooks and lifetime works of artists, architects, and sculptors. Their early works often show immature execution, yet they also reveal strong signs of content and technique that later appear in their masterpieces. Practice, exercise, and explicit training are necessary for this intelligence to advance. As ideas are structured graphically in one's mind and a hierarchy of sorts is created from seemingly unrelated information (Ausubel, 1978), the novice advances toward more sophisticated and coherent imaging skills.

Notables

Leonardo da Vinci's sketchbooks leave no doubt that he qualifies not only as a true visionary, but also as a person with a strong visual/spatial intelligence. He sketched thousands of drawings of scientific phenomena, architectural renderings, and renowned anatomical drawings. His visual/spatial intelligence was so finely tuned that his work is unsurpassed even today. Other visual/spatial notables include Frank Lloyd Wright, Auguste Rodin, and Pablo Picasso.

Personal Profiles

Everyone possesses visual/spatial intelligence to some degree. Yet, some are not as tuned in as others to this channel of images, pictures, and graphics. They do not use a lot of metaphorical language, and they often write out directions rather than drawing a map. In general, these people rely on other intelligences to describe or understand the world. On the other end of the spectrum, there are some who have a more fully developed visual/spatial intelligence. They see through their mind's eye, visualizing phone numbers for quick recall, easily picturing how the kitchen will look with new wallpaper, or sketching thoughts in a concept map in order to see how ideas relate.

People reveal their visual/spatial intelligence in the language they use: "I see what you mean," "It looks good," "Show me," or "Do you see the big picture?" Visual/spatial intelligence is also noticeable in those who have a flair for matching outfits or a propensity for splashes of color or decorative jewelry.

I Hear It!

Those high in the visual/spatial intelligence might say things like "The movie was better than the book" or "The comics are the first thing I read in the Sunday paper." Theirs is a world of images, pictures, and graphics. They are able to see themselves five years from now and set long-term goals; they remember faces and places, not streets and numbers.

Implications

It is disturbing to see cuts in school programs involving the arts. The visual and performing arts must share center stage with other academic and vocational activities. Training, practice, and exercise in the visual/spatial intelligence is as important as these other activities, and all children deserve the opportunity to hone their skills and talents in this area.

For learners to massage this intelligence, classroom environments must reflect the value placed on it. Paints, crayons, pastels, clay, paper, paste and glue, markers, sand, water, scissors, tape, computer software, and color copiers are the tools of artists. From the primary classroom to the college lecture hall, these tools must be accessible for all to use, experiment with, play with, and mess around with as they envision their world.

Logical/Mathematical Intelligence

Pictured in the icon as a graph representing specific data, the logical/mathematical intelligence encompasses an entire range of reasoning skills. From the logic of Sherlock Holmes to the wisdom of Winston Churchill and from the cleverness of the Big Bad Wolf to the sound deductions of Archimedes, the logical/mathematical intelligence charts the data, information, and facts in the human mind.

Looks and Sounds Like

The following are all examples of what the logical/mathematical intelligence looks and sounds like: the reasoning of a scientific hypothesis, the logical progression of a computer program, the dichotomous classification of a species, the sequence of operations in mathematical equations, the cause-and-effect cycle of societal trends, the predictability of a plot in a novel, the patterned complexity of the periodic table of the elements, and the layered textures of an archeological dig. All of these things are sights and sounds of this incredibly *rigid*, yet incredibly *expansive* intelligence. Within this paradoxical intelligence, order reigns supreme.

Development

Beginning with concrete manipulatives and hands-on learning, youngsters soon grasp the concept of one-to-one relationships and numeration. They advance from concrete to representational ideas in the form of symbolic language, working equations, and formulas, and they learn about abstraction through the world of logic and numbers.

Reasoning is the fourth "r" of the developing mind's critical skills of reading, 'riting, and 'rithmetic. As learners construct knowledge and grapple with new ideas, they use their logical/mathematical intelligence to make sense of

IRI/Skylight Publishing, Inc.

their world. It is the logical/mathematical mechanism in the mind that seeks order by analyzing and compartmentalizing discrete pieces of information into chunks of meaning that can be abstracted into practical applications.

Notables

Perhaps the most frequently mentioned of all logical/mathematical notables is Albert Einstein. His theory of relativity, $E = mc^2$, symbolically represents a complex series of computations that embody a theory of the universe. Others include Polya (1945), who delineated the logic of the mind in his steps to problem solving, as well as Socrates, Plato, and Aristotle, who documented the logic of syllogistic language. More modern notables include Sherlock Holmes, Agatha Christie, and Secret Agent 007.

Personal Profiles

Personalities that exhibit a strong logical/mathematical intelligence enjoy lively discussions, relish the dialogue of controversy and argument, and are often comfortable with paradox and ambiguity. Students adept in this "frame of mind" understand the abstraction of calculus and the logic of statistics. They debate articulately, embrace the study of law, and are eager to analyze, chart, graph, and mathematically extrapolate data to its reasoned ends. They delight in opportunities to deduce and like nothing better than an end to a dilemma that resembles a neatly wrapped package.

Implications

The implications of this intelligence call attention to the need for rigorous curricula and vigorous instruction in the area of critical thinking, mathematical reasoning, and logic. Manipulating objects and working with concrete materials are important to this intelligence. It is also important to gradually move toward the symbolic realm of math, music, or language to secure abstract ideas. Discerning fact from fiction in literature, observation from inference in scientific investigation, and pure data from biased representation are exercises completed by the logical/mathematical mind. Encapsulated in this intelligence are the microskills of analysis, including comparison, classification, sequencing, and prioritizing. The ability to analyze, evaluate, and logically surmise are the essence of this intelligence.

Verbal/Linguistic Intelligence

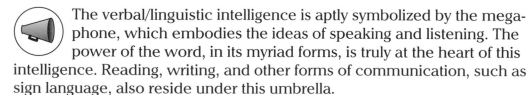

The verbal/linguistic intelligence is aptly symbolized by the megaphone, which embodies the ideas of speaking and listening. The power of the word, in its myriad forms, is truly at the heart of this intelligence. Reading, writing, and other forms of communication, such as sign language, also reside under this umbrella.

Looks and Sounds Like

Art and science are the culturally valued targets of receptive language (listening and reading) and expressive language (speaking and writing) that are

I Hear It!

I Hear It!

embedded in the verbal/linguistic intelligence. In the realm of receptive language, the verbal/linguistic intelligence looks like someone reading Fitzgerald's *The Great Gatsby*, Hemingway's *The Sun Also Rises*, Tolstoy's *War and Peace*, or listening to a presidential campaign speech. On the other hand, expressive language sounds like someone giving directions over the phone to a friend or writing out a grocery list. Signs of this intelligence also include dialogue, arguments, whispers, laughter, handwritten invitations, letters of correspondence, and poems and essays.

Development

Youngsters or novices imitate the sounds, rhythms, and tones of the language they hear, stringing words together into decipherable fragments and then into fully discernible sentences of proper syntax and sense. Oral language is most often followed by written language—nonsense or serial writing that eventually becomes phonetically spelled words, simple sentences, and fully developed paragraphs. While this is the developmental journey of a young learner, older learners are often introduced to language in oral and written forms simultaneously. Yet, the developmental sequence is still evidenced in the progress from simple to complex forms.

Vygotsky (1986) says that thinking is embedded in the language we use and Piaget (1972) uses formal learning stages to signal the development of abstract levels of thinking. These mindful abstractions are communicated through language.

Notables

Of note in the verbal/linguistic intelligence is John Fitzgerald Kennedy and his famous call to action: "And so, my fellow Americans, ask not what your country can do for you; ask what you can do for your country." Or Martin Luther King Jr.'s resounding refrain, "I have a dream . . ." or the words of Neil Armstrong, "That's one small step for man, one giant leap for mankind." Words like these become emblazoned in one's memories—not as a written message, but as spoken rhetoric of power and strength and vigor.

Personal Profiles

While the verbal/linguistic intelligence may not be considered a strength of everyone, most claim success with some aspect of it. For example, a student may have finely developed listening skills, yet may be less adept at speaking and articulating ideas. Or, one may sense a real comfort zone in reading, yet feel somewhat inadequate writing down his or her thoughts. Still, there are obvious connections within the complex tapestry of language as suggested by the idea that writers are readers first.

Implications

What does all this mean? It simply points to one of the critical "frames of mind" that Gardner postulates—the verbal/linguistic frame. And, implied in the exploration of this frame is the need to recognize, appreciate, and refine

IRI/Skylight Publishing, Inc.

the skills attributed to this intelligence: reading fact and fiction; writing memos, notes, invitations, letters, essays, novels, short stories, and news releases; speaking formally (speech, debate, presentation) and informally (conversations and dialogues); and listening to messages, music, and media.

Musical/Rhythmic Intelligence

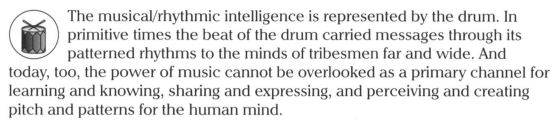

The musical/rhythmic intelligence is represented by the drum. In primitive times the beat of the drum carried messages through its patterned rhythms to the minds of tribesmen far and wide. And today, too, the power of music cannot be overlooked as a primary channel for learning and knowing, sharing and expressing, and perceiving and creating pitch and patterns for the human mind.

Looks and Sounds Like

In a June 1982 article in *Psychology Today* titled "The Music of the Hemispheres," Gardner stated that musical ability is packaged in the brain in more varied ways than verbal or spatial skills. So, too, is the intelligence, which can be seen by strolling through the halls of a school that integrates the curriculum with multiple intelligences.

In one classroom, students memorize their multiplication facts by using a steady rhythm and beat: "3 x 3 = 9, 3 x 4 = 12, 3 x 5 = 15. . . ." Rote memorization of rules of grammar, spelling, or even arithmetic seems to be easier for some through singsong phrases such as the following:

> "Con-junction is a junction."
> "'I' before 'e' except after 'c'."
> "Yours is not to reason why; just invert and multiply."

In the music classroom, students learn melodic sequences that eventually form songs. In the kindergarten room, children find their spots on the rug when transitional music is played by the teacher. Music is played in the gym as part of the PE department's "strive to be fit" aerobics program. A steady rhythm is tapped out by students learning keyboarding in the computer room. And in the English-as-a-second-language (ESL) room, students learn folk songs as their model for language development.

Development

The musical/rhythmic intelligence, often regarded as an innate talent, is nurtured and developed in many ways. Typically, youngsters are exposed informally to music in their home environments through a variety of media. At some point, they may begin taking private lessons to learn a musical instrument, and they may join the school band or orchestra. This is how students develop lifetime skills to support their musical/rhythmic intelligence.

Notables

One of the most globally recognized and enduring musicians is Mozart. He describes his relationship to music and its composition in this way:

IRI/Skylight Publishing, Inc.

I Hear It!

When I am . . . completely by myself, entirely alone . . . or during the night when I cannot sleep, it is on such occasions that my ideas flow best and most abundantly. Whence and how these come I know not nor can I force them . . . . Nor do I hear in my imagination the parts successively, but I hear them *gleich alles zusammen* [at the same time, all together]. (Peter, 1977, p. 123)

Among those renowned in the musical/rhythmic intelligence are Italian operatic tenor Luciano Pavarotti, and violinist Isaac Perlman.

Personal Profile

It is clear that the profile of human potential is incomplete without the musical/rhythmic intelligence, and everyone possesses some degree of aptitude. Gardner is careful to point out that this intelligence meets the rigorous criteria he has set, which therefore qualifies it as an intelligence. Some prefer to consider musical ability a talent rather than an intelligence; nonetheless, it is easily trained and developed.

Implications

Since music, rhythm, and beat are regarded as the elements of one of the seven intelligences, it behooves us as educators to include them as an integral part of the curriculum. Youngsters need to give this intelligence the exercise and reinforcement it needs in order to develop and blossom. School districts that embrace Gardner's theory of seven intelligences must also embrace music and the other arts, for they are undeniably interconnected. J. David Bowick, superintendent of the Oakland Unified School District, explains:

> During my school days, music was the reason to learn, the access to learning, the joy in learning. For other ghetto kids with whom I grew up and for those whom I later taught, music, art, dance, drama, and other "frills" were the inspiration that led many of them up and out of poverty." (Bowick, 1984)

Bodily/Kinesthetic Intelligence

The bodily/kinesthetic intelligence is symbolized by a clapboard—the director's call for action. Action is the key to this intelligence. The body is the conduit for the mind, and muscle memory obtained from experiences is what defines the bodily/kinesthetic intelligence.

Looks and Sounds Like

To envision the bodily/kinesthetic intelligence, imagine the precision of high-flying acrobats in a circus ring or pirouettes performed by a prima ballerina; think of the strength and timing of a prize fighter or the massive, symmetrical, fully toned body of a weightlifter. Hear the sounds of the bodily/kinesthetic intelligence as a typist beats out a rapid and steady rhythm, a pianist's fingers

14

fly across a piano's keys, or a symphony performs a crescendo in dynamic, earth-shattering brilliance.

I Hear It!

Development

Perhaps the easiest way to describe the development of this bodily/kinesthetic intelligence is to compare it to Posner and Keele's (1973) accepted stages of skill development—novice, advanced beginner, competent user, proficient performer, and expert. These stages can be illustrated by describing the different stages of learning to snow ski.

Novices process pieces, but not necessarily in order. For example, they often learn to go down a hill before they know how to stop or control their downhill run. *Advanced beginners* put together various pieces and practice in sequence. They don't really care about the results; they just want to know if they did it right. As learners become more competent, they care about the relationship of skill to the whole experience. *Competent* skiers are able to put together strings of turns and eventually master the hill. They're in a comfort zone and it's fun. *Proficient performers* have forgotten exactly *how* they ski. Their performance is automatic. *Experts* have also forgotten everything about the step-by-step progression of skiing and often can't explain it to someone else. Instead, they *show* the person how to ski, oftentimes glossing over difficult points.

The stages of learning, while more noticeable in gross motor activities, also apply to fine motor developments such as writing, computing, auto repairing, and playing the trombone. In essence, the bodily/kinesthetic intelligence, whether used with gross motor or fine motor skills, grows and develops in fairly predictable ways.

Notables

The notables in this intelligence span myriad fields, one of which is dancing. A familiar name from this field is Mikhail Baryshnikov. His fantastic leaps across the stage seem to defy gravity, and his exquisite technique astounds audiences. Just as Baryshnikov's image is known to the world of dance, Michael Jordan's gravity-defying image is legendary in the world of sports. Other notables with a strong bodily/kinesthetic intelligence include Kristy Yamaguchi, Walter Payton, and Bo Jackson.

Personal Profiles

The "frame of mind" described in Gardner's concept of the bodily/kinesthetic intelligence is evidenced early on in the fine and gross motor skills of youngsters. In fact, a major focus of exemplary early childhood programs is in this kinesthetic arena. Yet, just as with the other intelligences, personal profiles for the bodily/kinesthetic intelligence run the gamut from naturally skilled and proficient learners to the poorly coordinated and obtuse performers.

There are those who can type quite proficiently and there are those who prefer to peck along with two index fingers. There are those who excel in a number of sports and those who choose not to participate in physically oriented activities. Some can play a musical instrument with no problem, while others claim to be "all thumbs." Of course, many people fall somewhere

I Hear It!

in-between the two extremes and learn to type competently, play a fair game of tennis, and pick away at their guitars.

Implications

The overriding implications for the full development of the bodily/kinesthetic intelligence lies in a rich classroom that invites hands-on investigations, immersion in experiential learning situations, and long-term, authentic projects that require manipulation and maneuvering. This intelligence flourishes beyond the classroom walls in outdoor educational trips, field trips, and excursions. Gardner suggests (1983) that through the bodily/kinesthetic intelligence students experience and learn in children's museums, which invite sensory exploration and discovery learning. As discussed in Dewey's (1938) seminal piece, *Education and Experience*, the bodily/kinesthetic intelligence requires fertile territory for growth and development. With this intelligence, needed environmental richness extends naturally from the gym, playground, and track into various playing fields, stadiums, and sports complexes.

Interpersonal/Social Intelligence

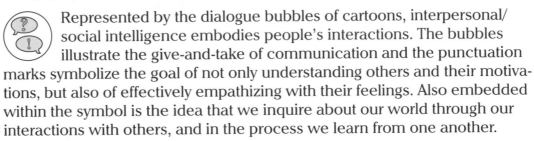

Represented by the dialogue bubbles of cartoons, interpersonal/social intelligence embodies people's interactions. The bubbles illustrate the give-and-take of communication and the punctuation marks symbolize the goal of not only understanding others and their motivations, but also of effectively empathizing with their feelings. Also embedded within the symbol is the idea that we inquire about our world through our interactions with others, and in the process we learn from one another.

Looks and Sounds Like

Interpersonal intelligence looks like a charismatic leader surrounded by an adoring crowd; a glib salesman spinning his or her pitch; a football team's trust, camaraderie, and synchronized play on the field; a teacher coaching a child in language skills; and a doctor holding the hand of a suffering patient.

Sounds of interpersonal intelligence include intimate conversations, arousing evangelic praises, lively debates, Socratic dialogues, structured articulations, phone conversations, shared secrets, political rallies, heated arguments, and cries of "surprise!" The sound of this intelligence is the sound of socialization.

Development

Interpersonal skills develop on a sliding scale ranging from isolation to skillful social interactions. Youngsters learn social behavior as they come in contact with others, first in their immediate family circle, then in peer situations, and then in public encounters. It seems, however, that the socialization process is dependent not only on the frequency of the interactions but also on the context and intensity of those interactions. For example, youngsters who attend nursery schools and have opportunities to interact with other children seem to adjust more easily to traditional schooling because they are more likely to know how to converse, share, and get along with their peers.

16

I Hear It!

It's interesting to track the socialization process of young children as they develop into fully functioning adults. Their development begins with the "me/mine" mentality of very young children, whose self-centered worlds revolve only around themselves. They then move into an adolescent phase and assume a posture of "me/them." Their lives become ruled by peer pressure and peer approval. As maturing adults, a "me/we" attitude prevails, and they pragmatically embrace a team-centered approach. There are, of course, many variations of this picture of social development, but, as Gardner states, "the child can come to know himself . . . only through coming to know other individuals" (Gardner, 1983, p. 247).

SOCIAL DEVELOPMENT

Young Child	Self-Centered—Me/Mine
Adolescent	Peer Centered—Me/Them
Adult	Team Centered—Me/We

Notables

Among the notables with obviously high interpersonal intelligences are missionaries who devote their lives to others, such as Mother Teresa, or religious leaders, such as Mahatma Gandhi. Also often noted in this category of interpersonal intelligence are the charismatic leaders in the political arena, including John F. Kennedy, Martin Luther King Jr., and Bill Clinton. Other personalities who qualify as examples of strong interpersonal intelligences are the ultimate interviewers, Phil Donahue, Barbara Walters, and Larry King, who all have a talent for getting others to open up.

Personal Profiles

Personalities are typically categorized as introverted or extroverted. Introverts are more comfortable turning inward and are often seen as asocial. Extroverts, on the other hand, seem to thrive on the company of others and are viewed as social butterflies. In reality, of course, most people fall somewhere in-between the two extremes. As with the other intelligences, the spectrum of personal attributes and preferences regarding interpersonal skills is extensive. Yet each has the potential to develop this intelligence to its fullest and call on it when needed.

Implications

Schools fostering the interpersonal intelligence are not didactic, behavioristic models of schooling in which teachers traditionally cover the content and information they want students to know; instead, these schools exemplify a constructivist model of schooling in which students are expected to make meaning in their minds of the subject matter. In this constructivist philosophy, interaction between the students and the teacher is enhanced and extended

I Hear It!

to include interactions among the students themselves. In essence, this intelligence thrives on active learning within the social context of the classroom.

Intrapersonal/Introspective Intelligence

Metaphorically, the intrapersonal/introspective intelligence is a personal valentine invisibly inscribed with the message "Be Mine." This intelligence also carries the message "Know thyself." Pragmatically, the intrapersonal intelligence represents a frame of mind in which learners internalize learning through thoughtful connections and then transfer it to novel situations through reflective application. It is with the intrapersonal intelligence that one has the ability to become acquainted with him- or herself.

Looks and Sounds Like

The manifestation of the intrapersonal intelligence is seen most vividly in personal diaries, daily journals, thinking logs, sketch pads, and notebooks. Self-reflection, self-awareness, and self-evaluation are often evidenced in these written formats, which evolve over time. Personal growth, acquisition of knowledge, and development of skills such as drawing and sketching are systematically traced through the pages of these continuing personal records. They provide fertile ground for meaningful reflection and powerful self-analysis and evaluation.

In another modality, the intrapersonal intelligence sounds like self-editing, such as, "No, I think I'm better at this," or the metacognitive monologue, "I must remember to talk more slowly and enunciate my words." As Dr. Art Costa, professor emeritus at Sacramento State University of California, has been heard to say that when you catch yourself talking aloud—to yourself— that's metacognitive. Metacognition is the act of planning, monitoring, or evaluating one's own behavior. Metacognition embodies the frame of mind Gardner labels as the intrapersonal intelligence.

Development

The intrapersonal intelligence develops, according to Swartz and Perkins (1987), in four incremental stages: *tacit, aware, strategic,* and *reflective. Tacit* behavior refers to using a skill or idea in an oblivious state. For example, young students may be able to read, but they seem totally unaware of the strategies they use—or even that they have an exceptional ability in this area. When students enter the next stage, *awareness*, they become cognizant of their strategies and/or their levels of performance. They are able to step back from the action and "freeze frame" their behavior. Subsequently, as they become more introspective, they advance to the *strategic* phase. In this phase, they consciously select particular models of behavior. For example, our readers might deliberately plan to "skim" or "scan" an essay for needed information because they know it is an efficient strategy for certain tasks. In turn, the *reflective stage* occurs when a student is able to reflect upon the degree of success or failure of the strategic method they used.

18

While the concept of intrapersonal intelligence seems to embody various stages or levels of proficiency, these stages are not locked into a chronological map. On the contrary, individuals embrace this introspective intelligence in similar patterns as Gardner's other intelligences. Although these patterns of occurrence are individually programmed to some extent, they are also dependent upon stimuli from the surrounding environment. If a culture values intrapersonal reflection, as many Eastern countries do, the intrapersonal intelligence is more likely to attract the attention and exercise it needs to develop and flourish.

Notables

Naturally, notables in the intrapersonal arena often include people in the field of psychology such as Freud and Jung; writers such as Emerson and Thoreau; artists such as Leonardo da Vinci; and philosophers such as Socrates, Plato, and Confucius.

Personal Profiles

The intrapersonal intelligence is present in varying degrees for each of us. There are those who seem totally unaware of their own behavior or how that behavior affects the people around them. Who among us has not been at a party, in the midst of a "braggart" or "blow hard," who drones on incessantly, unaware of a cool reception, total boredom, or a shrinking audience? On the other hand, there are those who are deeply reflective and acutely aware of their actions and words. Remember Dale Carnegie's message in *How to Win Friends and Influence People*? To paraphrase his intent—find out what the other party wants, then with that as your goal, proceed with the interaction.

Implications

The intrapersonal intelligence must be fostered and developed if real, significant, and long-lasting transfer of learning is to take place. For it is in the awareness, the strategic planning, and the reflective evaluation that students capture information and apply it in purposeful ways. Journals, logs, and portfolios for self-evaluation and dialogue with others help students articulate their strengths and weaknesses. They are necessary components of schooling that guide the development of the intrapersonal intelligence.

▌FROM THE FIELD
MULTIPLE INTELLIGENCES

While Gardner's theory of multiple intelligences is unequivocally the trunk of the mighty oak, branches of interpretive models continue to sprout. In an effort to take Gardner's theory into the practical realm of the classroom, a number of voices from the field offer strategies and frameworks for teachers and students. Among the authors, consultants, and strategists speaking from the field are Lazear; L. Campbell; Chapman; Armstrong; O'Connor and Young; Chapman, Bellanca, and Swartz; and B. Campbell.

I Hear It!

Lazear

David Lazear has four books based on the multiple intelligences theory: *Seven Ways of Knowing* (1991), *Seven Ways of Teaching* (1991), *Seven Pathways to Learning* (1994), and *Multiple Intelligence Approaches to Assessment: Solving the Assessment Conundrum* (1994). These books provide awareness, amplification, teaching, and transfer of the intelligences into classroom life and life outside the schoolroom walls. They also include assessment strategies for incorporating the seven intelligences.

L. Campbell

Linda Campbell's *Teaching and Learning through Multiple Intelligences* (1992) focuses on introductory models of the "other five" intelligences (visual/spatial, musical/rhythmic, interpersonal, intrapersonal, and bodily/kinesthetic), which are not focused on in schools.

B. Campbell

Bruce Campbell's work *The Multiple Intelligences Handbook* (1994) provides lessons and ideas that have evolved directly from his own classroom in Seattle. His "centers" approach offers opportunities for students to exercise all seven intelligences.

MULTIPLE INTELLIGENCES CENTERS

William Shakespeare	Linguistic
Albert Einstein	Logical/Mathematical
Martha Graham	Kinesthetic
Pablo Picasso	Visual/Spatial
Ray Charles	Musical
Mother Teresa	Interpersonal/Social
Emily Dickinson	Intrapersonal/Introspective

Chapman

In her book, *If the Shoe Fits...*, Chapman frames the seven intelligences in a metaphor of shoes and develops lessons and activities around them. For example, a fuzzy bedroom slipper represents the intrapersonal intelligence. Ideas for self-awareness and self-reflection are depicted with this shoe. A drum major's boot represents the musical/rhythmic intelligence, and a bunch of football cleats illustrates the teamwork required for the interpersonal intelligence. In this work, Chapman presents all seven intelligences individually and in integrated combinations as tools for problem solving.

Armstrong

From a more global perspective, or at least from beyond the schoolroom walls, Armstrong's *Seven Kinds of Smart* (1993) and *Multiple Intelligences in*

IRI/Skylight Publishing, Inc.

I Hear It!

the Classroom profile Gardner's intelligences through descriptions of them as they are used in everyday life. Included are exercises for readers to use their many intelligences.

O'Connor and Young

Targeting the K–3 classroom, O'Connor and Young use the multiple intelligences to design activities for primary units of study in their book, *Seven Windows to a Child's World* (1994). Using themes such as spring and winter, they plot appropriate lessons using various disciplines.

Chapman, Bellanca, and Swartz

Chapman, Bellanca, and Swartz provide a full spectrum of assessment strategies for all seven intelligences. Unlike Lazear's forms and formats, *Multiple Assessments for Multiple Intelligences* (1994) provides in-depth discussions that highlight a set of alternative assessments for each intelligence targeted.

■ FROM THE TOWER
FOGARTY'S MODELS OF CURRICULUM INTEGRATION

We have put schooling together in a manner that has appeared to work for many years. But, as we look at the demands of society today, we find it is a different world. Our students are coming to us fragmented and we continue the fragmentation in school. If our vision is one of a whole child, we need to look at ways to teach the *whole* child. Students don't often see the connections among separate and distinct subjects such as science, math, social studies, and literature. We need holistic ways to present information and get students involved in learning so they can apply what they've learned to their lives. Ultimately, we need to integrate the curricula. Several things have happened in education that dictate a more integrated look at schooling, including brain research that didn't exist before. Now, we have supportive evidence that shows how students learn.

Curriculum overload is another important issue. We continue to add things, but we seldomly take things out. How can we possibly teach everything when information today doubles every year and a half? One answer is restructuring schools from the inside out by reviewing the curriculum and setting priorities. We need to ask ourselves what it is that kids need to know for the rest of their lives. Then, we need to create models of schooling that focus on the *learner*.

The glory of the model for curriculum integration is that once again teachers become the designers. They can put curriculum and instruction together the way they think it makes sense. They know what to do. They're the experts. They've known for many years what to teach. There are many, many ways to integrate the curricula. Frequently, we integrate within a single discipline or we may integrate across disciplines. Sometimes, integration is simply within the mind of the learner.

IRI/Skylight Publishing, Inc.

I Hear It!

Having a class read a novel while teaching about the period in history in which the novel takes place is more powerful learning than just studying literature and history separately. Teaching a math unit on measurement makes an impact on more students and makes much more sense to them if that form of measurement is used in a cooking unit.

These are commonsense ways of putting our curriculum together. They are things we have done in the past, but they are done more deliberately now. Teachers can "selectively abandon" and "judiciously include" things in their curriculum while sifting out the valued goals embedded within various content areas. They can then begin to set priorities in an overcrowded and somewhat splintered curriculum.

Within a Single Discipline

Integrating curricula within a single discipline provides a platform for making connections from one day's work to the next, from one part of a project to the next, and from one idea to the another. A semester-long integrated art project at an inner-city school allows students to create symbolic representations in a permanent wall mural and to connect to the school community. An added benefit to this contribution is that their work is an indelible statement. Making these connections within a discipline is critical to integrating skills and concepts into meaningful life situations. The connection made within a single content area provides a needed context for deeper understanding. The integration of concepts leads to the transfer and application of skills in holistic and natural ways for lifelong use. Students who learn in connected ways see the big picture and have a sense about how ideas fit together. By enabling students to see that what they learn is connected to real-life experiences, they can see that their learning has greater meaning.

Webs across the Disciplines

Integrating curricula across disciplines may be as simple as resequencing subject matter or looking for a shared concept with another content area. In one classroom, where the preparation of pudding played an important role, students did activities that involved measurement and communication skills as well as the scientific concept of changing matter.

The curricula can also be integrated by selecting an overall theme and using it as an umbrella idea that connects various subject areas. The theme, which may evolve from a particular academic area, can be developed in the whole language classroom by using a traditional literature-based approach. Some themes may be schoolwide and web out to every classroom in the building. For example, one school took advantage of available resources with a U.S. postal theme, entitled "Wee Deliver," to involve every classroom. Each month a different class designed stamps and other classes delivered the mail. Underlying this theme were the skills of writing and communication.

Another thematic approach is the personal theme. In one model, individuals selected a theme that was significant to them and used that theme to connect to the content in a personal way. Personal themes can develop

22

naturally from children as they observe and interact with their environment and reflect upon their experiences.

Threads across the Disciplines

Designing lessons that encourage higher-level thinking naturally leads to integrated learning. Another way of integrating across several disciplines is to thread certain skills and concepts into several subject areas. Following are examples of schools and teachers weaving the thinking skills of theorizing, comparing, and contrasting into their lessons—lessons that allow kids to work together, rank ideas, justify decisions, and articulate thoughts freely.

One school selected problem solving as the skill to thread through every classroom and every subject matter content. Another school used both the study and application of technology as its thread to integrate curricula. They electronically connected every classroom to the cable network and even connected some classes to other schools by a FAX modem. Students here are motivated to write and communicate not only within the classroom, but also between schools. Technology here enables and connects.

Inside the Mind of the Learner

Children often have a lens of interest. Anytime we can tap into that interest we are ahead, because it can be an impetus for integrating learning. While teachers can redesign the curricula to make explicit connections between lessons, in the final analysis the true integration of ideas must occur inside the minds of the learners.

Model 1:   FRAGMENTED

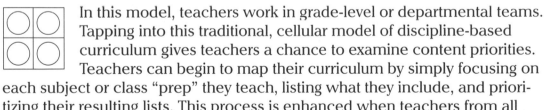

In this model, teachers work in grade-level or departmental teams. Tapping into this traditional, cellular model of discipline-based curriculum gives teachers a chance to examine content priorities. Teachers can begin to map their curriculum by simply focusing on each subject or class "prep" they teach, listing what they include, and prioritizing their resulting lists. This process is enhanced when teachers from all departments and grade levels form job-alike teams and discuss what's important in their curriculum. Decisions are made to "selectively abandon" some things in order to "judiciously include" others. Once the job-alike teams come to some agreement about curricular priorities, they are then well prepared to represent their grade level or department on an interdisciplinary team. Teachers who have the backing of their colleagues in their department or grade level bring confidence to their cross-disciplinary teams because they have done the preliminary work. Discussions within their own groups yield a significant degree of consensus, and the interdisciplinary team members become well grounded in their priorities.

Just one afternoon inservice devoted to grade-level or departmental meetings that are focused on setting curricular priorities can pay big divi-

TOWARD AN INTEGRATED CURRICULUM

Ten Views for Integrating the Curricula: How Do You See It?

1 Fragmented
Periscope—one direction; one sighting; narrow focus on single discipline

Description
The traditional model of separate and distinct disciplines, which fragments the subject areas.

Example
Teacher applies this view in Math, Science, Social Studies, Language Arts OR Sciences, Humanities, Fine and Practical Arts.

2 Connected
Opera glass—details of one discipline; focus on subtleties and interconnections

Description
Within each subject area, course content is connected topic to topic, concept to concept, one year's work to the next, and relates idea(s) explicitly.

Example
Teacher relates the concept of fractions to decimals, which in turn relates to money, grades, etc.

3 Nested
3-D glasses—multiple dimensions to one scene, topic, or unit

Description
Within each subject area, the teacher targets multiple skills: a social skill, a thinking skill, and a content-specific skill.

Example
Teacher designs the unit on photosynthesis to simultaneously target consensus seeking (social skill), sequencing (thinking skill), and plant life cycle (science content).

4 Sequenced
Eyeglasses—varied internal content framed by broad, related concepts

Description
Topics or units of study are rearranged and sequenced to coincide with one another. Similar ideas are taught in concert while remaining separate subjects.

Example
English teacher presents an historical novel depicting a particular period while the History teacher teaches that same historical period.

5 Shared
Binoculars—two disciplines that share overlapping concepts and skills

Description
Shared planning and teaching take place in two disciplines in which overlapping concepts or ideas emerge as organizing elements.

Example
Science and Math teachers use data collection, charting, and graphing as shared concepts that can be team-taught.

6 Webbed
Telescope—broad view of an entire constellation as one theme, webbed to the various elements

Description
A fertile theme is webbed to curriculum contents and disciplines; subjects use the theme to sift out appropriate concepts, topics, and ideas.

Example
Teacher presents a simple topical theme, such as the circus, and webs it to the subject areas. A conceptual theme, such as conflict, can be webbed for more depth in the theme approach.

7 Threaded
Magnifying glass—big ideas that magnify all content through a metacurricular approach

Description
The metacurricular approach threads thinking skills, social skills, multiple intelligences, technology, and study skills through the various disciplines.

Example
Teaching staff targets prediction in Reading, Math, and Science lab experiments while Social Studies teacher targets forecasting current events, and thus threads the skill (prediction) across disciplines.

8 Integrated
Kaleidoscope—new patterns and designs that use the basic elements of each discipline

Description
This interdisciplinary approach matches subjects for overlaps in topics and concepts with some team teaching in an authentic integrated model.

Example
In Math, Science, Social Studies, Fine Arts, Language Arts, and Practical Arts teachers look for patterning models and approach content through these patterns.

9 Immersed
Microscope—intensely personal view that allows microscopic explanation as all content is filtered through lens of interest and expertise

Description
The disciplines become part of the learner's lens of expertise; the learner filters all content through this lens and becomes immersed in his or her own experience.

Example
Student or doctoral candidate has an area of expert interest and sees all learning through that lens.

10 Networked
Prism—a view that creates multiple dimensions and directions of focus

Description
Learner filters all learning through the expert's eye and makes internal connections that lead to external networks of experts in related fields.

Example
Architect, while adapting the CAD/CAM technology for design, networks with technical programmers and expands her knowledge base, just as she had traditionally done with interior designers.

© Robin Fogarty, 1991*

*Extrapolated from "Design Options for an Integrated Curriculum" by Heidi Hayes Jacobs in *Interdisciplinary Curriculum*, ASCD, 1989.

dends. It is the first step toward the curriculum mapping necessary for integrating. Obviously, model 1 is not truly an integration of content, but rather a *preparation* for curriculum integration.

Model 1 Example

A technology teacher lists these things as elements or units for one year: (Other teachers may create similar lists for their disciplines.)

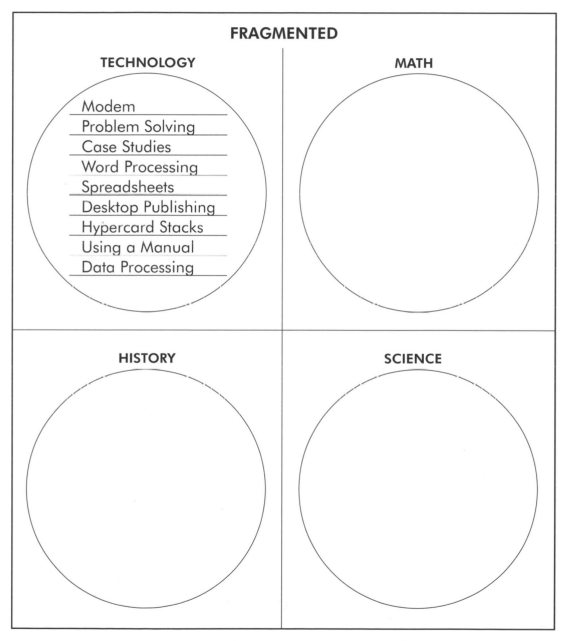

FRAGMENTED

TECHNOLOGY

- Modem
- Problem Solving
- Case Studies
- Word Processing
- Spreadsheets
- Desktop Publishing
- Hypercard Stacks
- Using a Manual
- Data Processing

MATH

HISTORY

SCIENCE

In the ensuing dialogue, the teacher ranks "Using a Manual" as number one. The argument is that students will use new technologies throughout their lives, and, therefore, will need to know how to do the technical reading required to use a manual skillfully. Yet, his counterpart argues that "Using a Manual" should be ranked as last. He claims that the software and hardware are becoming so sophisticated that they are self-correcting. He suggests that

I Hear It!

I Hear It!

the manual is, or will become, a less viable problem-solving tool. A third department member feels that technical reading should be included in the English curriculum.

All three teachers are experts, schooled and experienced in technology, and all three offer valid arguments. Yet, some level of consensus must reign if schools are to make reasoned choices and agree on priorities. While teachers are energized by these discussions, the real purpose is to groom the curriculum with a fine-tooth comb and appreciate subject-matter content in the larger context of natural and holistic learning.

Model 2: CONNECTED

The first time teachers teach a class or grade level, they will probably follow a curriculum guide or text. However, once they have taught the material, they will forever put it together in a way that makes the most sense to them, adjusting it to flow together in natural ways. Interestingly, teachers often manipulate their curriculum so automatically, so intuitively, that when you ask them about it, they have to think it through formally before they can articulate their reasons. Yet, the connections are always there, although implicit. Once they are ferreted out, the connections become obvious and explicit.

By using the connected model, specific units are taught one after the other because they have natural connections. These connections usually fall into two categories: themes or threads. Themes are big ideas or concepts like *patterns*, *change*, or *discovery*, while threads are more likely to be skills or tools that run through both units, like *thinking skills*, *social skills*, and *graphic organizers*. As teachers work to find natural linkages between specific content units, the actual connectors may be somewhat elusive. To facilitate the discovery of themes and threads, teachers should discuss their ideas with their colleagues. In the course of their dialogues, teachers will become reflective about their practice and will become better able to make explicit connections for their students.

Model 2 Example

The connected model is illustrated on the following page.

First, the teacher teaches a unit on Canada, our neighbors to the north. This he follows with another unit on Mexico, our neighbors to the south. Both units are connected through the concept of "conversations across cultures." This big idea of "conversation" is used to explore the ideas of dialogue, articulation, and sharing between and among various cultures. This concept of "conversation" is so fertile that it could be used as a thematic umbrella over a number of other cultures.

Often, connected models uncover themes and threads that are far-reaching and complex. It is important, however, to note that teachers put their curriculum together in a natural sequence, allowing the different topics or units to flow into one another. Once the connectors become obvious, it is easier to make the connections explicit to the students. The more overtly teachers can make the connections, the more holistic the content is for the students.

IRI/Skylight Publishing, Inc.

CONNECTED

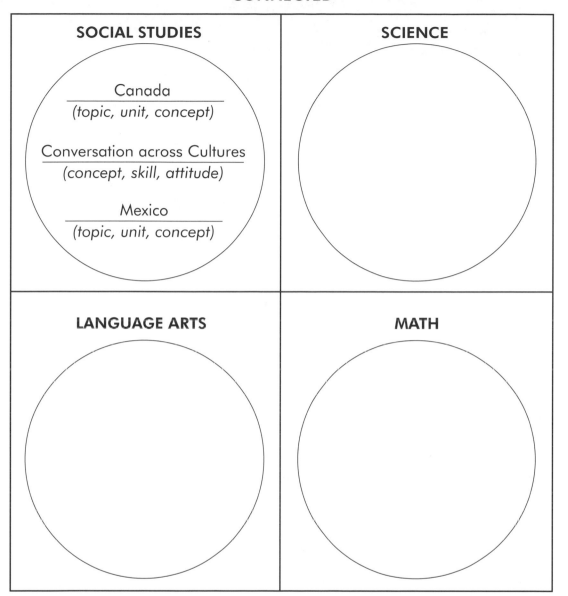

SOCIAL STUDIES

Canada
_____
(topic, unit, concept)

Conversation across Cultures
(concept, skill, attitude)

Mexico
_____
(topic, unit, concept)

SCIENCE

LANGUAGE ARTS

MATH

Model 3:   NESTED

Many teachers in today's classrooms use the nested model without knowing what it is called. With the current mandates for higher-order thinking, cooperative learning, and authentic assessments, the nested model offers an efficient and effective way to organize a somewhat overloaded curriculum.

If teachers ask the question, "What will kids need to know twenty-five years from now?" their answer invariably encompasses the genre called life skills—the skills of thinking, teamwork, and problem solving. To include these skills in meaningful ways, they must be infused into the context of purposeful assignments and projects. The nested model provides the framework for that kind of contextualized learning.

IRI/Skylight Publishing, Inc.

I Hear It!

LIFE-SKILL THREADS

THINKING SKILLS

Creative/Generative Skills

Hypothesizing
Generalizing
Predicting
Inferring
Brainstorming
Summarizing
Visualizing
Surveying
Imaging
Defining

Critical/Analytical Evaluative Skills

Classifying
Comparing
Contrasting
Prioritizing
Evaluating
Judging
Critiquing
Criticizing
Analyzing Bias
Justifying
Validating
Labeling

SOCIAL SKILLS

Communication Skills

Attentive Listening
Clarifying
Paraphrasing
Summarizing
Emphasizing
Sympathizing

Leadership Skills

Affirming
Encouraging
Accepting Others' Ideas
Including Everyone
Delegating
Empowering

Conflict Resolution Skills

Reaching Consensus
Learning to Agree/Disagree
Arbitrating
Mediating
Voting

SKILLS IN THE ARTS

Painting
Film
Design
Dance
Drama
Music
Sculpture

GRAPHIC ORGANIZERS

Webs
Mind Maps
Right-Angle Thinking
Venn Diagrams
Priority Ladders
Grids
Matrices
Cause/Effect
Fishbones
Thought Trees
Hexes
5Ws
T-Charts
M-Charts
Agree/Disagree

TECHNOLOGICAL SKILLS

Word Processing
Spreadsheets
Graphics
Problem Solving
Using a Manual
Hypercard Stacks
Programming
Modem
Internet
Voice Mail
CAD/CAM

Model 3 Example

The teacher in this example has created several hands-on activities designed to target the bodily/kinesthetic intelligence while learning about gravity. As the students execute various experiments, they are asked to compare and contrast the forces demonstrated and to think critically about their findings. Their results are then depicted in a Venn diagram, which graphically represents similarities and differences in the gravitational forces studied.

Many teachers might use this very lesson or a reasonable facsimile, however, to give this lesson transfer power, the teacher must talk about the skills of comparing and contrasting and encourage students to reflect upon their uses. Critical to the nested model are metacognitive monologue and reflective dialogue that name, label, and apply life skills within meaningful contexts. This is called purposeful learning and it helps students create and construct meaning in their minds, as well as provide them with lifelong tools for problem solving and decision making.

IRI/Skylight Publishing, Inc.

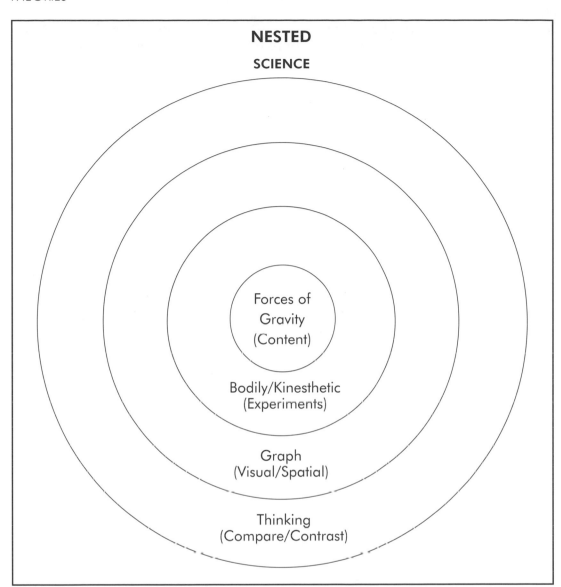

NESTED

SCIENCE

Forces of Gravity (Content)

Bodily/Kinesthetic (Experiments)

Graph (Visual/Spatial)

Thinking (Compare/Contrast)

Model 4: SEQUENCED

Sequencing curriculum content by beginning conversations across grade levels and across disciplines is a step toward curriculum mapping. In this model, teachers are asked to survey their content expectations for a semester or even a year. They are asked what units, topics, skills, and concepts are on the horizon for each subject area or class prep they teach. Then, with partners, teachers map out their subject matter and discuss the most logical or beneficial sequence for their content. Sometimes, just by being aware of the content targeted in other subject areas or disciplines, teachers can rearrange their content in order to make it coincide in a complementary way.

The benefits of two classes studying the same topic are many. Think about shared films, speakers, and field trips. Or think about complex projects that need chunks of time and teams of experts. Imagine what powerful learning it is for students to read a biography of Churchill while studying World War II or to learn about teamwork with their science lab partner while reading about

I Hear It!

dog sled teams in *Call of the Wild* in English class. One enhances the other as teachers learn to talk to each other about what they teach and when they teach it.

Teachers who take a long look at their curriculum content often find several natural match-ups that make sense. As a result, teachers are more than willing to resequence their curriculum, if possible. One note of caution, however, seems prudent. Sometimes after a genuine effort to talk with one another about content, teachers find that there are no natural linkages and that rescheduling would only result in contrived integration. However, even if no natural links are found, such conversations allow teachers to gain knowledge about other classrooms. With this kind of knowledge, connections are possible at another time or with another subject area. After all, once one knows, one can't *not* know.

Model 4 Example

Sequencing two topics from different disciplines may be as simple as studying Native American rhythms in music class while studying Native Americans in social studies. However, resequencing *content* may be more complicated. For example, a math department may use the scope and sequence of the science department to guide them in introducing various math skills. This way, math skills are more meaningful when learned within the context of real science applications. Although this may be harder to organize, the results make it well worth the effort.

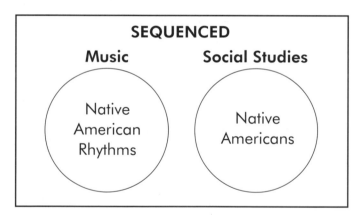

Model 5:   SHARED

In contrast to the sequenced model of curriculum integration, which requires a long look at the semester or year, the shared model dictates an in-depth view of a particular content unit.

This model requires an intense conversation with someone from another discipline or subject area. Teachers ask one another what they do *specifically* when teaching a certain unit. They describe in detail the activities and learnings targeted in a particular unit. After both parties are privy to the real meat of the two units, they look for those concepts and skills that are shared by the topics taught by each teacher. Themes and threads then begin to emerge.

The shared model looks for "roots running underground" or themes and threads that underlie all content. It is an authentic model for integrating

IRI/Skylight Publishing, Inc.

curricula through conceptual underpinnings. To share in curricula integration, two disciplines embrace a single idea simultaneously. Remember, the shared model of curriculum integration focuses on an in-depth look at two units in two disciplines, whereas the sequenced model fosters a long-term plan across two different subject areas in an attempt to resequence topics for greater alignment and integration.

Model 5 Example

The following anecdote illustrates the usefulness of model 5:

> Two high school teachers were talking at lunch one day. The social studies teacher lamented about his students' lack of enthusiasm for the unit on Egypt and complained that they weren't coming to class prepared and were uninterested and uninvolved. "The only thing that intrigues them about Egypt are the pyramids and the mummies," he said. His friend, the science teacher, listened sympathetically; then, he shared his story about how excited his students were about the biology unit he was teaching—the dissection of frogs. Right then, an idea flashed in his mind. "Hey, what if we take what's left of these little critters and have the kids make mummies of them?" he asked.

Using the high-interest topics of dissection and mummies, the teachers orchestrated a day to mummify frogs. In the process of planning their event, significant life skills and big ideas readily emerged, such as the thinking skills of sequencing and problem solving and the concepts of structures and/or systems. These ideas gave more depth and meaning to the biology lesson as well as to the social studies lesson.

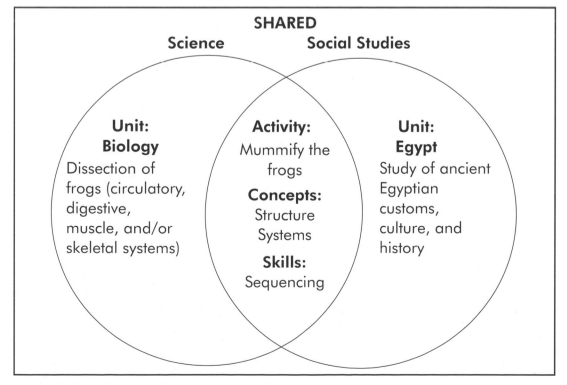

SHARED

Science   **Social Studies**

Unit: Biology
Dissection of frogs (circulatory, digestive, muscle, and/or skeletal systems)

Activity: Mummify the frogs

Concepts: Structure Systems

Skills: Sequencing

Unit: Egypt
Study of ancient Egyptian customs, culture, and history

I Hear It!

Model 6: WEBBED

Diversity, fashion, inventions, technology, family, and patterns are all big ideas used in the classroom. In fact, the webbed model of thematic teaching is frequently cited as the most commonly used model of curriculum integration. From the whole language classroom of the elementary schools to the thematic approach of middle school pods to the novel-based thematic instruction of the humanities department, themes provide viable umbrellas for instruction. Themes are used for two distinct purposes: to organize content and to ignite learning. Umbrella themes, or big ideas, act like magnets. Once they are in place, themes create magnetic forces that draw ideas for curriculum content and instructional activities.

Developing themes that have rigor and vigor requires a number of critical steps. A brief look at the steps are provided through the use of the acronym THEMES. (This process is developed extensively in chapter three.)

T—Think of themes to build a healthy bank of at least one hundred themes.

H—Hone the list by coding the ideas as topics, concepts, or problems. Topics may be subject-related, but concepts and problems seem to reach out to multiple disciplines.

E—Extrapolate criteria and discuss reasons and rationale for selecting a theme. Know why it's a worthy, fertile theme.

M—Manipulate the theme by generating key questions; explore the many dimensions; find a focus with a "hook" question that drives the thematic investigation.

E—Expand through activities; web the theme to multiple content areas and develop purposeful activities.

S—Select goals and assessments that target learning and report the results of the learnings.

Model 6 Example

A simplified example of the thematic model is illustrated using the theme of technology. Teachers embraced the theme of technology as a "school-to-work" initiative and students embraced it as a natural part of their daily lives. Within this theme, key questions emerged that led the investigation into several curriculum areas.

IRI/Skylight Publishing, Inc.

I Hear It!

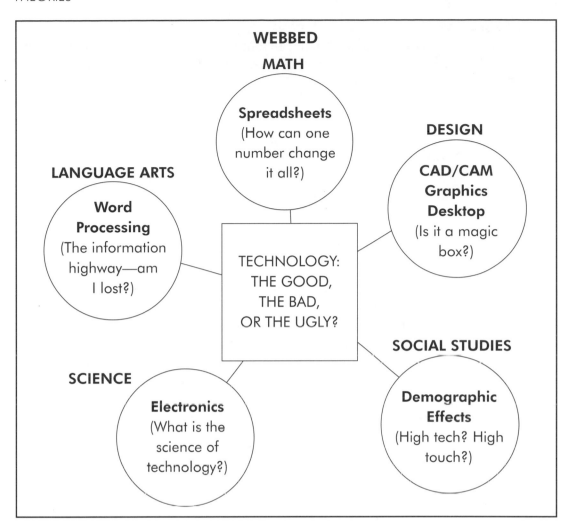

Several of the questions generated by the teacher team targeted investigations across the disciplines. For example, the key question, "Technology: the good, the bad, or the ugly?" opens the umbrella for a broad investigation into the pros and cons of technology. This becomes the "hook" question for students throughout the unit. The other questions lead to inquiry into various subject areas.

Social Studies
"High tech? High touch?" suggests a possible study in demographics about technology and its effects on society.

Science
"What is the science of technology?" opens the door for the study of electronics and computers.

Design
"Is it a magic box?" prompts an exploration into the design capabilities of computers, including CAD/CAM, desktop publishing, and multimedia.

IRI/Skylight Publishing, Inc.

I Hear It!

Language Arts

"The information highway—am I lost?" is a natural opening for starting the journey through the maze of technological devices for communication arts (FAX, E-mail, modem, Internet, etc.).

Math

"How can one number change it all?" is the bait for learning how spreadsheets make budget calculations a breeze.

Naturally, this unit can be developed beyond these areas as new questions evolve. Yet, as this unit stands, it presents an encompassing look at the multifaceted phenomenon called technology.

Model 7: THREADED

Sometimes curriculum integration focuses on integrating the life skills of thinking, cooperating, and organizing, rather than intertwining subject matter content. The threaded model does just that. It threads the life skills of the metacurriculum throughout discipline-based instruction. A familiar example prevalent in the schools is often referred to as "writing across the curriculum." While some critics may not regard this as "real" integration, there is no doubt that threading life skills into multiple content areas promotes easy transfer of such things as thinking, cooperating, and technology into relevant situations.

One plus of this threaded model is that it does not disrupt the status quo. In organizations with departmentalized structures, threading critical life skills into subject matter content provides a viable and visible integration of curriculum for students. They see the connective threads and some even comment on the similar things going on in each class. Another benefit of threading is the reality that teachers often incorporate thinking and cooperating into lessons and activities without actually teaching about the skills themselves. In essence, the content becomes the vehicle that carries the skills of thinking, cooperating, organizing, and multiple intelligences. Although a faculty or team must take time in the beginning to meet and decide upon common threads, the model does not require a lot of team time thereafter. With the threads in place, various teachers throughout the building can incorporate the threads as often as practical.

Model 7 Example

To thread skills into course content, one school selected analysis of bias as a thinking thread.

IRI/Skylight Publishing, Inc.

I Hear It!

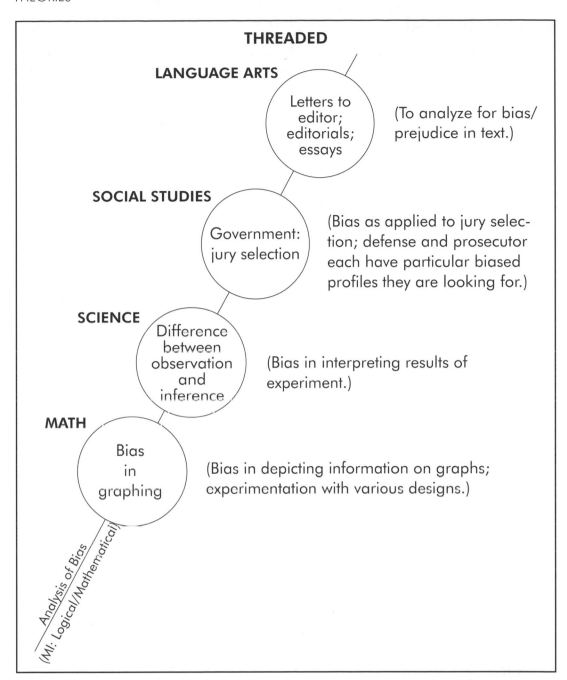

THREADED

LANGUAGE ARTS

Letters to editor; editorials; essays

(To analyze for bias/prejudice in text.)

SOCIAL STUDIES

Government: jury selection

(Bias as applied to jury selection; defense and prosecutor each have particular biased profiles they are looking for.)

SCIENCE

Difference between observation and inference

(Bias in interpreting results of experiment.)

MATH

Bias in graphing

(Bias in depicting information on graphs; experimentation with various designs.)

Analysis of Bias
(MI: Logical/Mathematical)

A quick look at the previous diagram shows how easily a thread weaves its way across various curricular content. In a math class, students learn to manipulate information on graphs and thus learn that bias can occur when interpreting what the graph indicates. The difference between observing and inferring is targeted in the science lab as students examine how bias can slip into the interpretation of data. In government class, the paradox involved in selecting a jury offers an ample opportunity to study bias. Students realize that the paradox of jury selection lies in the fact that in an effort to select an unbiased jury, lawyers end up formulating biased opinions of potential jurors. In a language arts class, students analyze essays for possible bias as they learn to examine the contextual framework of the essay, including who, what, where, how, and why. In all four cases, the thread fosters rigor as well as relevance for life.

I Hear It!

Model 8: INTEGRATED

The ultimate model of curriculum integration is often thought of as being a fully integrated, cross-disciplinary approach. In this design, teachers from several disciplines map their curriculum content. As each area of the map develops, a complex design unfolds in which commonalities begin to emerge. These commonalities, which often undergird all content, are discovered under the guise of concepts, skills, or attitudes. These "big ideas" are the themes and threads that connect to various disciplines.

Unlike the thematic approach of the webbed model that starts with a theme, here the integrated design starts with content and a theme or thread emerges. The process is inductive in nature, and it often takes some time and skill to unearth the commonalities. However, the process has great integrity because the content and curricular goals dictate the emergent theme. In this case, there is little question that the theme reaches out to different disciplines since it is derived directly from the content. While both the webbed and integrated models may result in thematic instruction, it is important to note that the process for each is quite polar—one is deductive and the other is inductive.

The cross-disciplinary or interdisciplinary approach in this model is, by all means, desirable; however, the sheer number of teachers involved may prohibit extensive use. Remember, however, that model 5, the shared model, replicates the process but with fewer subject areas. If this is the desired

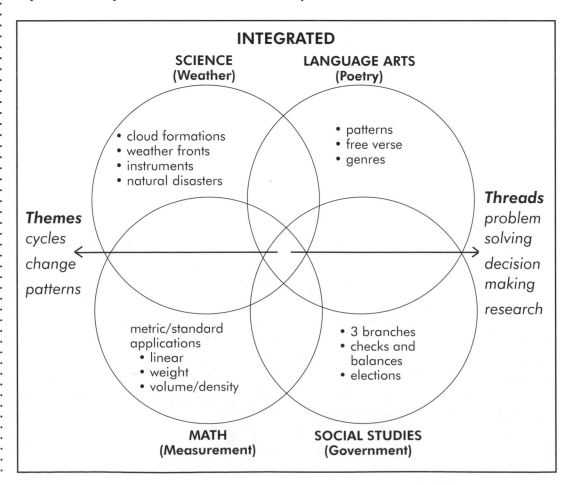

IRI/Skylight Publishing, Inc.

approach to curriculum integration, use it with a few or with many disciplines. Tailor the numbers to work for the situation. Then, once a theme is accepted, explore the theme with higher-order questions, expand them into activities, and select goals and assessments just as in the webbed model.

Model 8 Example

Beginning with content, goals, and objectives, the integrated model inductively reveals commonalities in the shape of themes and threads. For example, consider the following four disciplines and their typical units of study. In science, the focus is on weather. Cloud formations, weather fronts, instruments, and natural disasters are included in this study. In language arts, a unit on poetry exposes students to patterned and unpatterned genres of poetry. Social studies highlights the three branches of government, the system of checks and balances, and elections. And, finally, the units of measure in math concentrates on an in-depth comparison of the metric to the standard system. After some discussion, the actual content focus of each area is illuminated and the themes of *cycles* and *patterns* emerge. Several possible skill threads of problem solving and research emerge as well. All of these bubble up in the center, and these big ideas become candidates for integrative themes or threads in this inductive model.

Model 9: IMMERSED

Stepping beyond the external models of connection making orchestrated primarily by the teacher, model 9 looks at the internal connections learners make. True integration of learning is, after all, the construction of meaning in the mind by connecting new information to past experiences and prior knowledge. If a teacher can help students connect the idea of photosynthesis to other ideas about cycles, their understanding of the concepts—cycles in general and photosynthesis in particular—is enhanced. This "chunking" of information helps form concepts. Thus, in the process of constructing ideas and concepts in their minds, learners must make sense of the myriad stimuli bombarding the brain. They must find ways to take discrete bits of knowledge and facts and build meaningful chunks of information. Once the discrete data are aligned and integrated into meaningful concepts or ideas, the information can be more easily internalized.

Our mission as educators is to help learners make connections in their minds. Understanding that each learner brings different schemata to the learning situation, teachers in the constructivist classroom know that they have no easy task before them. They must devise thoughtful, instructional episodes that require students to use their minds to assimilate the ideas presented. Model 9 provides a framework for individual learners to immerse themselves in areas of personal interest and growth. In fact, the immersed model is designed to parlay the intense interests, prior knowledge, and past experiences of the individual learners into active learning of new material. In turn, the immersed model of integration fosters an ongoing application of

I Hear It!

learnings into novel situations. Model 9 promotes internal connection making through the interest and concept formation of the learners.

Interestingly, teachers must find ways to facilitate that connection making. To do this in a classroom with twenty-five or thirty kids, teachers find certain cognitive and cooperative strategies helpful. Specifically, in classrooms where teachers use cooperative learning and cognitive tools, such as graphic organizers, students' thinking becomes more accessible. For example, as students talk, discuss, dialogue, and articulate their thinking in cooperative interactions, teachers are able to hear the ideas and thoughts of the students. So, too, with the use of graphic organizers. As students present their ideas using Venn diagrams, flow charts, and matrices, teachers become privy to students' ideas. The thinking is visible for all to see and reflect upon.

Model 9 Example

The simplest way to describe an immersed learner is through a specific example that illustrates how an intense interest takes learning into a number of areas. In this example, the learner has an interest in books. In fact, as a youngster she was known as a bookworm. Intrigued by futuristic scenarios,

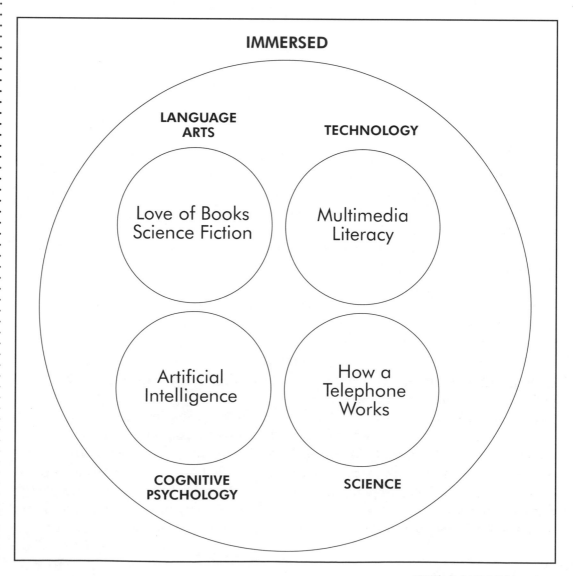

IRI/Skylight Publishing, Inc.

she developed an interest in science fiction novels. This immersed learner then entered the field of library science and was catapulted into the science of technology by breakthroughs in information science. She became computer literate and advanced in her chosen field. Her initial immersion into books and libraries acted as a conduit to other disciplines, directing her in the direction of artificial intelligences. Satellite communications and the functioning of the telephone became part of her curriculum. Then, seeking to find out how the mind works and how to connect certain forms of information in the library setting, she submerged herself in books on cognitive psychology, yet another field rooted in her initial area of interest. On and on it goes—the immersed learner reaches out across multiple disciplines and various content areas.

Model 10: NETWORKED

 A natural extension of the immersed model is model 10, the networked model. As learners pursue their fields of interests, they are pulled into peripheral areas, as if their interests were meandering paths. Learners begin to network as they explore the depth and breadth of their areas of interest. Following is an example of what a networked learner might experience:

> A small child, Maria likes rocks and constantly picks up pretty pebbles and stones. Eventually, she has a small collection. In her intermediate years, she establishes an impressive collection of mounted, labeled, and categorized rocks and minerals. Aware of Maria's intense interest, her teacher suggests she visit a local archeological site that offers week-long summer camp programs for young people. A week at the archeological dig leads this immersed learner into the heart of the networked model. She meets an archeologist, an anthropologist, and a geologist, as well as other nature and history enthusiasts. A true networked model is illustrated as Maria's interests in rocks and minerals lead her into the related areas of geology, archeology, and anthropology.

In the networked model, the learner's horizons expand as other fields are exposed and explored. Interestingly, the multidimensional aspects of the model often help learners zero in on particular areas of interest and expertise. Yet, the paradox remains. The learner's focus narrows as the learner's initial area of interest is broadened.

IRI/Skylight Publishing, Inc.

I Hear It!

Model 10 Example

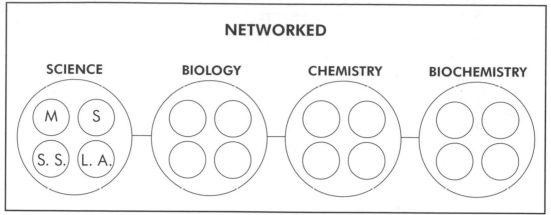

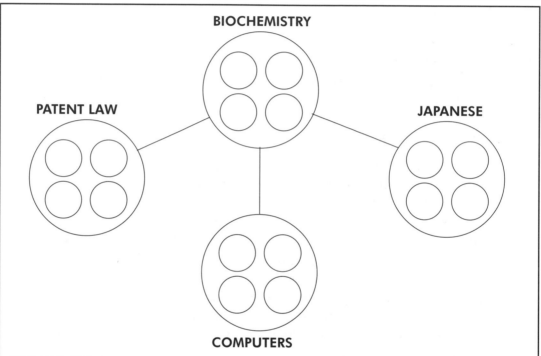

The figure above represents the initial integration process of an immersed learner who starts out liking science. By the time he reaches high school, his interest seems rooted in the specific field of biology; however, as his university work unfolds, this learner incorporates a chemistry minor into his program. Then, he focuses his doctoral studies in the area of biochemistry, with his dissertation work involving the theory of chemical bonding. Proceeding in his career, this immersed learner now enters into a never-ending network of professional contacts and even learns Japanese in order to understand and work with suppliers. Soon, he is involved in computer classes, which enable him to simulate investigations electronically before committing his time, effort, and resources to the lab. Continuing in the web of career opportunities, his expertise in biochemistry becomes so valued that he is offered an all-expense-paid internship in patent law. This learner, immersed in a love for science, is now on a path leading to a promising career as a patent attorney.

IRI/Skylight Publishing, Inc.

FROM THE FIELD
CURRICULUM INTEGRATION

I Hear It!

Although Fogarty's ten models for curriculum integration provide the underpinnings for the ideas developed within this work, there are other voices that provide new, different, and/or complementary directions for authentic integration. Among the proponents of integrated learning are Jacobs, Kovalik, Beane, and Vars. As integrated learning becomes a school focus, teams are encouraged to pursue these resources, as each offers a unique dimension to this complex issue of integrated learning.

Jacobs

Jacobs' *Interdisciplinary Curriculum: Design and Implementation* (1990) lays out a continuum of five options for curriculum integration. Beginning with discipline-based and parallel designs, Jacobs also highlights the multidisciplinary, the interdisciplinary, the integrated day, and the complete program.

Kovalik and Beane

Kovalik (1993) and Beane (1993) incorporate the use of higher-order questions to instill rigor into the thematic focus. While Kovalik stresses essential questions in integrating thematic instruction, Beane stresses the inclusion of student-generated questions. As students brainstorm issues and concerns about a theme, they search for essential questions to drive the thematic unit.

Vars

Vars' classic booklet from the middle school curriculum, *Interdisciplinary Teaching* (1992), focuses on this integrated approach. Vars' work provides a succinct and practical guide for not just the middle school staff, but for all interested in this idea.

Lounsbury

Another voice from the middle school movement is John Lounsbury. An editor of the 1992 edition of *Connecting Curriculum through Interdisciplinary Instruction,* he intertwines the development of interdisciplinary instruction with the idea of teaming. (He says the letters in the word *team* stand for "together everyone achieves more.") In *Doda* (1992), Lounsbury uses an interdisciplinary web to create thematic units such as "Chinese culture," "architecture," and "aviation."

Grady

Grady's approach to interdisciplinary curriculum uses themes as umbrella ideas to connect the disciplines. Her work at the Mid-continent Regional

Educational Laboratory (McREL) in Colorado utilizes the ideas of standards and benchmarks as guides to integrated thematic learning that targets high-level outcomes. Grady uses the ideas of developing "chunks" of integrated curriculum with the driving force of "critical content."

Just Do It!

JUST DO IT!

Study the fan design that represents integrating curricula with multiple intelligences.

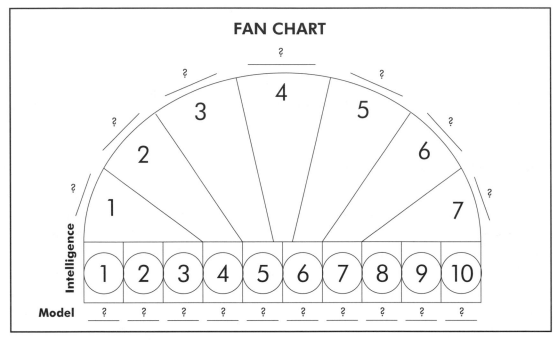

Figure 1.5

Label the seven intelligences and name the ten models of curriculum integration. After the fan chart has been completed, reflect on the pros and cons of combining the two. In the reflection that pursues, try to develop an understanding of the concept of integrating curricula with the multiple intelligences. Using a PMI chart (de Bono, 1976), speculate on how the three major elements of teams, themes, and threads are enhanced or obscured through these brain-compatible models for integrating curricula with multiple intelligences.

TEAMS, THEMES, AND THREADS

P(+) (Plus)	
M(−) (Minus)	
I(?) (Interesting)	

IRI/Skylight Publishing, Inc.

CAN WE TALK?

Using Gardner's seven intelligences, the following seven vignettes profile human potential. Among the examples are a six-year-old entering first grade, a college student majoring in education, and an adult learner. Read the seven scenarios. Understanding that humans each have a "jagged profile" as unique as their fingerprints, identify several "frames of mind" or "kinds of minds" for each vignette. Then, complete the chart in order to identify at least three of the seven intelligences presented in each story.

MULTIPLE INTELLIGENCES VIGNETTES: "FRAMES OF MIND"			
Character	*Frame 1*	*Frame 2*	*Frame 3*
Juanita (6 yrs.)			
Lupe (8 yrs.)			
Alicia (10 yrs.)			
Trevor (12 yrs.)			
Tracy (16 yrs.)			
Heather (20 yrs.)			
Ira (37 yrs.)			

FRAMES OF MIND—GRID TALK

After plotting the information culled from the vignettes, look for insights, reflections, and questions that surface about the multiple intelligences profiles of the human mind and the complexities presented in the scenarios. Notice that there is not *one* intelligence that is highlighted, but a number of different intelligences that interact with one another in each of the cases.

Juanita (6 years old)

Juanita is labeled "gifted" in the first grade. Not only can she read at the age of six, she has also completed the trilogy of *The Hobbit*. Her vast vocabulary is evident in her speech and writing, and she can spell "spaghetti" as easily as "cat." She loves both nonfiction and the classic literature her father intro-

Can We Talk?

duced her to. Juanita's verbal skills are extraordinary and her teachers are challenged to keep her moving forward in this area.

Accompanying Juanita's forte for verbalization is her naturally developed musical intelligence, an intelligence Gardner classifies as language related. Schooled in the Suzuki method from the age of three, Juanita is an accomplished pianist. Her repertoire of classical pieces is impressive, and one senses Juanita's immersion in her performances. In fact, when she plays the piano, she's happy all day. This musical intelligence spills over into her written work. She writes about the piano and illustrates many of her ideas with musical notes.

Paints, crayons, chalk, and pastels are the favorite tools of this image-conscious youngster. Illustrations fill her written works, regardless of their content. Her science paper is filled with progressive sketches of her beans growing in the window, and her morning sentences and stories are accented with detailed drawings that enhance her words. Even Juanita's printing and lettering are elaborated with scrolls, swirls, and squiggles, and decorative engravings border her daily work. Juanita's images are so strong that she converses with an imaginary friend and playmate, Bunny. Yet, when someone else acknowledges the existence of Bunny, Juanita giggles and says, "Oh, he's only pretend."

Lupe (8 years old)

Lupe, a third grader, is proficient at the highly complex game of Dungeons and Dragons. Beginning with the strategic logic of chess, Lupe quickly moved into the voluminous paraphernalia and many layers of the Dungeons and Dragons episodes. Also indicative of his logical reasoning is his fascination with nonfiction. Lupe often plows through encyclopedia entries, moving from the top of a page right on through to the last entry on the page. His ability with numbers is phenomenal. He makes computations in his head and calls out answers that are usually verified by his calculator.

Lupe's amazing sense of logic is complemented by his keenness for visualizing. Even at a young age, he took an unusual interest in his clothes and often selected colorful sweaters to wear with matching socks and coordinated shirts to assemble a look that was pleasing. Connected closely to his skillful and strategic logic in gamesmanship is his ability to visualize. By picturing possible moves of game pieces, he can "see" the outcomes. His mind's eye, in effect, directs his play.

Lupe prefers to be alone with his books, games, and creative toys. He likes to invent electronic devices and gadgets such as burglar alarms and experiment with chemistry sets and the like. Lupe is aware of his own inquisitiveness as well as his likes and dislikes. He appears comfortable with himself and often explains his motivations to his parents. Knowing himself at such a young age, Lupe shows that he has an unusual propensity for self-reflection.

IRI/Skylight Publishing, Inc.

Alicia (10 years old)

If there isn't music or rhythm where Alicia is, she creates her own. At the age of ten, she is taking keyboard lessons and willingly practices an hour every day after school. She loves music in school and has already starred in two musical performances. Alicia and her family live several miles from the nearest large city, which suits her just fine because her family sings and harmonizes all the way there and back.

Alicia's teachers know how much she loves music. When they see her tapping her toe or pencil, they often ask what song she's singing in her head. She is very proud of the perfect score she recently received on a name-the-states test. She gives credit to the song "Fifty Nifty United States," which lists every state alphabetically. Her teacher agrees that the song must have helped, because he noticed that during the test Alicia's head nodded in a steady beat before she wrote each answer.

When she is not creating or practicing her music, Alicia is off and running. Her parents enrolled her in dance at the age of four. She wants to learn to twirl the baton so that she can become the majorette for the band when she is older. Her favorite day at school is "Track and Field Day," where she enters almost every event. She especially enjoys jumping the hurdles. Settling down seems to take longer for Alicia than some of her classmates, and sitting for long periods of time is sheer torture! She loves being teacher's helper and volunteers to help set up centers, perform science experiments, play class-room instruments, and anything else that involves active learning.

When Alicia's pencil isn't tapping out a beat, it is usually drawing or doo-dling. She loves making collages and mobiles and understands best when her teacher uses graphics such as semantic maps and Venn diagrams. Alicia has found that "making pictures in her head," as she calls it, helps her to under-stand and remember what she is learning. She first discovered the powerful effect of visualizing when she had to memorize a piano solo for recital. She had practiced and practiced, but when she sat down on the piano bench, her mind went blank. She couldn't even remember the name of her solo. Alicia looked straight ahead, wishing there were some music in front of her. Sud-denly, she could "see" it, every page of it, in her head, and by the time she finished playing her solo flawlessly, she even remembered its title!

Trevor (12 years old)

Trevor is a seventh grader who is just as proud of his collection of doodles and pictures as he is of his good grades. Many of his drawings are done during school in classes that are lecture-based or "just plain boring," as Trevor puts it. Others are a result of long hours of detailed work on sketches and designs. While his classmates make simple book covers, Trevor creates covers with intricate and complex geometrical designs or cartoon characters.

Trevor is drawn to classrooms that are picture rich. Slides, mobiles, pho-tos, overhead transparencies, and other visuals that reinforce the lesson make all the difference in his motivation and understanding. He is easily frustrated by an overdose of words, whether he's reading, writing, or listening

Can We Talk?

IRI/Skylight Publishing, Inc.

Can We Talk?

to them. His frustration about long writing assignments quickly changes to excitement, however, when he is encouraged to include visuals. He doesn't seem to mind doing required research or writing if he can express himself through his drawings and pictures. Trevor's teacher can identify Trevor's reports without his name because they always have one picture on the front, one on the back, and several throughout.

Trevor spends most of his free time putting together and painting models. Watching him work is truly a "moving" experience, because he begins at a table, then lies on the floor, then stands. He loves math class this year because, as he says, the teacher "keeps us really busy when we learn. We move around to different centers and use manipulatives."

Trevor is definitely not a social butterfly. He couldn't care less about having a wide circle of friends. Instead, he has a small group of close friends and is happy to spend time alone. His mental and physical well-being are very important to him, as is his academic achievement. Trevor tried out several groups and organizations in school before he settled on OM (Odyssey of the Mind). He seems to have found his niche. The sponsor says that when the group is working on a problem, Trevor seems to be able to visualize what is needed to solve it. Then he goes off by himself and makes a prototype, which the group refines and develops.

Tracy (16 years old)

Tracy, a high school junior, is on the pompom squad and in the swing choir. She takes dance lessons and also helps teach dance to young children. Tracy operates video equipment for her parents and sets the VCR when anyone in the family wants to record something. She loves to go on errands, whether for teachers or her parents, especially if it means driving the car.

Tracy seems to have an endless supply of energy when she is interested and motivated. She is always ready to pitch in on special school and classroom projects. At other times, when she has been sitting too long or when the entire class is engaged in quiet reading, she gets fidgety. Only the teachers who understand Tracy know to suggest that she stand up or move.

Music is a large part of Tracy's world. In addition to being on the pompom squad and singing in the swing choir, Tracy plays the piano, sings in the concert choir, and knows every song from the musical her school put on last year. Her current kick in preferred style is country, but that changes fairly regularly. She begs to see every musical production that comes to town, and she can sing or rap to every commercial. If it were up to Tracy, music would be piped into every classroom as a background to learning. It's never off in her bedroom!

Tracy loves people. Almost everything she is a part of involves others. Interacting with people is second nature to Tracy. Not long ago, a boy in one of her classes asked her, "Who are you, anyway? You talk to everybody!" She spends hours on the phone and doesn't feel that a weekend is a success unless she is invited to at least one party. She likes to study with friends and worries when there is conflict. She is the unofficial peacekeeper within each of her groups. Cooperative learning activities and all-group discussions are definitely her cup of tea.

46

Heather (20 years old)

If ever there were a "perfect coed," Heather would be it. A twenty-year-old college student at a large university, she never even seemed to be homesick when she left for her first year of school. Now a sophomore, she has many friends, both male and female, and every one of her teachers knows and likes her. She was recently in charge of a community service event for her sorority. The event needed a high percentage of participation in order for it to be successful and Heather pulled it off. Speaking of sororities, Heather shares her room with three other girls and loves it. She says the only problem they have is in divvying up phone time. Because of her high grades, Heather qualified for several honors classes. She particularly likes English because it involves a lot of group discussion and problem solving. She plans to major in elementary education and special education.

In high school, Heather was on the soccer team and the cheerleading squad. Now, in college, she jogs and walks every day and is actively involved in campus activities. Last year she was a dancer in a charity production on campus. She likes to sit on her bed to study, with her books and papers spread around her; however, she must get up and move regularly. Her class schedule suits her because she has time to move about during the day.

Heather's strengths in reading, writing, and speaking have helped her fit into both educational and social settings easily. She loves to read and comprehends what she is reading without really trying. When speaking, she uses metaphors, humor, and wit, which isn't usually so well developed in a person her age. She is sensitive to language and responds in tears when she interprets someone's remarks as critical, sarcastic, or belittling. People like being around her because she is careful of others' feelings in her conversations.

Ira (37 years old)

Ira is grounded by an unusual insightfulness, which is partially a result of his self-exploration into his own spirituality. This exploration has lead Ira to understand what motivates him. He is clear on what he values and where those values are rooted. This introspective nature spills over into others also, and Ira's intuitive and knowing ways are sought out by trusting family members and friends alike. His advice is valued because it seems to echo an inner voice.

Linked to his introspective nature is his acuity for language. He is a voracious reader and loves to create fictional works of his own. Readers invariably remark about the striking and memorable quality of his written words.

Related to Ira's inward nature is his natural ability to run long distances. In contrast to his love of running marathons is his fondness and skill for team sports. Ira displays above-average athletic abilities from years of playing basketball, baseball, and football. His propensity for athletics is so keen that even now in his adult years he is able to attack new sports such as swimming, skiing, rollerblading, and tennis with the same grace and ease that punctuated his youth.

Interestingly, Ira's gentle way with people is often noted by others. Although he is somewhat shy upon meeting people, he somehow manages to

Can We Talk?

put others at ease. They seem to sense a genuineness that creates the loyalty and friendship of people whom he has encountered throughout his life.

In his school career, Ira formed a lyrical opera club. He also has a fondness for the rhythm of rap music. Both opera and rap music are entwined with the language of lyrics.

Ira's writings are frequently punctuated with images and extended metaphors: "You're like a bicycle, as soon as you stop moving, you fall down." This visualization skill surfaces in another realm. Trained as a chef, Ira has an uncanny sense of presentation. He serves the simplest foods in ways that are pleasing to the eye.

While often overshadowed, another intelligence manifests itself frequently in Ira's exceptional memory for facts, data, and information. At a moment's notice, he can rattle off sports statistics, historical sequences, and film trivia ad infinitum. In addition, the logic he brings to an argument or point of view is more often than not, right on target.

Frames of Mind Key:
Juanita—Verbal/Linguistic, Musical/Rhythmic, Visual/Spatial; Lupe—Logical/Mathematical, Visual/Spatial, Intrapersonal/Introspective; Alicia—Musical/Rhythmic, Bodily/Kinesthetic, Visual/Spatial; Trevor—Visual/Spatial, Bodily/Kinesthetic, Intrapersonal/Introspective; Tracy—Bodily/Kinesthetic, Musical/Rhythmic, Interpersonal/Social; Heather—Interpersonal/Social, Bodily/Kinesthetic, Verbal/Linguistic; Ira—Intrapersonal/Introspective, Verbal/Linguistic, Bodily/Kinesthetic

IRI/Skylight Publishing, Inc.

WHAT'S IN IT FOR ME?

What's in It
for Me?

Input

Reflection on the seven intelligences and the ten models for curriculum integration is the key to the chapter. Think about these two complementary frameworks in this way:

> **Attention to Multiple Intelligences = Diversity of Instructional Strategies**
>
> **Attention to Integration Models = Holistic, Connected Curricula**

Reflection...

Think about and then respond in writing to the following:

I think the instructional unit of mine that taps into the multiple intelligences is . . .

Reflection...

Think about and then respond in writing to the following:

I integrated curricula when I . . .

_____

_____

_____

_____

_____

_____

_____

_____

_____

_____

_____

_____

IRI/Skylight Publishing, Inc.

SHOW ME!

CHAPTER 2

Teams

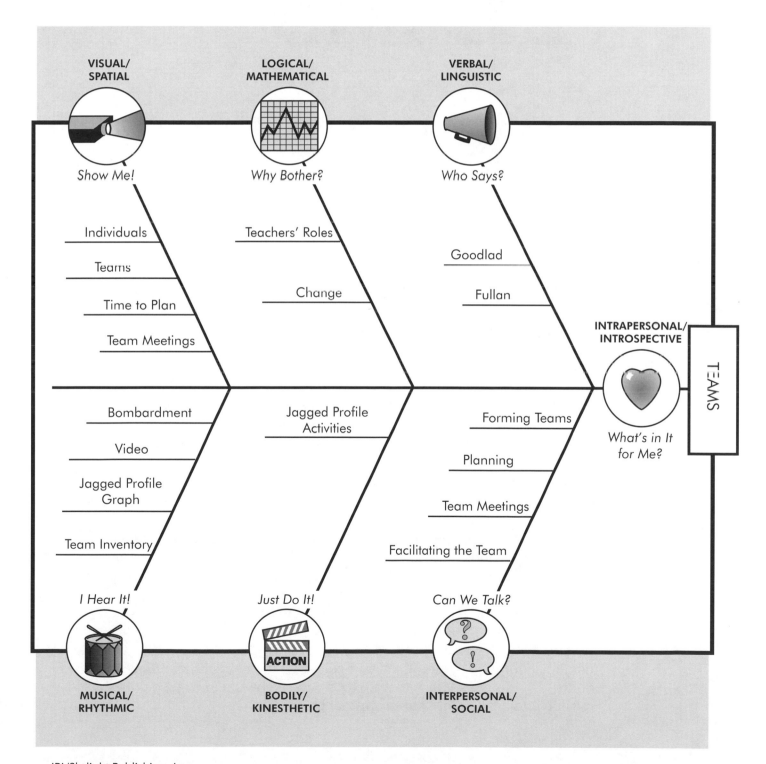

VISUAL/ SPATIAL
Show Me!

Individuals
Teams
Time to Plan
Team Meetings

LOGICAL/ MATHEMATICAL
Why Bother?

Teachers' Roles
Change

VERBAL/ LINGUISTIC
Who Says?

Goodlad
Fullan

INTRAPERSONAL/ INTROSPECTIVE
What's in It for Me?

TEAMS

Bombardment
Video
Jagged Profile Graph
Team Inventory

Jagged Profile Activities

Forming Teams
Planning
Team Meetings
Facilitating the Team

I Hear It!

MUSICAL/ RHYTHMIC

Just Do It!
ACTION

BODILY/ KINESTHETIC

Can We Talk?

INTERPERSONAL/ SOCIAL

IRI/Skylight Publishing, Inc.

CHAPTER

2 TEAMS

Society is always taken by surprise at any new example of common sense.

—*Ralph Waldo Emerson*

Why Bother?

WHY BOTHER?

If integrated learning is becoming a reality in our schools, it is because teachers are talking to each other, thinking and planning, and reflecting and evaluating (Schlechty, 1990; Barth, 1990). Teachers' roles change from total autonomy in their own classrooms to professional collaboration with staff outside of their classrooms. The isolation of teachers is well documented in *School Teacher* (Lortie, 1975), in which teachers are kings of their castles, sovereign rulers of their roosts. One joke about this shift from isolation to collaboration is that teaching is the second most private behavior. Behind closed doors, no one really knows what teachers are doing. In collaborative models, doors have to open and teachers must converse, share, and plan together.

In order to begin a professional dialogue among learned colleagues, a series of questions needs to be answered: Do we want to organize our schools by teacher teams and student clusters, as Goodlad (1984) suggests? If so, how do we create teams, build trust, assemble clusters, and get them started? Once the teams are functioning, how do we keep them working productively and help them overcome obstacles? How do we facilitate team meetings with effective process strategies? How do we help teams resolve conflicts, come to agreements, and celebrate their successes? Only when we address these questions can we experience a change from discipline-based curricula to a more integrated approach.

IRI/Skylight Publishing, Inc.

WHO SAYS?

Teacher teams are essential for meaningful school reform (Goodlad, 1984; Fullan, 1991). Districts and boards across the continent are striving to restructure schools with a learner-centered focus. As a result, an integrated, holistic curriculum design has appeared boldly on many agendas (Virginia, Wisconsin, Kentucky, Michigan, Iowa, British Columbia, and Ontario). Building teacher teams is part of the "chunking" process of school reform. Chunks of time, clusters of kids, and teams of teachers are much like the ad hoc teams that Peters and Waterman (1982) use in their landmark book, *In Search of Excellence*, to describe "skunkworks" set up by innovative employees who make things happen in particular areas. Skunkworks are small teams of people—manageable chunks of an organization—who "just do it."

If we are to integrate curricula in our nation's schools, maybe we too must recognize and honor the skunkworks, the existing teacher collaborators who are already making it happen. Or, perhaps we must decide to create more manageable chunks in an organization (Goodlad, 1984). Consider radically reshuffling the deck by putting the staff into teacher teams and assigning clusters of students to the teams for long-term, innovative approaches to the business of schooling. While this is part of the middle school concept, Goodlad (1984) heralds the idea of student clusters or schools within a school for K–12. The decision to reorganize into "schools within a school" is the first in a series of decisions that will lead to more integrated learning. Teacher teams and student clusters set the stage for professional dialogues that supersede any real integration of curricula. When teachers know that they are responsible for the total learning experience of a group of students, they rally to the cause. Teachers start sharing and planning in creative ways that cross the curricular lines, and they involve the learner in rich learning episodes (Jacobs, 1990; Merenbloom, 1991; Little, 1981). Learners become the focus of team planning and are a common denominator for various subject matter contents and curricular concerns.

I Hear It!

I HEAR IT!

TEAMS RAP

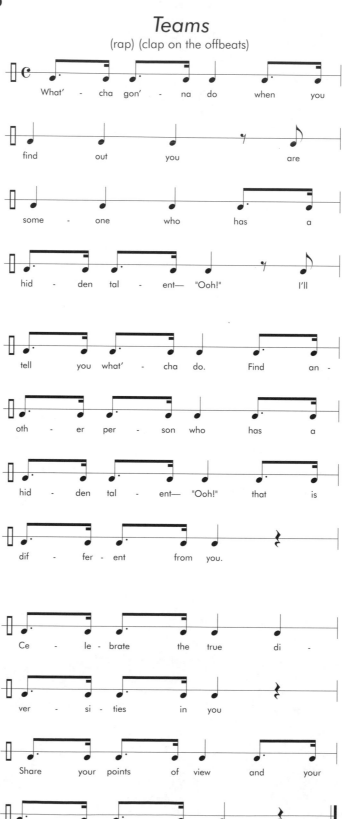

Teams
(rap) (clap on the offbeats)

What' - cha gon' - na do when you
find out you are
some - one who has a
hid - den tal - ent— "Ooh!" I'll
tell you what' - cha do. Find an -
oth - er per - son who has a
hid - den tal - ent— "Ooh!" that is
dif - fer - ent from you.
Ce - le - brate the true di -
ver - si - ties in you
Share your points of view and your
vi - sion will come through!

IRI/Skylight Publishing, Inc.

LIST OF WORDS (BOMBARDMENT)

One easy way to remember the seven intelligences is to group a few together. For example, Gardner groups them together in the following way:

GARDNER'S GROUPINGS

Word Related	Verbal
	Musical
Object Related	Mathematical
	Bodily
	Visual
Personal	Interpersonal
	Intrapersonal

Others group the intelligences according to the letter they begin with:

LETTER MNEMONICS

V	Visual
	Verbal
M	Musical
	Mathematical
I	Interpersonal
	Intrapersonal
and	Bodily

Armstrong (1993) suggests another organizer for listing the "seven kinds of smart." He uses simple language that is easy to remember:

I Hear It!

SEVEN KINDS OF SMART

Word Smart *1*

Music Smart *2*

Logic Smart *3*

Picture Smart *4*

Sports Smart *5*

People Smart *6*

Self Smart *7*

Of course, for a visual learner the seven intelligences can easily be understood through icons. In this case, the projector represents the visual, the graph the logical, the megaphone the verbal, the drum the musical, the clapboard the bodily, the conversation bubbles the interpersonal, and the heart the intrapersonal.

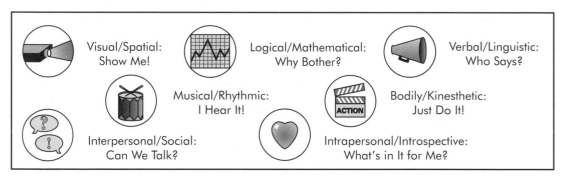

Visual/Spatial: Show Me!

Logical/Mathematical: Why Bother?

Verbal/Linguistic: Who Says?

Musical/Rhythmic: I Hear It!

Bodily/Kinesthetic: Just Do It!

Interpersonal/Social: Can We Talk?

Intrapersonal/Introspective: What's in It for Me?

VIDEO—COMMON MIRACLES

To learn more about the multiple intelligences and to understand the theory based on current brain research, the video *Common Miracles: The New American Revolution in Education* with Peter Jennings (Guilbault & Paul, 1993) is a useful tool. The most informative part of the video is from the beginning to the scene where a young girl says, "It takes time to think." The remainder of the video is naturally of value; however, if time is limited, this part of the video is most important.

JAGGED PROFILE GRAPH

Each intelligence is explored here through immersion. As you proceed, pause to try out the ideas. Experience the reaction to each of the seven intelligences and prepare a "jagged profile" graph as pictured in figure 2.1. To make a graph, simply fold a piece of notebook paper in half and then fold it in half two more times. You now have an accordion fold with eight sections. Label the first seven sections from left to right as indicated in the figure.

IRI/Skylight Publishing, Inc.

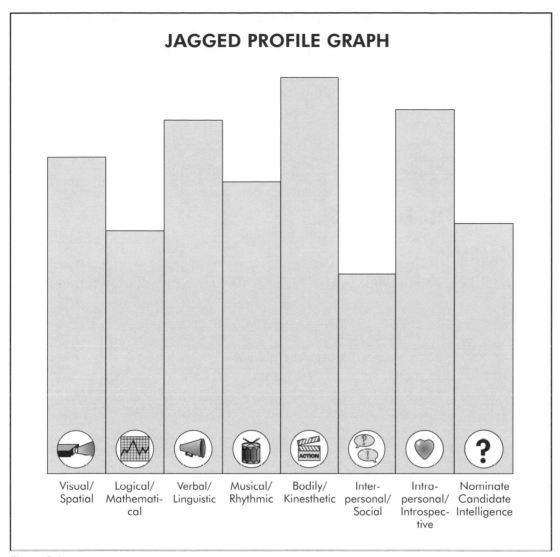

Figure 2.1

Notice that the activities for exploring each intelligence have a number of consistent elements. Each is introduced with an icon, a question or statement, and a random list of associations. There is a lead activity and a follow-up, or optional activity, to try with each intelligence as well as two carefully selected quotes. One quote suggests words uttered by someone strong in that particular intelligence, while the other quote is from someone who is perhaps weak in that intelligence. The exploration of each intelligence closes with a cartoon depicting some aspect of the intelligence.

While some may want to try all the ideas surrounding one intelligence, others may want to dip in and out more quickly. If this is the case, one can simply sample the quotations and select the one most fitting. However, to truly experience the intelligence targeted in each activity, immersion in the activities is recommended. In either case, use your accordion-folded paper to create your own personal "jagged profile" graph. To do this, systematically mark the column at the same point—high, low, or middle—after you have inventoried a particular intelligence. Then, tear off the remaining top section of the column. When you finish all seven, you will have a bar graph represent-

IRI/Skylight Publishing, Inc.

ing your jagged profile. Justify your marking of each intelligence with a brief note, indicating your thoughts or point of reference. For example, one might mark the visual/spatial intelligence high and justify it with the remark "prefer maps, doodle, draw pictures." These notes are for later reference, when the individual profiles are blended into a team inventory.

Just Do It!

JUST DO IT!

JAGGED PROFILE ACTIVITIES

Visual/Spatial

Read the list of associations and mentally add other words that pop into your mind.

VISUAL/SPATIAL

Images	Mind's Eye
Graphics	Imagination
Drawings	Visualization
Sketches	Dreams
Maps	Nightmares
Charts	Films
Doodles	Videos
Pictures	Photographs
Space	Collages
Puzzles	Statues
Designs	Art
Looks	Architecture

Lead Activity—Paired Opposites

Picture "cold" in your mind. What do you see? (An object, a color, the word "cold," etc.?) Now, picture the paired opposite of "cold," which is "hot." What do you see this time? Name other paired opposites and visualize each (e.g., happy/sad, tall/short). Using colored markers, draw what you pictured for "cold" on a plain sheet of paper. Then, draw "hot" on the other side.

Optional Activity—Down Memory Lane

Visualize in your mind's eye the following ideas. To do this, think of the object suggested and try to picture it in your mind. Visualize the following:

IRI/Skylight Publishing, Inc.

Your bedroom door. Does it open into the bedroom or out into the hallway?

The ketchup bottle in your refrigerator. Is it half full, low, or full? What does the top look like?

A zebra. Are the strips horizontal or vertical?

The sides of a yellow pencil. How may sides are there?

The buttonholes on a man's shirt. Are they vertical or horizontal?

A penny. Which way is Lincoln facing?

The Statue of Liberty. Which hand is raised?

Look at the face in figure 2.2. Close your eyes, see if you can remember what you saw. Test yourself. Peek at the figure again. Now, close your eyes and see it in your mind. Turn the face upside down. Look at the new face and remember the first face you saw. Draw the smiley face without looking. Visualize, in your mind's eye, the first face.

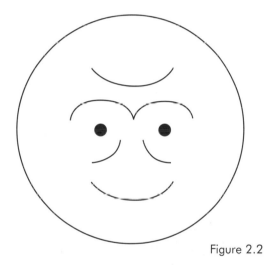

Figure 2.2

Quotes

Read both quotes below. Decide which one you are more likely to agree with.

I shut my eyes in order to see.
　　　　　—Paul Gauguin

Bad artists always admire each other's work.
　　　　　—Oscar Wilde

59

Just Do It!

"I'm imagining a triple scoop of rocky road on a waffle cone..."

Now that you have completed these activities, mark your graph and justify your marking. Tear off the remainder of the bar.

Logical/Mathematical

Read the list of associations and mentally add other words to the list.

LOGICAL/MATHEMATICAL

Reasoning	Proof
Logic	Conclusion
Deductive Thinking	Judgment
Inductive Thinking	Evaluation
Facts	Assessment
Data	Critique
Information	Rebuttal
Spreadsheets	Reliable
Database	Valid
Sequencing	Analyzing
Ranking	Organizing

IRI/Skylight Publishing, Inc.

Just Do It!

Lead Activity—Patterned Accents

"Patterned accents" is a logical sequencing activity. Count from one to twelve, maintaining an equal volume for each number and keeping a steady beat.

Below are several lines of the numbers one through twelve. Practice them one at a time, saying louder any number that has a caret over it. When you can read each line successfully, start at line one and read straight through line to six.

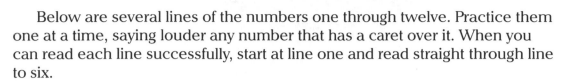

(1) 1̂ 2 3 4̂ 5 6 7̂ 8 9 1̂0 11 12

(2) 1̂ 2 3̂ 4 5̂ 6 7̂ 8 9̂ 10 1̂1 12

(3) 1̂ 2 3 4 5̂ 6 7 8 9̂ 10 11 12

(4) 1̂ 2 3̂ 4̂ 5 6̂ 7 8̂ 9̂ 10 11 1̂2

(5) 1 2̂ 3 4̂ 5 6̂ 7̂ 8 9 1̂0 11 1̂2

(6) 1 2̂ 3̂ 4 5̂ 6 7 8̂ 9 1̂0 1̂1 12

Create patterns using the lines. How many other patterns can you create and perform?

Optional Activity—Horse Cents

Try the following activity as an additional exercise for the logical intelligence:

> A man buys a horse for $50 and sells it for $60. He buys the horse back for $70 and then sells it again for $80. Did he earn or lose money, and how much? Or did he come out even?

Quotes

Read both quotes and decide with which one you identify.

> *Try to know everything of something, and something of everything.*
> —Henry P. Brougham

> *A conclusion is the place where you got tired of thinking.*
> —Martin H. Fischer

IRI/Skylight Publishing, Inc.

Just Do It!

"Of course you think it's easy. You've been at this a lot longer than I have."

After you have completed these activities, mark your graph, justify your marking, and tear off the remainder of the bar.

Verbal/Linguistic

Read the list of associations and mentally add other words.

VERBAL/LINGUISTIC

Bulletins	Newspapers	Foreign Languages
Debates	Plays	Reading
Dialogues	Poems	Papers
Memos	Speeches	Spelling
Essays	E-Mail	Talks
Newsletters	Speaking	Words
Narratives	Grammar	Lyrics
Writing	FAXes	Wordsmiths

Lead Activity—Admiration

Do the "admiration" exercise. Think of someone you admire (a favorite athlete, entertainer, educator, politician, author, musician, etc.) and write three things about that person.

IRI/Skylight Publishing, Inc.

Just Do It!

Optional Activity—Sense of Humor

Try following the cues, step by step, to develop a thoughtful paragraph.

1. Name someone you believe has a good sense of humor (fictional, historical, or personal).
2. Tell two traits of this person that suggest a good sense of humor.
3. Describe someone who does *not* have a good sense of humor.
4. Tell how the two are different.
5. Write a concluding sentence.
6. Title your piece "Sense of Humor."

Now, read over your written comments.

Quotes

Read the quotes below and identify with one or the other.

Language is the light of the mind.
—John Stuart Mill

Language—a form of organized stutter.
—Marshall McLuhan

VERBAL/LINGUISTIC

"I got a thesaurus for my birthday. I was surprised, amazed, astonished, astounded, awed, dumbfounded, shocked, stupefied, staggered, stunned..."

At this point, mark your graph, justify your marking, and tear off the remainder of the bar.

Just Do It!

Musical/Rhythmic

Read the list of associated words and add others that occur to you.

MUSICAL/RHYTHMIC

Adagio	Opera
Timbre	Rhythm and Blues
Baritone	Rap
Pacing	Melody
Commercials	Rhythm
Classical	Tunes
Folk	Rock
Allegro	Soprano
Jazz	Choir
Jingles	Symphony
Madrigals	Tenor
Beat	Chorus
Music	Timing

Lead Activity—My Name Is Joe

Hi, My Name Is Joe

Hi! My name is Joe. I've got-ta
wife and three kids. I work in a but-ton fact-to-
ry. One day my boss came to me and said,
"Joe, are you bus-y?" I said, "No."
He said, "Turn the but-ton with your right hand."

(© 1991 World of Music. Used by permission.)

Learn the "Hi, My Name Is Joe" chant. On the last line, begin turning the imaginary button to the beat of the chant with your right hand. Continue this motion throughout the repeat of the chant, which repeats several times. The last line changes each time, but your actions should be cumulative. At the end of verse two, both hands turning to the beat, and so on.

Verse 2:   "Turn the button with your left hand."
Verse 3:   "Turn the button with your right foot."
Verse 4:   "Turn the button with your left foot."
Verse 5:   "Turn the button with your right elbow."
Verse 6:   "Turn the button with your left elbow."
Verse 7:   "Turn the button with your head." (optional)

IRI/Skylight Publishing, Inc.

Optional Activity—Tune In

Just Do It!

> *Hum,*
> *Sing,*
> *Clap,*
> *Whistle*
> *a tune . . .*

Hum, sing, clap, or whistle a tune that is familiar to you as you tune in to your musical/rhythmic intelligence.

Quotes

Review the quotes and select one that seems appropriate for your intelligence in the musical/rhythmic arena.

> *I produce music as an apple tree produces apples.*
> —*Camille Saint-Saëns*

> *I know only two tunes: one of them is "Yankee Doodle,"*
> *and the other isn't.*
> —*Ulysses S. Grant*

Don't forget to mark the graph as you plot your jagged profile.

Just Do It!

Bodily/Kinesthetic

Read the list of associated words and add words of your own.

BODILY/KINESTHETIC

Act	Jump
Activity	Twist
Action	Twirl
Experiment	Assemble
Try	Disassemble
Do	Form
Perform	Reform
Play	Manipulate
Drama	Touch
Sports	Feel
Throw	Operate
Toss	Immerse
Catch	Participate

Lead Activity—Nursery Rhymes

Make a list of as many nursery rhymes as you can think of in one minute. Select one nursery rhyme to act out. Decide how you will act out your nursery rhyme, practice it, and then try it out.

Optional Activity—Mirror Image!

Find an exercise program shown on television. Now, follow the routine as closely as possible. Pretend you are mirroring the images on the screen.

Quotes

Read both quotes and select the one that suits you.

You can't think and hit at the same time.
—Yogi Berra

I hate all sports as rabidly as a person who likes sports hates common sense.
—H. L. Mencken

IRI/Skylight Publishing, Inc.

Just Do It!

BODILY/KINESTHETIC

" …I can explain!"

Again, remember to continue plotting your jagged profile.

Interpersonal/Social

Read the list of associations and mentally add other words.

INTERPERSONAL/SOCIAL

Interact	Stutter
Communicate	Socialize
Converse	Meet
Share	Greet
Understand	Lead
Empathize	Follow
Sympathize	Gangs
Reach Out	Clubs
Care	Charisma
Talk	Gadabout
Whisper	Crowds
Laugh	Gatherings
Cry	Twosomes

Just Do It!

Lead Activity—The Moral of the Story Is...

Fables are make-believe stories that have a moral at the end. Many of these morals have become clichés (e.g., "Don't count your chickens before they hatch" or "Satisfaction will come to those who please themselves"). List as many clichéd morals as you can. Create a short fable using one of the morals on your list. Now, act out your fable. Use movement, environmental sounds, instruments, etc.

Optional Activity—Doors and Windows

In social situations, do you see yourself as a door or a window? Justify your answer by elaborating on why you made your choice and describe the *kind* of door or window you are in social situations (e.g.,"I'm a revolving door because I'm always on the move in social groupings").

Quotes

Read both quotes and select the one that appeals to you.

> *By thought, I embrace the universal.*
> —Blaise Pascal

> *I hate free from all prejudices. I hate everyone equally.*
> —W. C. Fields

INTERPERSONAL/SOCIAL

"We are the committee to investigate the coincidence between the school lawns being mowed on one day and 'spinach' being served for hot lunch the next day."

Continue to plot your jagged profile.

IRI/Skylight Publishing, Inc.

Intrapersonal/Introspective

Read the list of associations and mentally add words.

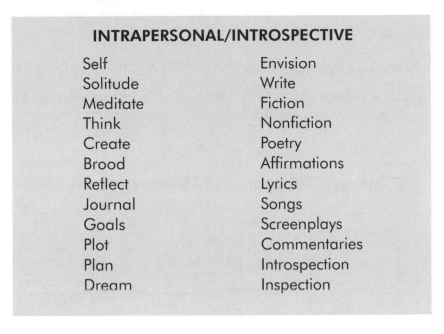

INTRAPERSONAL/INTROSPECTIVE

Self	Envision
Solitude	Write
Meditate	Fiction
Think	Nonfiction
Create	Poetry
Brood	Affirmations
Reflect	Lyrics
Journal	Songs
Goals	Screenplays
Plot	Commentaries
Plan	Introspection
Dream	Inspection

Lead Activity—Self-Portraits

Take a few minutes to complete this portrait activity.

1. Get a large sheet of newsprint or butcher paper and colored markers.

2. Use a pencil to draw a full-body portrait of yourself.

3. Draw a line down the middle of the portrait, separating the drawing of your body into two equal parts. Go over the pencil outline with a different color for each half.

4. Out to the left side of your head write "professional." To the right side your head write "personal."

5. On your left arm, draw something you really like about your professional life. Do the same for your personal life, on the right arm.

6. On your left leg, draw something you wish were different in your professional life. Do the same for your personal life, on the right leg.

7. Think of something you do well that positively affects both your professional and personal life. Then draw that over the middle line, toward the upper torso.

8. Think of something about your character that positively affects you professionally and personally. Draw that over the middle line toward the lower torso.

IRI/Skylight Publishing, Inc.

Just Do It!

9. Think about something you would like to change about yourself professionally but need to give yourself permission to act on. Draw that at the left side of your torso. Do the same for your personal life, and draw it at the right side of your torso. Finish decorating your portrait.

Optional Activity—Linear Psychology

Look at the shapes in figure 2.3. Without reading the descriptions, select one that is most representative of you. Then, read the description to see if you agree or not.

LINEAR PSYCHOLOGY: PREDOMINANT BEHAVIORS

Box
- get things done
- highly organized
- love data and information
- have difficulty making decisions when data is not conclusive
- procrastinate

Triangle
- leader
- focused at all three corners
- highly confident
- outspoken
- love to tell boxes what to do
- assertive and successful

Rectangle
- a box moving toward a triangle
- transitional
- eager to learn
- open minded
- exciting

Circle
- filled with harmony and peace
- love people
- relationship oriented
- creative thinker
- have difficulty with triangles

Squiggly Line
- sex craved
- party animal
- overactive imagination
- short attention span
- enjoy helter-skelter life

Figure 2.3

Quotes

Select the quote that depicts your level of intrapersonal intelligence.

Just Do It!

> *One of the greatest necessities in America is*
> *to discover creative solitude.*
> —*Carl Sandburg*

> *All mirrors are magical mirrors; never can we*
> *see our faces in them.*
> —*Logan Pearsall Smith*

INTRAPERSONAL/INTROSPECTIVE

"Maybe I shouldn't have 'assessed' my schoolyard pranks."

Finish plotting your jagged profile.

Candidate Intelligence

Gardner (1983) often claims that there are at *least* seven intelligences and admits there may be more. For column number eight, you may want to nominate a candidate intelligence and rate yourself on it. Simply identify a plausible intelligence such as "humor," discern an activity that uses it, and then rate yourself and justify the marking. Now, all of the bars on your jagged profile graph should be marked and torn. What kind of profile do you have?

IRI/Skylight Publishing, Inc.

Just Do It!

THE SEVEN INTELLIGENCES

"Well, we always encouraged him to use all his potential."

Can We Talk?

CAN WE TALK?

Review the talents of each member to create an inventory of each team's talents or to form a well-balanced team. To do this, teams should explore both professional credentials and hidden talents. Before jumping into the inventory, however, think about the teams and how teams are best formed or reformed.

FORMING TEAMS: TOP DOWN OR BOTTOM UP?

Who forms the teams? Do teachers have a voice in the makeup of the team or cluster, or are the decisions made from above? Let's look at an option that reflects the best practices currently in effect. For example, one middle school may not choose a top-down or a bottom-up model. Instead, it might take the middle road. Before forming teams, the staff members participate in an informal sociogram in which they list staff members with whom they prefer to work. Armed with that information, the principal organizes the members into base teams of four or six, whose members are diverse in gender, areas of expertise, years of experience, professional credentials, and teaching styles.

IRI/Skylight Publishing, Inc.

In this example, teams, team facilitators, or team coaches are formed for a three-year cycle of student clusters, which span the sixth, seventh, and eighth grades. The teams follow their clusters from grade to grade, thereby guaranteeing long-term relationships for teacher-team building as well as holistic, integrated learning experiences for the students. Sample teams from this scenario might include staff from the following disciplines:

Team X: Math, science, social studies, art, PE, and reading

Team Y: Computers, math, social studies, language arts, science, and gifted

Team Z: Music, science, math, language arts, social studies, and L.D.

The teams are formed with as much diversity as possible in academic areas, since each team is ultimately responsible for the total curriculum content of their student cluster. Teams may, at times, bring in an expert from another team if they need special consultation or content-specific instructional ideas.

BEGINNING THE CONVERSATION: IT'S A START!

The following are three distinct types of interactions. The first is characterized by high-powered, team-building antics that give a jump-start to the groups, which motivates them to trust one another and operate with a common focus. The second type of interaction begins the conversation and then steadies the pace so that the team's diverse talents may be appreciated. Finally, the third type of interaction settles the team into a comfortable cruising speed for the year's plans that lie ahead. All of these interactions are appropriate for the upcoming journey of curriculum integration.

Team Building

Consider holding a staff retreat before the first year of curriculum integration and focus on team-building activities that create a sense of familiarity and trust. Staff members might be involved in several activities with a skilled facilitator to create a bond (Fullan, 1983). They can create team names, symbols, and mottoes or slogans (Scearce, 1993). For example, one team might call themselves "The Wrestling Team" because they are wrestling with ideas. They can make a symbol of a wrestler's arm lock and create a motto such as "We wrestle with ideas." They can also create a song to the tune of "Row, Row, Row Your Boat." While these antics might seem superfluous to some, the humor, collegiality, and sense of "teamness" that result speak for themselves (Williams, 1993).

Team Inventory

A second tier of retreat activities may focus on beginning conversations among team members that reveal their areas of expertise. Now is the time for

Can We Talk?

team inventory. Attention should be given to both formal and informal strengths and interests. For example, while one team member might be valued for her skills as a mathematics teacher, her hobby of flying Piper Cubs might also spark other possibilities. Another teacher on this team might reveal a pen name and authorship of several published pieces, as well as academic expertise in American literature. All talent areas should be mentally logged for future reference. Or, the team might incorporate all its members' talents into a poster.

Shared Vision

This team inventory may be followed by still a third tier of retreat interactions in which the teams work on a shared vision that relates to the school or district mission. For example, one team might use the inductive model of goal setting called "cardstorming" as described by Williams (1993). At this point, the teams might outline significant outcomes implied in their team vision. These outcomes might include a long-term integrated project such as an opera production that highlights learning in languages, arts, and teamwork.

APPRECIATING TEAM TALENT

Use the chart titled "100 Ways to Say You're Great" to finish the poster activity. Hang up the poster and the chart for future team meetings.

IRI/Skylight Publishing, Inc.

100 WAYS TO SAY YOU'RE GREAT!

Great! Good Job! Atta Girl! Swell! Wonderful! What a Great Idea! You Did It! I'm Pleased! Unbelievable! Awesome! A-OK! Nice Job! Way to Go! Thumbs Up! Pat on the Back! Nod! Smile! Grin! Hug! Super! The Best! None Better! I Love It! You're It! Special! Dynamite! That's It! Fine! Super Duper! No Match! You've Got It All! You're the Best! No Competition! Right On! I'm Proud of You! Keep It Up! Never Give Up! Drive On! Smooth! Sweet! Too Much! Absolutely the Best! #1! Front Runner! Second to None! Yea! Yes! Whoa! Whoopie! Top Notch! The Greatest! A Peak Performance! You're a 10! Go For It! Just Do It! Ya! Yep! I Knew It! I Knew You Could Do It! I'm in Your Corner! You're a Winner! Congratulations! It's a Done Deal! Optimal! Extra Sharp! Supercalifragilisticexpialidocious! You're on the Way! Star! Stellar! Spectacular! Beautiful! Precious! It's a Take! Got It! You've Done It! Not Again! I'm Excited! I Never Doubted You! Be There! Hmm! Good! No Finer! Over the Top! That's It! I Knew You Could! You Can! You Will! You Must! Fabulous! You're the Greatest! Be Good! Don't Stop Now! I'm Proud as a Peacock! You're My Man! You've Hit the Target! Bull's Eye! Smooth Sailing! Feeling Good! You're It! The Apple of My Eye! Stupendous! Wow!

IRI/Skylight Publishing, Inc.

Can We Talk?

TEAMING CONFERENCE

An added element to the long-range goal of building teams for curriculum integration is the idea of a team conference. Just as the retreat serves a special purpose in the initiation of teamwork, so too, does the teaming conference. It is a high-profile event that permits massive training opportunities in skills and strategies that all school teams need. It highlights sessions on leadership, cooperative skills, process strategies, trust-building techniques, thematic teaching, thinking skills, learning styles, multiple intelligences, total quality, and the development of significant goals and assessment procedures.

A teaming conference acts much like a leadership academy that offers specific targeted training. Teams attend sessions of their choice to meet their immediate needs and concerns. For example, one team may want to have an in-depth session on thematic instruction, while another team may need training in cooperative learning. The conference allows teams to share the responsibility of deciding what kind of training they need.

A teaming conference also offers opportunities for sharing ideas and networking with other teams. After all, teams learn as much from other teams as they do from facilitators. This conference idea gives working teams assurance that ongoing support and training are there for the long run. It is but one platform for team growth and development. However, to avoid a one-shot, smorgasbord approach to staff development (Joyce and Showers, 1983), additional opportunities for ongoing sharing and training are part of the larger plan.

PLANNING

A school doesn't operate without planning. There must be a plan and there must be support and ownership from all levels. And, there must be time to plan—time that is carved out of an already overloaded schedule. Adapted from a list published by the NEA Center for Innovation, the following page provides food for thought as teams struggle with the challenge of finding time to meet.

IRI/Skylight Publishing, Inc.

FINDING TIME TO PLAN

Purchased Time
Summer writing; vacation

Borrowed Time
Add 15 minutes for 4 days, gain
1 hour on 5th day

New Time
Teacher incentives; motivate
use of own time

Tiered Time
Layer with existing functions
such as lunch and
breakfast meetings

Common Time
Schedule block time for
teacher teams

Found Time
Serendipitous times that
occasionally occur: student
teacher, visiting dignitary,
assembly, snow day

Freed-Up Time
Parent volunteers, senior
citizens, visiting artists, etc.;
create time

Rescheduled Time
Revise calendar year and/or
daily timetable

Better-Used Time
Rethink faculty and department meetings
already on schedule—use memo, notes,
or bulletins when possible

Released Time
Inservice, institute, and
professional development days

From *The Learner-Centered School,* p. 51–52. (Extrapolated
from *Time for Reform* by Purnell and Hill.)

IRI/Skylight Publishing, Inc.

Can We Talk?

"Whoa! … This can't be right!"

By being creative with the possibilities suggested in this list, time can be made available for team meetings and planning—if it is a priority.

Select two of the ideas from the list to think about and let your ideas percolate. Then, write an action plan for finding time to plan using the team's ideas. Be creative and innovative. Make it happen.

TEAM MEETINGS

Teams also need help finding ways to conduct effective meetings. Specifically, they need to learn how to set agendas, make decisions, and how to come to a consensus. Teams must decide what kinds of things can be done before and after a team meeting (or outside the context of a meeting entirely) to keep their time spent together as short and as productive as possible. In addition, teams need to discuss strategies and team-generated guidelines that will govern their work together. For example, a team may agree on the following guidelines:

√ Begin meeting on time
√ Review the agenda
√ Stay on task
√ Come prepared
√ Participate (everyone)
√ End meeting on time

Teams also need specific methods and processes for gathering ideas, analyzing input, reaching agreement, and implementing and evaluating results.

IRI/Skylight Publishing, Inc.

GROUP PROCESS CYCLE FOR TEAM MEETINGS

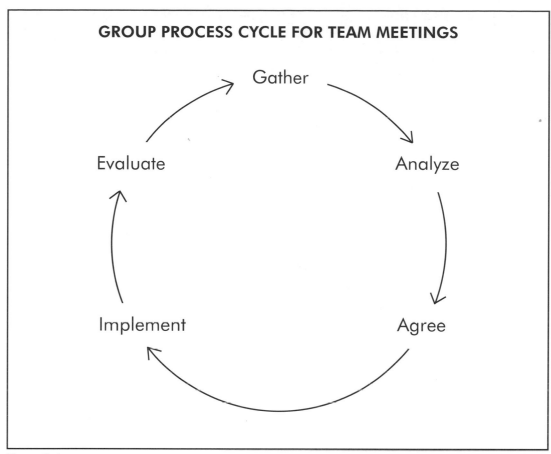

Figure 2.4

To visualize this process in action, imagine a team meeting early in the fall to begin integrating curricula through a thematic instructional unit. The following agenda is set at the beginning of the session.

1. State Purpose: Select a theme.

2. Gather Ideas: Brainstorm lists.

3. Analyze: Categorize lists.

4. Agree: Select one theme (discuss).

5. Implement: Go back to the classroom and have students generate questions about the theme.

6. Evaluate: Identify pluses and minuses of the session.

7. Set Time: Gather student questions and meet again.

The team meeting might go as follows:

> The meeting starts on time. The team selects arbitrary roles for the process: recorder, reporter, observer, encourager, and discussion leader. Team members brainstorm one hundred theme ideas. To reflect on the ideas, they categorize the one hundred themes into topics, concepts, or problems. This discussion of criteria reveals several considerations, including relevancy, availability of resources, and keen interest of both

Can We Talk?

students and teachers. The team agrees to select three candidate themes: a topic theme (e.g., natural disasters), a concept theme (e.g., change), and a problematic theme (e.g., pollution). They also decide that the first step toward implementation is to take the three ideas to the students and have them generate essential questions for each. The team plans to gather evidence leading to a final theme selection by examining the students' questions. After briefly discussing the process they used for the meeting, they set the next meeting for a week later and adjourn at the agreed-upon time.

Of course, each meeting differs. Some are whole-team meetings, while others involve only members who need to meet for particular reasons. Most meetings are scheduled for the designated block of time, but some are arranged by the participants on their own time. Meetings are the backbone of team planning and effective teams know they need to maximize this time together. They organize time for specific member input and for follow-up that can easily be done away from the meeting. Emergency meetings are kept to a minimum, but the team meets as it needs to. Sometimes they meet to resolve conflicts or to poll the groups if disagreements are obvious. However, team members need to remind each other that too many meetings and too much time can take their toll. Remember, there is life after school. Be reasonable. As one teacher says, "Integrating curricula is so entangling, it's like spaghetti; once you get in, you can't get out. Teachers need an out!"

GUIDE ON THE SIDE: FACILITATING THE TEAM

Facilitation involves a number of different tasks, including making schedules, calling meetings, finding resources, resolving conflicts, and orchestrating celebrations. Scheduling may mean formally meeting with the "authorities" and building in a block of time for teams to meet (Merenbloom, 1991; Goodlad, 1984). However, it can also mean simply helping the teams carve out informal chunks of time to begin a conversation about curriculum integration.

Once teams are formed and are functioning at a basic level, they need ongoing skill training in group processes, coaching, and support, and they need genuine feedback on their meetings. This is where the facilitator takes on the role of "guide on the side" (Schlechty, 1990). The facilitator may (1) guide the choice of models for curriculum integration, knowing what level of sophistication various teams have (Fogarty, 1991; Jacobs, 1990); (2) coach the team in process skills (Williams, 1993; Scearce, 1993; Fullan, 1993; Joyce & Showers, 1983), including consensus-seeking strategies and conflict-resolution techniques (Williams, 1993); and (3) provide valid feedback and appropriate support, as indicated by the growth of the teams (Joyce & Showers, 1983).

The site facilitator or team coach is always a visible, accessible resource person to whom teams may look for help. This may be the school principal, staff developer, or teacher on staff who is available for frequent interactions.

IRI/Skylight Publishing, Inc.

Can We Talk?

Teams may also seek expert opinions from outside consultants and specialists, such as guest speakers, relevant materials, networking opportunities, or any number of other viable services. While a facilitator may not be able to fulfill all of these roles, he or she can certainly be there to move the process along, especially if the team is not yet ready to take on certain responsibilities.

Team facilitators are needed as troubleshooters to help out groups when they are "landlocked" over an issue (Williams, 1993). Although teams are taught conflict resolution skills throughout the year in ongoing staff development programs, teams sometimes need an outside mediator (or arbitrator) if they are to continue to function and develop (Williams, 1993; Schmuck & Schmuck, 1988). "Guide on the side" implies that the "sage leaves the stage" (Schlechty, 1990) and takes a parallel position to the team itself. However, there are moments when an unbiased decision is the only way to free up a logjam. The facilitator also ensures that teams celebrate their successes in some way (Scearce, 1993; Johnson, 1979; Schmuck & Schmuck, 1988). This is sometimes overlooked, but it is a crucial element if teams are to develop a long-term involvement.

IRI/Skylight Publishing, Inc.

What's in It
for Me?

WHAT'S IN IT FOR ME?

Reflection...

Think about and then respond in writing to the following:

My thoughts about our team:

Strengths:

Possible Weaknesses:

IRI/Skylight Publishing, Inc.

SHOW ME!

CHAPTER 3

Themes

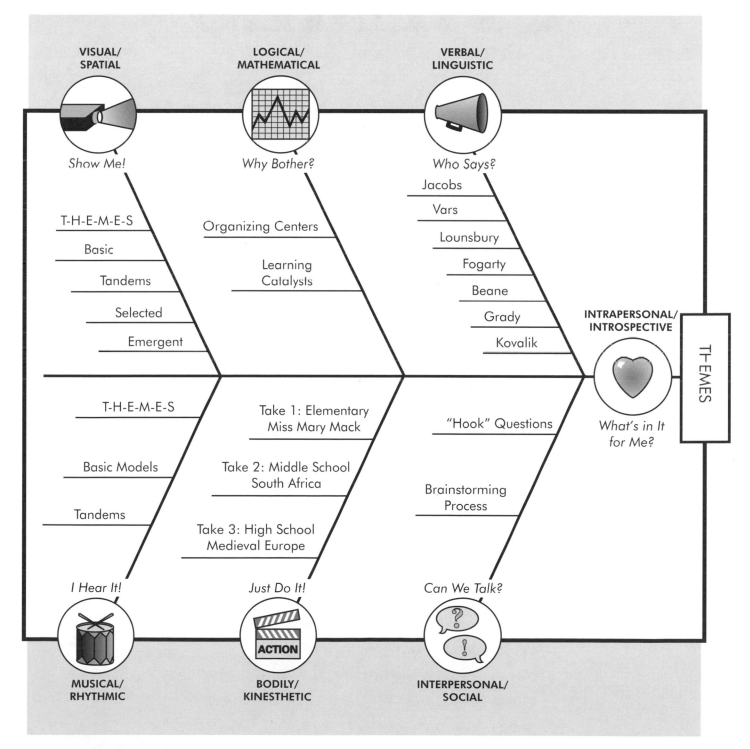

VISUAL/ SPATIAL

Show Me!

T-H-E-M-E-S

Basic

Tandems

Selected

Emergent

T-H-E-M-E-S

Basic Models

Tandems

I Hear It!

MUSICAL/ RHYTHMIC

LOGICAL/ MATHEMATICAL

Why Bother?

Organizing Centers

Learning Catalysts

Take 1: Elementary Miss Mary Mack

Take 2: Middle School South Africa

Take 3: High School Medieval Europe

Just Do It!

BODILY/ KINESTHETIC

VERBAL/ LINGUISTIC

Who Says?

Jacobs

Vars

Lounsbury

Fogarty

Beane

Grady

Kovalik

"Hook" Questions

Brainstorming Process

Can We Talk?

INTERPERSONAL/ SOCIAL

INTRAPERSONAL/ INTROSPECTIVE

What's in It for Me?

TH-EMES

IRI/Skylight Publishing, Inc.

CHAPTER

3

THEMES

The larger the island of knowledge, the longer the shoreline of wonder.

—*Ralph Waldo Emerson*

Why Bother?

WHY BOTHER?

Probably the most common form of curriculum integration is the thematic learning unit. From preschool classrooms to college-level practicums, themes act as umbrellas. They range from primary topics such as *bears*, *dinosaurs*, and *gardens* to themes that appeal to older groups such as *the environment*, *the solar system*, and *the human mind*. Themes provide highly visible **organizers** for curriculum design, making it easy for teachers and teacher teams to coordinate curricular content, and themes **ignite learning** for students. They act as a hook. Let's explore these ideas a bit more.

THEMES AS ORGANIZING CENTERS

The following are organizing centers that can help teachers find appropriate themes:

> **Topics:** dinosaurs, bears, rain forests
>
> **Concepts:** patterns, discoveries, relationships
>
> **Events:** field trips, musicals, spaghetti dinners
>
> **Projects:** inventions, murals, quilts
>
> **Novels:** *To Kill a Mockingbird, The Old Man and the Sea*
>
> **Films:** *Twelve Angry Men, Star Wars, Gettysburg*
>
> **Songs:** "Scarborough Fair," "We Are the World"

IRI/Skylight Publishing, Inc.

Topics

Topics tend to be subject related, concrete, and more narrow than conceptual themes. Topical themes encompass science topics such as the *solar system, mammals,* or *simple machines,* as well as social studies topics that include the *Civil War, Canada,* or *deserts.* Sometimes topics evolve from an art focus, such as *doodles* or *native crafts,* while other topics are rooted in technology, like *computers* or *codes.* Still other topics emerge from literature. Among typical literature-based topics are *heroes, mysteries,* or *travel,* and more generic topics such as *biographies* or *discoveries.*

Concepts

Concepts are broader ideas than topics. They are more abstract and global in nature. The distinguishing element of conceptual themes is their ability to reach out to many disciplines and defy subject matter boundaries.

Patterns is a conceptual theme that branches out to all content. This theme abounds in math (permutations, geometric designs, tessellations and algebraic notations, numeration and repeating decimals, and numeric progressions) and in science (periodic table of elements, branching patterns, waves, sand, cloud patterns, and genetic compositions). The same is true of patterns in history (history repeats itself), economics (cycles of the stock market), and geography (ocean currents, tectonic plates, continental shelves, and coral reefs). Naturally, art is rich with patterns (color, texture, design, and style) as is music (rhythm, beat, melody, and tempo). Patterns in health, patterns in business, patterns in technology. There are even patterns in physical education and sports (the pick-and-roll pattern in basketball or the figure eight in skating). The concept of patterns is rich and fertile and includes all aspects of the school curricula. Candidate themes include *cycles, change, harmony, diversity, relationships, fear, love, hate, prejudice, tolerance, courage,* and *responsibility.* Each has the ability to stretch across several disciplines and areas of subject matter content.

Events

Events act like a magnetic field, organizing all activities toward a forceful center. An event might be simple, such as a *spaghetti dinner* for the class, a *reception for the old-folks home,* or a *guest speaker.* However, it may also be large scale, such as a *fashion show,* a *three-day outdoor educational trip,* a *school play,* a *musical,* or an *eighth grade trip to Washington, D.C.* Regardless of the size or magnitude of the event, it rallies the same energetic effort from all it touches.

Sometimes an event is deliberately planned to be a high-profile culmination of a curriculum project. For example, one school organized a literature-based unit for fiction reading called "Up, Up, and Away!" As students read, they collected tokens for each book. The goal for the school was one thousand books (one thousand tokens). The pay off? If they reached the magic number, the principal would sit all day in a hot air balloon above the school. Needless to say, it created all kinds of reading activity.

Why Bother?

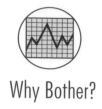

Why Bother?

Projects

Some projects can be almost overwhelming, such as *building a house* or a *solar-powered car*. Some projects are a little more manageable, such as *creating a package* that can protect an uncooked egg dropped from a height of eight feet or *producing a school newspaper* or *yearbook*. Other projects can be simple in comparison, such as *science fair projects, piñatas, jack-o-lanterns,* or *windowsill gardens*. Whatever the project, big or small, long or short, it has the power to elicit every student's focused energy.

Novels and Films

There is nothing as compelling to a diverse audience as a good novel or first-rate film. The story line, setting, characters, plot, subplots, major and minor themes, and, of course, climax all provide fertile ground for exploring ideas. Imagine the exciting curriculum ideas that could be inspired by *Moby Dick, Old Yeller, The Phantom Tollbooth, Twelve Angry Men,* or *Journey to the Center of the Earth*. The possibilities for meaningful thematic units are limitless.

Songs

Songs, along with drama, sculpture, dance, and other art forms, are the memory of a culture: Its victories and tragedies, its heroes and villains, its hopes and despair are all common themes of songs handed down from generation to generation within every culture. Songs' stories, settings, characters, and plots are no less exciting than those of novels or films. They are a perfect centerpiece for the integrated curriculum, both for what they are and what they can do as a bridge to other learning.

Songs such as "Shenandoah," "I've Been Working on the Railroad," and "Home on the Range" each tell a story about a time, a place, a group of people in the history of the United States. "Follow the Drinking Gourd" captures students' interest and imagination as they learn that it is an African-American song about slavery and the Underground Railroad. Consider the lessons that could develop from songs such as "Abraham, Martin, and John," "Fifty Nifty United States," "It's a Small World," "Free at Last," "Lift Ev'ry Voice and Sing," "I'm in the Army Now," "One Tin Soldier," "Waltzing Matilda," "So Long, Frank Lloyd Wright," and many, many more. These lessons capture the interest and imagination of students, motivating them to learn about and understand the world, both past and present. Lessons such as these offer yet another dimension to integrating the curriculum through multiple intelligences.

THEMES AS CATALYSTS

Students are another primary reason for using themes in the K–12 or college classroom. Themes ignite learning for students and provide highly visible, all-

IRI/Skylight Publishing, Inc.

encompassing umbrellas for curriculum and instruction. As students immerse themselves in a thematic unit, they realize how all of the activities connect under the umbrella of the theme. Themes as catalysts have kid appeal and are relevant, purposeful, meaningful, holistic, and contextual.

Kid Appeal

Keeping in mind the fact that themes ignite student interest, it becomes paramount that theme selections have "kid appeal." In fact, why not involve the students themselves in the selection of themes? Let them brainstorm lists of ideas to provide genuine impact in the selection process. Imagine the excitement the *atomic bomb* as a theme would generate. This topic has much more kid appeal than the concept of *nuclear energy*. Although topical themes may be selected because they are compatible to students' interests, the bigger ideas can remain the curricular focus for planning.

Relevant, Purposeful, and Meaningful

Themes not only provide the motivation or hook for students, they also make learning more relevant. Once students see the connection between things they're learning in class and things they're using in life, learning at school becomes purposeful and meaningful. Thus, by connecting lessons to situations outside of the classroom, students realize the relevance of academic tasks. They understand that calculating an area is not a mere exercise, but rather an equation that can help them determine such things as how much paint to buy to repaint their bedrooms.

Holistic and Contextual

Combining integrated learning with applied learning is similar to marrying academia to vocational education, tech prep to academic subjects, or the practical to the theoretical. It is exciting and relevant for kids. It also provides a holistic model of instruction and curriculum that fosters learning in context. Students can learn one-to-one correspondence by passing out straws. They can learn about the Pythagorean theorem as it applies to cutting rafters for a house. And, they can learn about writing by publishing a school paper. Through application, academic content is easily integrated with situations outside of the classroom. Learning is automatically and meaningfully transferred from learning the text to learning the *context*. Not only is contextual learning more helpful for students, it's also an efficient model for teachers. By embedding learning in relevant, holistic contexts, skill building is enhanced through applied problem solving. In summary, contextual learning, supported by thematic teaching, provides an efficient and often time-saving model for curriculum design.

Who Says?

WHO SAYS?

Voices from the field that promote thematic teaching span the United States. There is Jacobs in New York, Lounsbury in Florida, Beane and Fogarty in Illinois, Vars in Ohio, Grady in Colorado, and Kovalik in Washington. While each presents an experienced voice with practical and easy-to-implement ideas, each also has his or her own tenor.

JACOBS

Jacobs' design options for interdisciplinary curriculum feature six ideas: discipline-based, parallel, multidisciplinary, interdisciplinary, integrated day, and complete programs. Several of the options support the use of themes as organizing centers. Jacobs' *Interdisciplinary Curriculum: Design and Implementation* (1990) provides a collection of essays delineating the process of developing thematic units. Perkin's article "Selecting Fertile Themes for Integrated Learning" is included in this especially rich anthology. Perkins' examination of two themes (transportation and argument and evidence) reveals the keys to fertile themes.

VARS

Vars' *Interdisciplinary Teaching: Why and How* (1993) is a classic middle school book. Originally published as a monograph in 1987, Vars second edition provides an expanded resource. Specifically, thematic units are targeted through the core curriculum and feed off student issues and concerns. Curriculum themes, according to Vars, incorporate content, skills, and concepts as well as personal and social concerns. The result is often a problem-centered thematic unit such as *maturing, production and consumption,* or *policy making.*

LOUNSBURY

Another voice from the middle school movement is John Lounsbury. An editor of the 1992 edition of *Connecting Curriculum through Interdisciplinary Instruction,* he intertwines the development of interdisciplinary instruction with the idea of teaming. (He says the letters in the word *team* stand for "together everyone achieves more.") In *Doda* (1992), Lounsbury uses an interdisciplinary web to create thematic units such as "Chinese culture," "architecture," and "aviation."

FOGARTY

Fogarty's ten views of integrated curricula also provide options or models similar to Jacobs'. Fogarty's (1991) models include ten ideas: fragmented, connected, nested, sequenced, shared, webbed, integrated, immersed, and networked. To read more about Fogarty's work, refer to chapter one.

IRI/Skylight Publishing, Inc.

BEANE

Beane (1993), yet another familiar voice from the middle schools, is a long-time advocate of curriculum integration. His belief that themes, questions, and activities should be generated by the students themselves puts an authentic learner-centered focus on thematic instruction. Stressing the idea of students generating essential questions to frame a theme is a major component of Beane's work.

GRADY

Grady's approach to interdisciplinary curriculum uses themes as umbrella ideas to connect the disciplines. Her work at the Mid-continent Regional Educational Laboratory (McREL) in Colorado utilizes the ideas of standards and benchmarks as guides to integrated thematic learning that targets key goals. Grady uses the ideas of developing "chunks" of integrated curriculum with the driving force of "critical content."

KOVALIK

ITI: The Model: Integrated Thematic Instruction is a major work by Kovalik (1993). Based on brain research, teaching strategies, and curriculum development, Kovalik's model uses a yearlong theme as the "heart and soul" of the classroom. The yearlong theme is a big idea with a "kid-grabbing twist" (Kovalik & Olsen, 1993). Using theme titles such as "What Makes It Tick?" or "You Can't Fool Mother Nature," Kovalik illustrates ways to evaluate a theme, identify key points, and find multiple resources. Skills and concepts are targets for thematic instruction.

I HEAR IT!

Themes
(to the tune of M-O-T-H-E-R)

T is for the themes we think of daily.

H is for the honing of our lists.

E means we extrapolate criteria.

M means we manipulate the theme.

E expands activities and learning.

S is for selecting key goals.

Put them all together, they spell THEMES.

They open up the world for me.

I Hear It!

IRI/Skylight Publishing, Inc.

I Hear It!

T-H-E-M-E-S

Hundreds of Themes

Dinosaurs; The Future; Man vs. Nature; Whales; Myths; Robots; Time After Time; The Dawn of Civilization; Inventions; Friendship; Bears; Environment; Up, Up, and Away; Old Favorites; America the Beautiful; Our Canadian Neighbors; Across the Sea; Simple Machines; Shoes; Win or Lose?; Animals; Long Ago; Change; Patterns; Survival; Why Man Creates; Biases; Media; Biography; The Renaissance; How Dry Is the Desert?; The Ice Age; The Solar System; Water; Friend or Foe?; Cultural Diversity; Sound; Light; Insects; Cemetery Study; The Mind; Birds; Under the Sea; Around the World; Pyramids; War; War and Peace; Native Americans; The Circus; Hats; Shapes; Statistics; The Shrinking Globe; Conflicts; Transportation; Argument and Evidence; Beginnings; Perseverance; Family Treasures; Pilots and Passengers; Connections; When Time Began; 2020; Profiles in Courage; Fear; Trade; Exploration; Discovery; Love; Citizenship; Food, Clothing, and Shelter; The Community; Zoos; Nature's Fury; Dreams and Nightmares; Skyscrapers; Volcanoes; Earthquakes and Other Natural Disasters; The Weather; Heroes; Male vs. Female; Creatures; Craters; Submarines; Fish; Seashells; Colors; Rainbows; Reptiles; Technology; Television: Good or Evil?; Tragedy; Romance; Space; Spiders; Pioneers; Halloween; Holidays; The Wild West; Careers; Wisdom; Courage; Authority; Nutrition; Wellness and Fitness; Global Economy; Latin America; Natural Wonders; Death and Dying; Pets; Decisions; Mysteries; Magic; and Mammals.

Themes are fun, inviting, and doable, and they make learning exciting for students and for teachers. Themes also organize content and create manageable chunks of connected ideas. But, there are many questions about how we can make these themes work for us. How do we infuse integrity into our thematic units? How do we manipulate themes for real accountability? How do we align themes with our valued goals? How do we think about themes before plunging in? The answer to these questions is as simple as T-H-E-M-E-S.

IRI/Skylight Publishing, Inc.

THEMES

Think of themes	Generate; brainstorm 20–30 ideas; gather and collect in an ongoing manner.
Hone the list	Sort the themes into 3 categories: concepts, topics, problems; sift and select 3 (one from each category).
Extrapolate the criteria	Reflect and project reasons why a theme is valued; develop criteria to use it again.
Manipulate the theme	Reflect on possible questions: pose a question as the thematic focus; refine into a higher-order question with a "how" or "why."
Expand into activities	Generate viable activities; list relevant learning episodes; include activities for all the multiple intelligences and the various curriculum areas.
Select goals and assessments	Delineate aims and objectives; align activities to the valued goals; determine assessment strategies.

Figure 3.1

IRI/Skylight Publishing, Inc.

Think about themes by generating a lengthy list. As a faculty or team, brainstorm an initial list of twenty, thirty, or fifty ideas. Post the list on large paper in the teacher's lounge. Commit to doubling the list by the end of the week. Then start "stealing" ideas from everywhere. Gather ideas from books, journals, neighboring districts, other teachers, old units, and textbook concepts. Collect as many different ideas as possible. Think of the various disciplines and themes in your studies. Create a list with the students, and assign another list for homework to get the parents involved. Do whatever it takes to compile a longer list of "candidate" themes than the one listed earlier. Challenge yourselves: try to add to the list without duplicating any words already listed.

Hone the list. Just because you've brainstormed, collected, gathered, and listed one hundred themes does not mean that all of them are great (at least for your purposes). Sort out the ideas by dividing them into a list of three distinct sections. Label the sections as topics, concepts, and problems. Discuss or define what a *concept* is, which things are *topics*, and where the *problems* are. Or, sort out the ideas on the list and see what defining elements occur in the sorting process. Then, categorize the ideas as topics, concepts, or problems. With your colleagues and/or teammates, select three "champion" themes—one from each of the categories (e.g., a topical theme—*dinosaurs*; a conceptual theme—*systems*; and a problematic theme—*How Does Man Survive?*) Display the champion themes for all to see. Use whatever method necessary to reach an agreement on the three. Then, take a moment to reflect on how your team finally reached its decision.

Extrapolate criteria. Think about tug-of-war discussions that have resulted in champion themes. Recall the reasons, rationale, and persuasive arguments that convinced everyone a particular theme had merit or was better than another. Justify your choices. Know why one theme stands out above the rest. Dialogue with team members and discover their reasons for choosing certain themes. List the emergent criteria on large paper and post them next to the champion themes. Be clear about the criteria for selecting themes, because they are revisited each time a new theme is needed. Then, select one of the three themes to work with further.

Manipulate the theme. Massage the theme. Reflect on possible questions that naturally occur. What do you want to know? What are the essential questions—the questions that pique interest and invite investigation? Capture the questions of the children. Pose questions of value and notice how the thematic focus is transformed and raised to higher levels. Search for questions that provoke the mind and incite emotion. Think about how, why, and where. Transpose the theme into a question that evokes curiosity and intrigue—a question that drives the theme and brings all on board. Don't hurry through this part. As Francis Bacon once said, "A prudent question is one-half of wisdom." Process the theme by postulating all kinds of questions; refine them until a final question takes shape.

Expand into activities. Hook into a theme (and a question) and produce activities that are triggered by this theme. "Web" the theme out to the various curricular areas: math, science, social studies, language arts, art, music, health, PE, and technology (Fogarty, 1991). Think of more activities for integrated learning than can be done. Include activities that involve the multiple intelligences. Create a fun and exciting atmosphere as you recall, borrow, and invent appropriate and appealing activities for students. And, of course, include student choices and interests in an expanded and elaborated web.

Select key goals and assessments. Armed with the valued learner goals that comprise aims and objectives, take time to focus on the traditional curricular areas in the web—math, science, social studies, etc.—and examine each of the activities for alignment with expected goals. Use this step to "selectively abandon" and "judiciously include" activities. Once you have an organizing theme or question, you can literally generate hundreds of activities. The task now is to refine the thematic unit with only those activities that truly target significant goals. Each activity, in whatever subject area, needs to be rich enough to provide fertile ground for thoughtful learning and mindful production. Once the activities are refined and aligned, an assessment is easily made with authentic measures such as portfolios and performances.

IRI/Skylight Publishing, Inc.

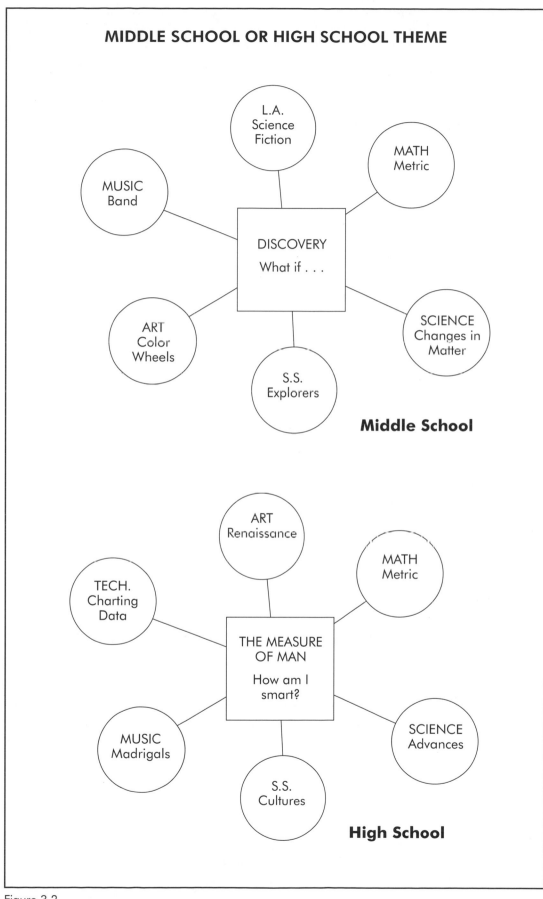

MIDDLE SCHOOL OR HIGH SCHOOL THEME

Middle School

- L.A. Science Fiction
- MATH Metric
- MUSIC Band
- DISCOVERY What if . . .
- ART Color Wheels
- S.S. Explorers
- SCIENCE Changes in Matter

High School

- ART Renaissance
- MATH Metric
- TECH. Charting Data
- THE MEASURE OF MAN — How am I smart?
- MUSIC Madrigals
- S.S. Cultures
- SCIENCE Advances

Figure 3.2

IRI/Skylight Publishing, Inc.

I Hear It!

More Themes

Sports; You; Skeletons; Music, Ballet, and Drama; Games Around the World; Antarctica; Fair-Weather Friends; Hobbies and Collections; Collectibles; Superheroes; Presidents; Choices; Honesty; Farms; Industrialization; The Paper Chase; Science Fiction; Family Living; The Computer Age; The Arts; Islands; The Written Word; News; The City; Opera; Famous Battles; Newspapers; Headline News; Superstitions; Legends; Texas; Mexico; Egypt; Favorite Places; Oregon Trail; Cluster; The Moon; Hemingway; The American Dream; The Young and the Old; Bridges; Currency; Language; A Picture Is Worth a Thousand Words; Caring; Animals at Work; Critics' Choices; Film; Human Connections; Archeology; Humor; Drugs: Beneficial or Harmful; Addiction; Plants; Senses; Magnets; Both Sides of the Issue; The Research Search; Famous People; Fame or Fortune?; Competition; Cooperation; Leadership; Tongue Twisters; Fables; Tall-Tales; Riddles; Controversy; Gardens; Witches, Ghosts, and Goblins; A Sign of the Times; Flowers; Celebrations of Life; Anecdotes; Afterthoughts; The Universe; Truth; Moral Dilemmas; Ethics; Pigs; Rain Forests; Evolution; Night and Day; Why Do People Develop Habits?; There's No Place Like Home; The Ugly American; Tourists; The Sky Above; Pollution; Handicaps; Fantasy; The Middle East; Faces; Clowns; Masks; Faulkner; The American Novelist; Leverage; Debate; Cartoons; The Changing Tide; Megatrends; Warm Fuzzies; Creative Features; Frogs, Toads, and Princesses; Fairy Tales; The World of Work; Ways of Knowing; Man Through Art; Happiness; Picture This; Every Ending Is a Beginning; Short Cuts; Fashion; Prey; Talk, Tales, and Tidbits; Seasons; Wheels; and Whatchamacallits!

BASIC MODELS

Selected and Emergent Themes

Themes may be deductively developed with a selected theme, or they may be inductively developed with an emergent theme. The critical difference between a selected theme and an emergent theme is in the initial process of finding it. The *selected theme* is chosen from a bank of theme ideas, while the *emergent theme* evolves from conversations about various content units represented by different disciplines. To illustrate the differences in process, we will look at a few vignettes that exemplify how themes, both selected and emergent, come about.

Selected Theme

Deductive Process/Webbed to Subject Matter: *How Courage Is Like the Rain: A Philosophy Study for the Senior Cluster*

IRI/Skylight Publishing, Inc.

ILLUSTRATED THEMES

Think of themes

Friends
The World
Animals
Harmony
The Arts

Argument and
   Evidence
Inventions
Cultures
Neighbors

People, Places,
   Things
Old Favorites
Time After Time

Hone the list

TOPICS	CONCEPTS	PROBLEMS
Dinosaurs	Patterns	Hostages
Bears	Cycles	Health Care
Environment	Conflict	School
Plants	Change	Funding

Extrapolate the criteria

CRITERIA FOR A FERTILE THEME

1. Relevant to students
2. Many resources available
3. Broad enough for all curriculum areas
4. Intrigues teachers and students

Manipulate the theme

Environment—Feast or Famine?
Citizenship—How Am I a Good Citizen?
Creativity—Why Does Man Create?
The American Dream—Fantasy or Reality?
Desert—How Dry Is the Desert?

Expand into activities

Select goals and assessments

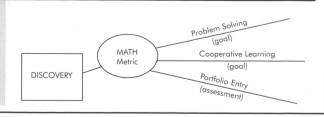

Figure 3.3

IRI/Skylight Publishing, Inc.

I Hear It!

Courage? What does it mean? What comes to mind? Hero. Sudden. Unexpected. Save a child. Train track rescue. *Profiles in Courage.* Inner self. Recognition. War hero. Medals. Purple Heart. Strength. Cowardice. *Catch-22.* Moral courage lion. *The Wizard of Oz.* Stand up! Stand out! Famous. High dive. Risk. Bungee jump. Untested. Undetected. Under pressure. Surprise, like a summer shower. Rain.

The brainstorm flows through its natural cycle: a burst of ideas, a lull, reignited associations, silliness, novelty, and a final winding down. The teacher pounces on the final word, "rain," and asks, "How is courage like rain?" Heads together, pens poised, the small groups discuss possible comparisons and one team writes on a large piece of poster paper. As the student writes, he thinks out loud: "Courage is like rain because both . . . hmm . . . both can happen suddenly; they can come upon you unexpectedly and . . . Wait, I've got it . . . they often result in a change for you. If you get caught in the rain and get wet, you change your clothes. If you act in a courageous way it may change how you feel about yourself."

So goes the latest scenario in the senior cluster. Staffed with a teacher team that consists of a guest artist, a visiting attorney, a guidance counselor, and a literature teacher, this philosophy study targets students from the senior cluster levels: incoming freshmen through graduating seniors. Designed around the discipline of philosophy, interdisciplinary approaches to subject matter expose students to content through dilemma and to the paradox and ambiguity of universally compelling philosophical issues: truth, justice, equality, authority, wisdom, courage, life, death, and love. Each is selected as a theme to study.

Themes can be explored in myriad domains. For example, in an experiment with authority, students can read about historically renowned figures of authority such as Hitler, Stalin, and McCarthy. They can compare these historical figures with authority figures in their own lives. In turn, literature can become a springboard for historical simulations, real-life role plays, personal journals, and depictions of authority through visual and performing arts. Following is an example of how a theme is explored by a teacher and students.

LIT. TEACHER: Courage is like rain . . . isn't that a fresh idea? Let's explore some of the ideas a bit further. For example, what do you mean when you say courage is unexpected? Give us a real illustration.

STUDENT: Well, when you step on the high dive and you look down, you're really afraid of the fall. Yet, you prepare, just

IRI/Skylight Publishing, Inc.

I Hear It!

as you've done in practice many times before; you proceed through your rituals of standing at the invisibly marked spot, stepping deliberately through the approach, focusing yourself mentally, and performing the precision dive with skill and grace. That's courage, if you ask me.

LIT. TEACHER: I agree. That's certainly a grand display of physical courage. What else?

STUDENT: Standing up for what you believe in, in front of your friends, when you know you're in the minority. I think that shows courage.

LIT. TEACHER: Tell us more about that.

STUDENT: Maybe you like classical music because you've had to learn it and play it in orchestra, but your friends want to listen to hard rock or rap. Even though it's a simple example, we can really pressure each other to the point that it does take courage to stick to your own ideas.

LIT. TEACHER: That's so true, isn't it? How about one more example of courage?

STUDENT: Cowards can be courageous. My grandpa says that a lot of guys in the war ended up as decorated heroes, but they weren't all that heroic in the beginning. Once their plane was shot down or they found themselves in prison camp, their courage got them through.

STUDENT: Yeah! It's like when someone rescues a kid from a fire or rushes into the street and throws a child from the path of a car—the courage just happens suddenly, unexpectedly. And someone who seems more like a coward in other situations proves himself a hero with courage.

Various subjects are integrated in this example. The fertile themes of courage, trust, and love are transformed into an investigative question and then easily "webbed" out to various disciplines for appropriate instructional activities. In turn, they are aligned with key goals (Fogarty, 1991) (see fig. 3.4).

To evaluate the study of courage, students are required to respond to certain questions for their portfolio or performance assessment. Presentations are as varied as their presenters. Creativity flourishes and debate is lively as students grapple with something unknown to them. After all, who really *knows* how common courage is?

IRI/Skylight Publishing, Inc.

COURAGE

Assignment:

Please prepare an answer to the essential question "How Common Is Courage?" You may use one or any combination of the following expressive forms:

- Art
- Music
- Drama
- Writing
- Speaking
- Other

You may work by yourself or in collaboration with one or two others.

Presentations begin next week. You will have 25 minutes to present and 5 minutes for feedback. Please sign up for a time.

IRI/Skylight Publishing, Inc.

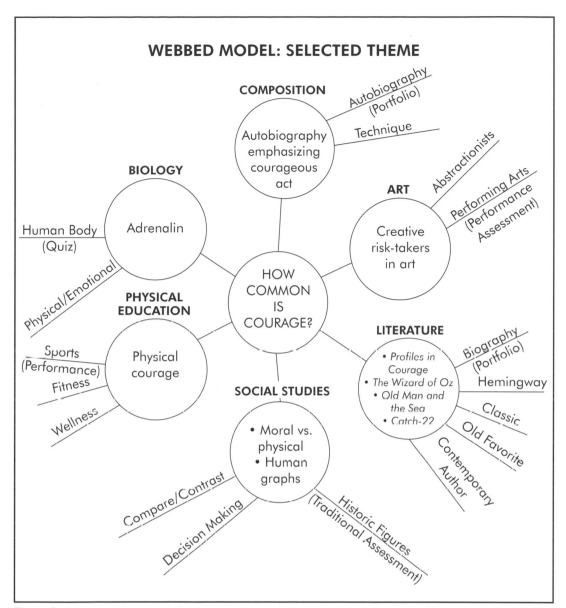

WEBBED MODEL: SELECTED THEME

Figure 3.4

Emergent Theme

Inductive Process/Start with Subject Matter Content: *Somebodies Who Make the Rainbow Real: Organic Learning in the Primary Cluster*

Strips of orange construction paper in a coffee can; a large black marker; a round reading table with several little chairs; shoebox "fish" games about the room; a line of students around the teacher. Words are rehearsed and called out to classmates as they approach the front of the line: Butterfly, the Refrigerator, Raggedy Ann and Andy, Piano, Garden, Girl, Prickly, Whale, and Dumbo. These words are what Sylvia Ashton-Warner (1963) calls the organic words that make up the "key vocabulary" of each learning child. In a language experience approach to reading, or whole language in the primary classroom, this New Zealander models a fully integrated learning environment that can be anchored by just one word as illustrated in the following poems:

IRI/Skylight Publishing, Inc.

I Hear It!

Deep Inside of Me

I start with just one word
One special word
Way down deep inside of me.
A word I love
A word I fear
One I can see and touch and hear.
I start with just one word
One special word
Way down deep
Inside of me.

Piano

Can Do! Can Do!

Now, I tell just what
That one word can do.
Popcorn pops,
Jackrabbit hops,
Grass grew.
Birdie flew.
Bluebird sings,
But, bee stings.
Now, I can tell just what
That one word can do.

bumble bee

Add-a-Few

Hmm, now that I have two
Why not
Add a few?
I tell its color
And shape
And size.
I create a picture of words
For your eyes.
Hmm, now that I have two
Why not add a few?

...NOW, I TELL
JUST WHAT
THAT
ONE WORD
CAN
DO! ...

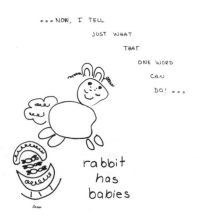

rabbit has babies

IRI/Skylight Publishing, Inc.

A Story to Tell

By gosh, by golly, by gee

I've got a whole story

Way down deep

Inside of me.

A story of love, or one about fear,

One I can see

And touch and hear.

By gosh, by golly, by gee

I've got a whole story

Deep down inside of me.

I Hear It!

Billy is camping in the forest and it is scarey.

Indeed, Indeed, Indeed

I've got all the words I need.

Words that name and

Words that can do

And words to describe.

Yes, all those words

That are way down deep

In my inside.

Indeed! Indeed! Indeed!

I have all the words I need.

The angel flies up in the air and she is singing a tune.

Inside of Me

Believe it or not

All those words that I've got

Can be set free from way down deep

Inside of me.

They can be thought about

Or better yet, said right out.

And if I write them down

I'll have a story to say and see

A real story, to really read

From way down deep inside of me.

Peacock has lots of feathers. Peacock is in the zoo. People like to see the peacock. Peacock opens its feathers and they are SO PRETTY!

A key word from inside a child's inner world can help him or her unlock the mystery of reading and open the door to numerous related activities that integrate the arts and academics into meaningful, holistic tasks. Following is an example of children choosing their own words:

IRI/Skylight Publishing, Inc.

I Hear It!

Emily slowly traces with her finger the word *butterfly* after the teacher writes it on an orange strip. "The easel," she responds to the teacher-initiated question of how she wants to study her word today. "I'm gonna paint my butterfly in beautiful, bright colors." Erin chooses to "water write" her word on the blackboard, while Matt forms his word out of seashells on a red mat. Effie uses dusty pastel chalks to print the word *girl,* and Eric traces the word *Dumbo* in wet sand.

Following the announcement of study time, the children settle down with their handmade orange stapled booklets, which match their orange word cards, and begin their sentence writing:

"Butterfly is beautiful!"	(Emily)
"Piano is magic."	(Erin)
"Garden can grow."	(Matt)
"Girl is pretty."	(Effie)
"Dumbo can fly."	(Eric)

Some ask the teacher to help them write their sentences, others quiz each other for words they need to fill the page. When the sentences begin to string together and form stories, the children receive sticky dots for punctuating their ideas. The teacher helps the children add headings and titles, and their writing develops. The buzz begins as partners share their stories.

This activity is done every morning for a month. The orange word booklets are then taken home to the parents, who know that the goal is for the child to read the sentence booklet to anyone and everyone who will listen, including goldfish, grandparents, and neighbors. For every reading, a signature is collected on the inside cover to be tallied Monday morning. At the end of the year, these students will have nine sentence booklets with color-coordinated cards for each month of the school year. They will also have a shoebox filled with their requested words. With the focus on authentic assessment (Burke, 1993), these artifacts provide ongoing evidence of the students' development. In fact, the final assessment tool is a tenth booklet containing a page from each of the previous booklets.

Although the activities in this primary classroom resemble those of many early childhood programs, there are several key elements to outline: (1) this is an ungraded class of four-, five-, and six-year-olds; (2) the curriculum is fully integrated (Fogarty, 1991) through a language arts focus, with music, art, math, science, and social studies creeping into daily activities; (3) the program provides a platform for genuine investigations and class projects; and (4) the parents are an integral part of the activities and the assessment process.

Interestingly, the integration of curriculum permeates every aspect of this classroom, and the students learn from one another. They learn not only their own words, but also the vocabularies of other children. They alphabetize,

IRI/Skylight Publishing, Inc.

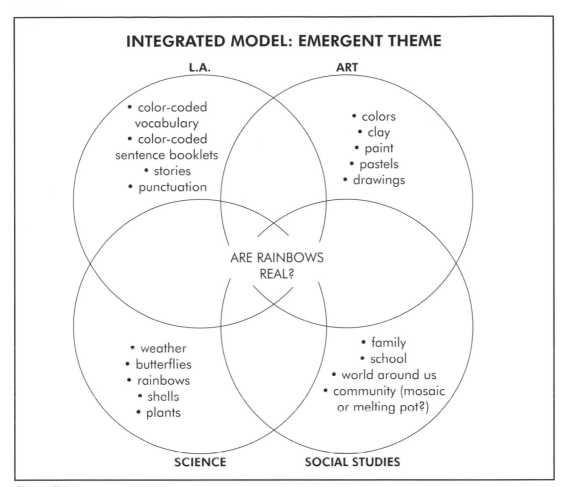

INTEGRATED MODEL: EMERGENT THEME

L.A.
- color-coded vocabulary
- color-coded sentence booklets
- stories
- punctuation

ART
- colors
- clay
- paint
- pastels
- drawings

ARE RAINBOWS REAL?

SCIENCE
- weather
- butterflies
- rainbows
- shells
- plants

SOCIAL STUDIES
- family
- school
- world around us
- community (mosaic or melting pot?)

Figure 3.5

categorize, and prioritize words as they internalize learning through reading, writing, listening, and speaking. The rainbow is one example of the serendipitous effects of the shoebox curriculum (see fig. 3.5). After one student paints a rainbow, several children want his word, too. In fact, the idea of the rainbow becomes contagious, and a special event is planned: the entire class paints a rainbow and displays it on a windowed wall.

Selected Themes Webbed to the Multiple Intelligences

In the themes of courage and rainbows, the big idea was connected to traditional subject matter content such as math, science, social studies, language arts, art, music, physical education, etc. Using similar approaches to thematic instruction, both selected themes and emergent themes can be connected to the seven intelligences (see fig. 3.6).

To connect a lesson to the multiple intelligences, teachers commonly use a single, fertile theme such as *responsibility* or *cooperation*. Common topics, such as *the individual and society*, *the community*, or *the Renaissance*, connect students' learning. Although these themes are often connected to traditional subject matter content, they can also be connected to multiple intelligences. By connecting themes using the seven "frames of mind" (verbal, visual, bodily, mathematical, musical, interpersonal, and intrapersonal), the disciplines become more flexible.

IRI/Skylight Publishing, Inc.

I Hear It!

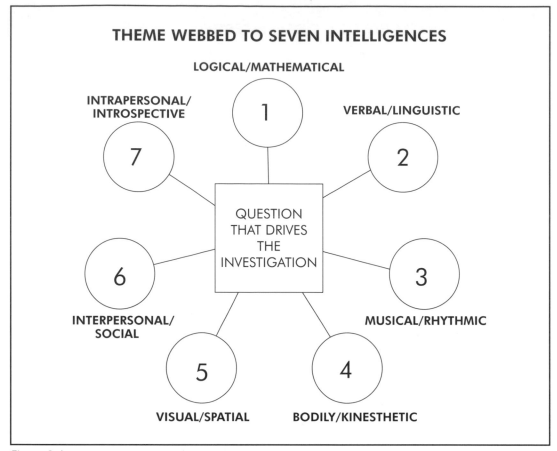

Figure 3.6

Two brief examples of the webbed, or selected, theme (deductively derived) are included here. One classroom scenario describes thematic instruction using a science topic: "The Cell: What Is the Mystery?" The sixth grade activities are developed through a focus on the seven intelligences.

In cooperative groups, students design a working model that demonstrates the process of cell diffusion. Each team uses its combined creativity to build and explain its invention. A glimpse into this very active classroom reveals energy and enthusiasm as the students engage their bodily/kinesthetic, logical/mathematical, and verbal/linguistic intelligences (see fig. 3.7).

The teacher announces, "Remember, your model must show the sequence of what happens when a cell membrane acts as a guard, letting certain things in and keeping other things out."

The teacher suggests to a group of students that they compare their model to actual cell diffusion. "Use your organized ideas on the Venn diagram to help you explain your model with your visual/spatial intelligence," the teacher says.

"We used golf balls and marbles," another group of students say. "The marbles, because of their smaller size, slip through the tube easily, while the golf balls are effectively stopped."

IRI/Skylight Publishing, Inc.

I Hear It!

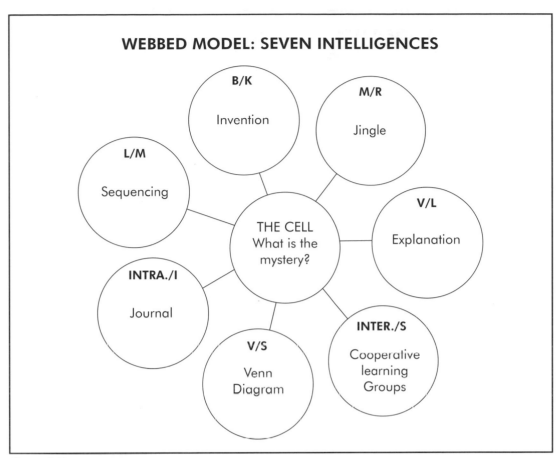

WEBBED MODEL: SEVEN INTELLIGENCES

B/K — Invention

M/R — Jingle

L/M — Sequencing

V/L — Explanation

THE CELL
What is the mystery?

INTRA./I — Journal

V/S — Venn Diagram

INTER./S — Cooperative learning Groups

Figure 3.7

"It's just like you said, the cell diffuses some things and stops or guards against others," says a student.

"Yeah! It works just like it's described in the science book," another student says.

Pleased with the students' apparent understanding of the concept of cell diffusion, this sixth grade teacher assigns the next part of the project: "For tomorrow, you are to present a jingle that explains and advertises your inventive models of cell diffusion. Be as creative as you can and use rhythm, beat, and melody to advertise your model."

"O.K.! Now, we need to find a familiar song and then write the lyrics to fit the melody," says a student in one group.

"How about something everyone knows, like 'Jingle Bells?'"

"That might work. Listen: cell diffusion, cell diffusion, cell diffusion all the way. Oh, what. . . ."

IRI/Skylight Publishing, Inc.

I Hear It!

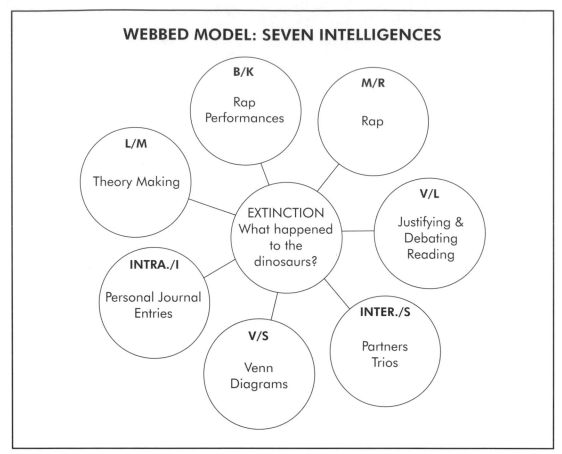

Figure 3.8

"I've got another idea. Let's each work on this at home. Then we can come in a little early and pick and learn the song that we like best. This way, we'll all have to know how cell diffusion works—because we'll have to put our ideas in the song."

The teacher comments while passing by the group, "That's a good idea. I'm really proud of the way this team has shown its use of all seven intelligences."

In another example, a fifth grade group demonstrates thinking and theorizing by using the multiple intelligences as a web for their theme: "Extinction: What Happened to the Dinosaurs?" (see fig. 3.8).

"Well, this is just a theory, but our group thinks that the continental shift [draws diagram on the board] brought with it colder climates, which in turn affected the food supply."

"Yeah, and when the food chain was interrupted, the dinosaurs eventually died out."

"That seems pretty logical. Does any other group have a plausible cause for the extinction of the dinosaurs?"

IRI/Skylight Publishing, Inc.

"Our team thinks that the plant-eating dinosaurs ate poisonous berries, and as they died off, the meat-eating dinosaurs soon had no food source."

"We think that the dinosaurs were caught in a plague of some sort. Maybe a bug bit them—like the mosquitoes that spread malaria—and the sickness eventually wiped out the entire population."

In an effort to create logical theories, students use a number of multiple intelligences in a natural flow of learning: the logical/mathematical intelligence is used in their reasoning sequences, the verbal/linguistic is used in the justification process, the interpersonal/social intelligence is used in cooperative learning groups, and the visual/spatial intelligence is used with Venn diagrams that compare and contrast theories. The intrapersonal/introspective intelligence is used in journal writing, a process that helps students reflect on their learning and apply ideas from class discussions to their readings. At the end of the unit, each group uses their musical/rhythmic intelligence to create a rap song about their theory-making process, such as the following:

We can synthesize,

We can prioritize,

We can dramatize, and

We can even hypothesize.

But most of all—

We love to theorize!

Theorize! Theorize!

That's our favorite exercise.

Emergent Themes Start with the Multiple Intelligences

By using the shared or integrated models (Fogarty, 1991) to find emergent themes, multiple intelligences can replace traditional disciplines. In this case, the content, activities, goals, aims, and objectives are categorized within a particular frame of mind. For example, in figure 3.9, the thematic project that emerged was the visual and performing arts. By slotting activities into each of the seven intelligences, a central or emergent idea evolves. Figure 3.10 illustrates an overview of the integrated learning designs of the school described in the following paragraphs.

As students study a social studies unit on cultures and symbols, cave art is displayed in an actual-sized papier-mâché cave located in the art gallery on the third floor. Music fills the air,

I Hear It!

IRI/Skylight Publishing, Inc.

I Hear It!

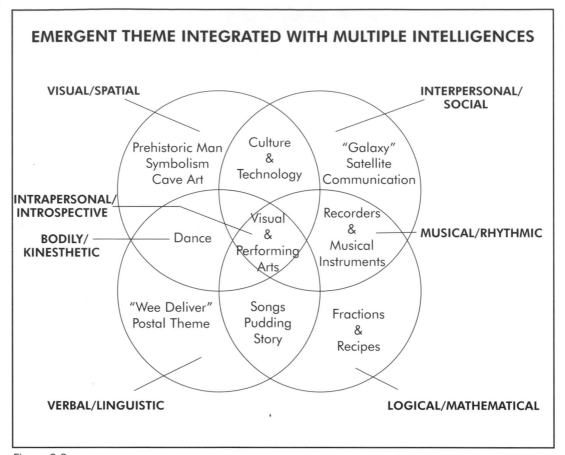

EMERGENT THEME INTEGRATED WITH MULTIPLE INTELLIGENCES

- VISUAL/SPATIAL
- INTERPERSONAL/SOCIAL
- INTRAPERSONAL/INTROSPECTIVE
- BODILY/KINESTHETIC
- MUSICAL/RHYTHMIC
- VERBAL/LINGUISTIC
- LOGICAL/MATHEMATICAL

Prehistoric Man Symbolism Cave Art

Culture & Technology

"Galaxy" Satellite Communication

Dance

Visual & Performing Arts

Recorders & Musical Instruments

"Wee Deliver" Postal Theme

Songs Pudding Story

Fractions & Recipes

Figure 3.9

and students learn the songs and dances of the studied cultures.

In another room, the sound of recorders drifts into the hallway. Young students, paired to share music stands, gingerly play these simple instruments as an introduction into the formal band program.

"Wee Deliver," a schoolwide theme sponsored by the U.S. Postal Service, dictates "zoning" the halls of the school à la the federal zip code system: Disney Town 16025, Star Park 11789, and Curiosity Heights 31452. The theme creates a natural forum for continued and purposeful writing across the curriculum and across the grade levels. Stamps designed by children from different classrooms are featured each month.

Student workers are interviewed by other students for positions in the post office, which entail early morning sorting and delivery routes. Student responsibilities include training new inductees and releasing new stamps. Although this began as a one-year theme, the principal emphasizes that the school's postal service is now an integral part of the children's lives, and

IRI/Skylight Publishing, Inc.

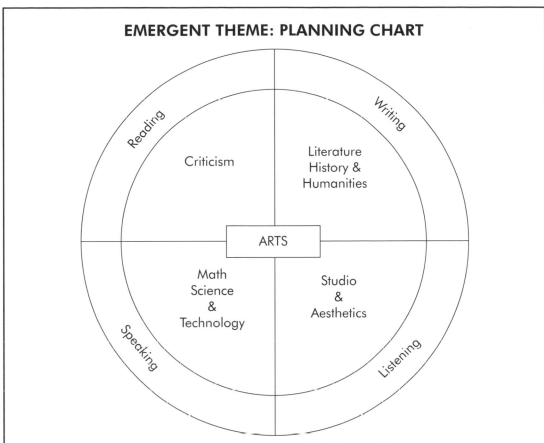

EMERGENT THEME: PLANNING CHART

Reading

Writing

Criticism

Literature
History &
Humanities

ARTS

Math
Science
&
Technology

Studio
&
Aesthetics

Speaking

Listening

Figure 3.10

it will continue each year in tandem with other selected themes.

Technology is an additional integrative thread at the school. Cable hookups throughout the school begin in the teacher's resource room. Branching out from a central source are a magic cable and wire branch, which resemble the tentacles of an oversized octopus. This center is referred to as the Heart Room of the school: the programming pulses through the classrooms. The satellite dish on the flat-roofed school proclaims the school's commitment to technology as an integrative thread. One third grade classroom, as part of the Galaxy Project, communicates by FAX with twenty-nine schools across the United States. Regional and cultural diversities are natural outgrowths of study in this high-tech communication network.

The impetus for the school's mission is embedded in the concept of integration of the arts; however, science, technology, and mathematical reasoning fall easily under this organizational umbrella. Mathematical concepts, logic, and relevant scientific application are part of everything children do. In one lesson,

IRI/Skylight Publishing, Inc.

I Hear It!

students use their knowledge of fractions to create pudding from a converted recipe, which in turn acts as a springboard for a science experiment on the changes of matter. In another classroom, students calculate what their weights would be on various planets. At the same time, they are reading a book about other cultures, their climates, and the interdependency of humans.

As in any K–8 school across the continent, children's artwork covers the walls; but, the decoration in this school goes one step further. In addition to a large, third-floor art gallery that houses an array of ever-changing exhibits and displays of authentic children's art, the lunchroom also acts as a gallery. Modeled after a fine-dining establishment, soft music serenades the student patrons. Upon entering the main dining room, one can see two large pictures adorning the back wall and a painting of a muscle man on the side wall. Half-walls, spotted with potted plants, divide the space, and the seating arrangements are carefully sectioned, as in a well-managed restaurant.

This school is the result of a mission made possible by the creativity, ingenuity, and hard work of an unstoppable team of dedicated teachers, parents, and staff. While the integration of the arts is a mission *possible,* it is also a dynamic, ever-evolving concept. Figure 3.11 illustrates the flexibility of using multiple intelligences as a means for finding emergent themes.

INTRODUCTION TO TANDEMS—THEMES

Just as the tandem bicycle is a bicycle built for two, tandem models of integration are constructed using two basic models: the basic webbed model and another model that complements it. Examples of possible combinations include the following: *webbed and threaded*; *webbed and nested, connected, sequenced, shared, immersed,* or *networked*; and *webbed and shared* or *integrated.*

Tandems Rap

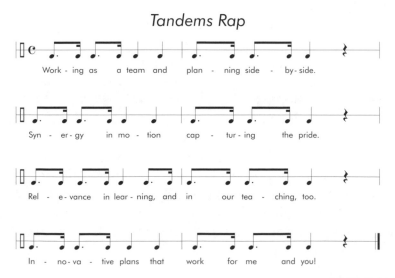

Work - ing as a team and plan - ning side - by-side.

Syn - er - gy in mo - tion cap - tur - ing the pride.

Rel - e - vance in lear - ning, and in our tea - ching, too.

In - no-va - tive plans that work for me and you!

IRI/Skylight Publishing, Inc.

I Hear It!

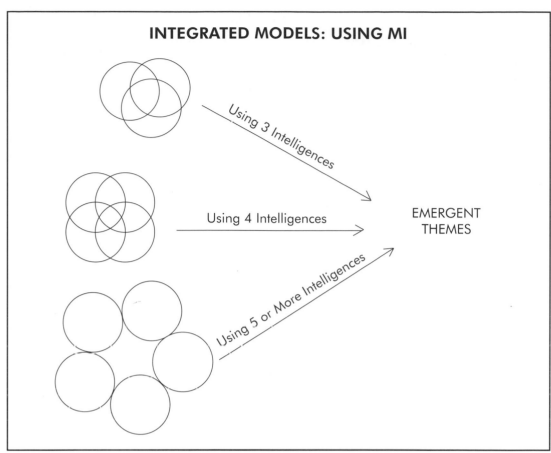

Figure 3.11

Tandem: Webbed and Threaded

Themes and threads are natural combinations. The tandem model for this design is shown in figure 3.12. A completed example of a thematic unit with a life skill thread might comprise an umbrella theme of communication with the key question "Can We Talk?" (see fig. 3.13).

While communication provides a thematic focus, the research thread provides an additional focus on a skill. Curricular activities are designed to be relevant to the communications theme. In addition, the life skill of research is threaded through the various activity modules. By including the research thread, the activity centers become more rigorous and, perhaps, more self-directed.

Tandem: Webbed and Other Models

Themes in combination with other models—connected, nested, sequenced, shared, immersed, and networked (Fogarty, 1991)—offer several opportunities for relevant and creative designs of curriculum integration. Just as in the highly popular webbed/threaded model for developing concepts or themes and skills or threads, other tandem combinations are used effectively from the K–college classroom (see fig. 3.14).

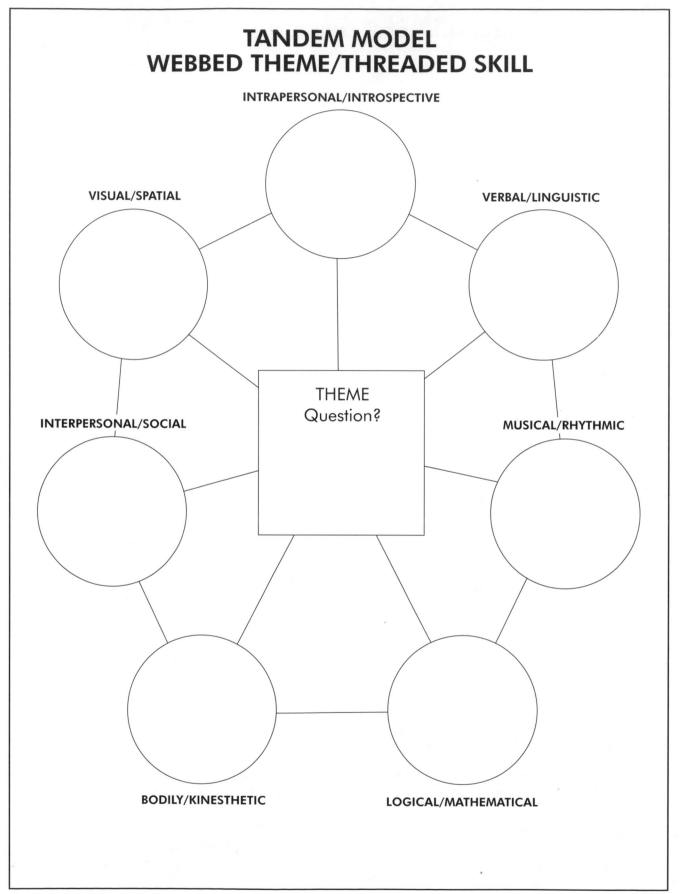

TANDEM MODEL
WEBBED THEME/THREADED SKILL

INTRAPERSONAL/INTROSPECTIVE

VISUAL/SPATIAL

VERBAL/LINGUISTIC

THEME
Question?

INTERPERSONAL/SOCIAL

MUSICAL/RHYTHMIC

BODILY/KINESTHETIC

LOGICAL/MATHEMATICAL

Figure 3.12

IRI/Skylight Publishing, Inc.

I Hear It!

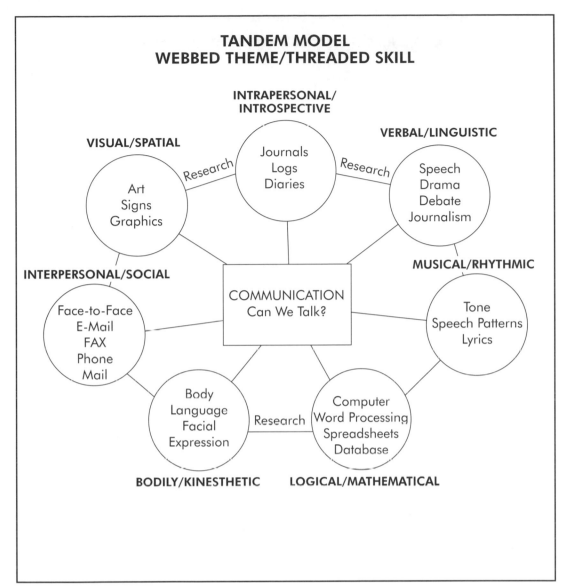

TANDEM MODEL
WEBBED THEME/THREADED SKILL

INTRAPERSONAL/
INTROSPECTIVE

VISUAL/SPATIAL

VERBAL/LINGUISTIC

Journals
Logs
Diaries

Research

Research

Art
Signs
Graphics

Speech
Drama
Debate
Journalism

INTERPERSONAL/SOCIAL

MUSICAL/RHYTHMIC

COMMUNICATION
Can We Talk?

Face-to-Face
E-Mail
FAX
Phone
Mail

Tone
Speech Patterns
Lyrics

Body
Language
Facial
Expression

Research

Computer
Word Processing
Spreadsheets
Database

BODILY/KINESTHETIC

LOGICAL/MATHEMATICAL

Figure 3.13

The webbed/nested tandem of "Fashion: Whose Statement Is It?" (see fig. 3.15) can be webbed to family and consumer education, art, and language arts. Yet, within each discipline, appropriate skills can also be conveniently nested into content lessons. In the webbed/sequenced tandem, the theme "Cultural Diversity: Who Do You Think You Are?" (see fig. 3.16) can be webbed to several disciplines. Activities can be coordinated to support the theme of cultural diversity and the music teacher can resequence his lessons on ethnic music to coincide with the curriculum of the social studies classes.

Similar ideas can be developed with other tandems as sketched in figure 3.14. This universal tandem web shows a number of possible designs. The final solution is dependent on the creative interactions of the teachers and their content.

IRI/Skylight Publishing, Inc.

WEBBED TANDEMS WITH OTHER MODELS

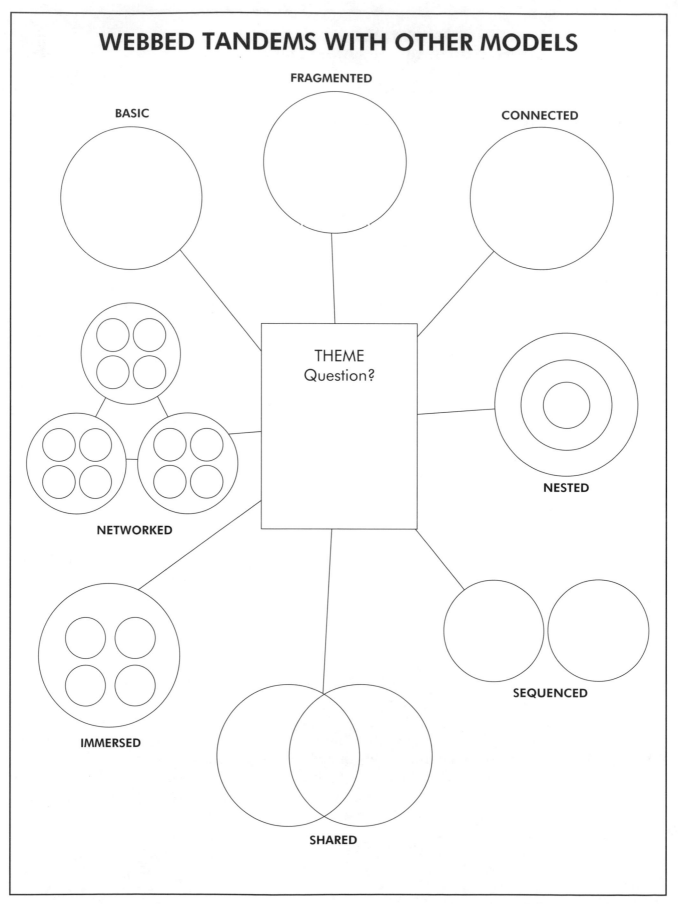

Figure 3.14

I Hear It!

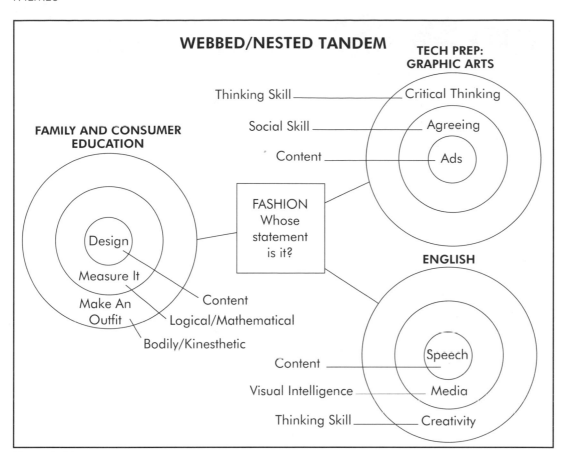

Figure 3.15

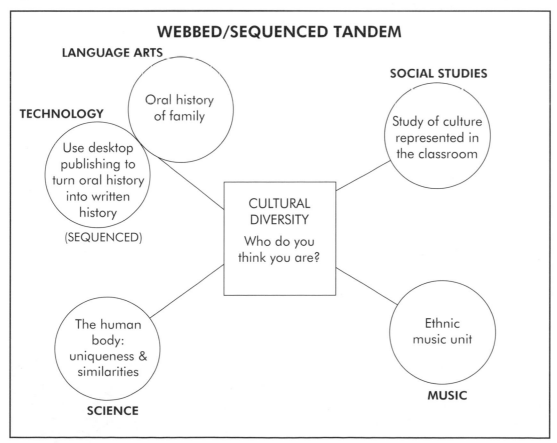

Figure 3.16

Just Do It!

JUST DO IT!

Elementary Lesson

"MISS MARY MACK"
Multiple Intelligences Web

There is mounting evidence that a growing number of schools are using Gardner's seven intelligences as activity satellites for integrated studies. Teachers who are familiar with the theory of multiple intelligences and its implications for education are more likely to use the intelligences as cognitive organizers for student activities. The multiple intelligences approach to thematic learning looks like the following lesson.

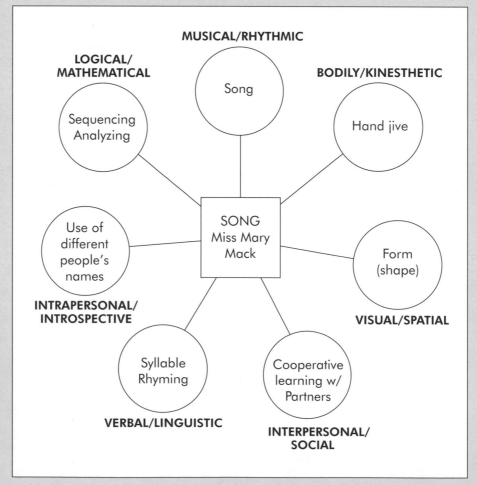

Figure 3.17

IRI/Skylight Publishing, Inc.

Just Do It!

Miss Mary Mack
(American play-party song)

1. Miss Mar - y Mack, Mack, Mack, all dressed in black, black, black with sil - ver
2. She asked her mother, mother, mother for fif - ty cents, cents, cents to see the

but - tons, but - tons, but - tons all down her back, back, back.
ele - phants, ele - phants, el - e - phants jump the fence, fence, fence.

Miss Mary Mack: Can You Jive to This?

Teach the song, then add a hand jive. Have the children stand and face a partner, then teach them the first part of the hand jive:

 Pat your legs with both hands.
 Clap your hands.
 Tap your partner's hands with both of your hands.
 Clap your hands.

On a flip chart, draw a circle to represent this first part.

Instruct everyone to perform the above pattern with you a total of four times.

Teach part two of the hand jive:

 Pat your legs with both hands.
 Clap your hands.
 Tap your partner's right hand with your right hand.
 Clap your hands.

On the chart, just to the right of the circle, draw a square to represent this second part. Instruct everyone to perform this part four times.

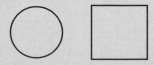

Draw another circle to the right of the square, and ask the students which motions they think they should do. (Part one.)

117

IRI/Skylight Publishing, Inc.

Just Do It!

Instruct everyone to practice the first three parts, as indicated by the circle, square, circle, repeating part three four times. Next to the second circle, draw a triangle. Ask the students if they think this part will be the same or different from what they've already done. (Different)

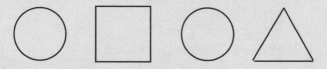

Teach the new part of the hand jive:
    Pat your legs with both hands.
    Clap your hands.
    Tap your partner's left hand with your left hand.
    Clap your hands.

Instruct everyone to practice this part, again performing it four times. On the chart, draw one more circle, this time to the right of the triangle.

Instruct the students to figure out and practice the entire hand jive with their partners.

Assessment: Traditional
Ask the students how they would label the form of the hand jive. (Same, Different, Same, Different, Same. [In music, this form is called a rondo.])

Assessment: Performance
Instruct everyone to perform the hand jive with their partners while singing the song. Perform the jive to the "slow" beat of the song at first. Later, students may perform it double-time.

Assessment: Portfolio
Have the students discuss what they learned with their partners. Direct them to discuss ways the hand jive could be changed and still reflect the rondo form.

IRI/Skylight Publishing, Inc.

Just Do It!

Miss Mary Mack: A Play on Words?
Language Arts Extension

Lesson Name: Miss Mary Mack
Targeted Intelligences: Integrated
Content Focus: Language Arts
Materials: Large chart paper and/or butcher paper
Colored markers or paints

Reinforcing Reading through Visualization and Movement

On a large chart, print the words of the song and draw lines over them as
indicated.

   —   —   —
Miss Mary Mack, Mack, Mack,

       —   —   —
All dressed in black, black, black,

       — —   — —   — —
With silver buttons, buttons, buttons,

       —   —   —
All down her back, back, back.

       — —   — —   — —
She asked her mother, mother, mother

       —   —   —
For fifty cents, cents, cents

       — — —   — — —   — — —
To see the elephants, elephants, elephants

       —   —   —
Jump the fence, fence, fence.

1. Have everyone say the words together in the rhythm of the song, as a rap.
2. Repeat step 1, this time add a hand clap for each line above the word or
   syllable. (For instance, "Mack" will have one clap, while "button" will have
   two.)
3. Repeat step 2. This time trace (rather than clap to) the line above the word
   or syllable as you say it.

Rhyming Words

Ask the students what they noticed about the words "Mack," "black," and
"back." (They rhyme.) On a large chart, make a list of these rhyming words.
Then, ask the students to name other words that rhyme with those same words.
As they call out words, add them to the list. Ask the students to name other
colors that have just one clap (or syllable). (Blue, brown, pink, white, green,
gray, etc.)

Just Do It!

Assessment: Traditional

Cooperative Learning—Using What We've Learned

Put the students into cooperative groups and instruct them to create a new verse for the first four lines of "Miss Mary Mack," using a one-syllable color, as below:

> Miss Mary Moo, Moo, Moo,
> All dressed in blue, blue, blue,
> With silver buttons, buttons, buttons,
> On her shoe, shoe, shoe.

Give each group a large sheet of chart or butcher paper and colored markers or paint, and instruct them to create a picture of their new rhyme. When the pictures are finished, the group members should sign them.

Assessment: Performance

When all the groups have finished their pictures, hang them around the room; then, have the groups take turns performing their rhymes for the rest of the class. After each group finishes, ask the group members what they liked best about:

1. making up a new rhyme;
2. creating a picture for the rhyme;
3. working in their group; and
4. their performance.

Ask the rest of the class what they liked most about the group's picture and performance and what they would do differently or change in any of the above four categories.

Making Our Learning Personal

At the top of four separate large sheets of paper, draw the following:

—   — —   — — —   **?**

Ask the students to remember which words in "Miss Mary Mack" had just one line over them (Mack, black, back, cents, fence). List those words under the single line. Ask the students which words had two lines (buttons, mother). List those words under the two lines. Ask the students which word had three lines (elephant). Write elephant under the three lines.

Have everyone clap and say each person's first name. Ask the students to help you put each name on the correct list. (Anyone's name that does not fit the three patterns from "Miss Mary Mack" goes on a "?" sheet for a future lesson.) Ask the students why they think some of the names, even those with two sounds, go on the "?" list. Put these lists up around the room so that the children can refer to them.

IRI/Skylight Publishing, Inc.

Just Do It!

Creating with Names

Circle one name from the one-syllable list and one from the two-syllable list. Instruct the students to say the first verse of "Miss Mary Mack" (the first four lines) with you, but this time insert the name chosen from the one-syllable list instead of "Mack," "black," and "back," and insert the name chosen from the two-syllable list for "buttons." Repeat this step several times, inserting different one- and two-syllable names.

Middle School Lesson

AFRICA—SOUTH OF THE SAHARA
Subject Matter Web

Using subject areas and multiple intelligences simultaneously as base camps for curriculum integration produces holistic and natural curricular connections for relevant student learning. The mind moves back and forth from the known to the unknown, and teachers can accommodate this phenomenon by combining discipline-based structures with the cognitive model of the seven intelligences. In this case, the known is the discipline-based and the unknown is the cognitive model of multiple intelligences. The following illustration in figure

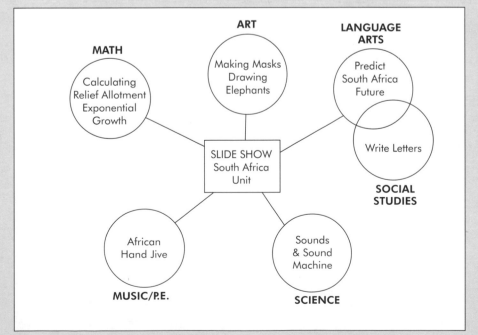

Figure 3.18

IRI/Skylight Publishing, Inc.

Just Do It!

3.18 demonstrates what the planning graphic might look like in this complex model of a thematic approach to learning, which focuses on subject orientation and multiple intelligences.

Create a slide show that features the diversities of Africa. Use pictures from magazines, journals, and books, and use music ("Africa" by Toto). Using a flip chart or chalkboard, have the students help you make a semantic map of the diversities they saw in the slide presentation.

Ask the students what sounds they think they would hear in Africa (birds, snakes, different animals, cars, etc.). Divide the students into several groups, and assign to each group one of the sounds suggested above. Walk from one side of the classroom to the other and instruct the groups to make their sound only while you are walking in front of them. Then, walk to the front of the class and "conduct" all the groups to make their sounds at the same time, first softly, then louder and louder, and then softly again. Discuss how they felt about this activity and what they heard.

Cooperative Learning

Have each group make an animal kingdom mural of the animals south of the Sahara in Africa. They can either find their pictures or draw or paint them. Instruct each group member to research one of the animals (assignments can be made through group consensus) and write a short report about that animal, making sure to include such information as whether or not the animal is becoming extinct and why and where the animal lives. Each report should be given orally to the class.

Study South Africa's political history. After the students learn about Apartheid, instruct them to compare Nelson Mandela to someone in American history who is also considered to be a hero. How are they alike? How are they different? What difference did each make in the history of their countries?

Learn about exponential growth by reading "The Hero's Reward" (upper grades). Hand out copies of the checkerboard (see fig. 3.19); then, read the story and instruct the students to figure out both the number of kernels and the number of boxes for several of the days. Discuss the concept of exponential growth and how else it can be used.

Draw an elephant. Read the following information to the students:

There are two basic kinds of elephants—African and Asian (or Indian). It is rather easy to tell one kind from another.

Asian elephants have smaller ears than African elephants. They have a high forehead with two rather large "bumps" on it. The back of the Asian elephant bends up in the middle, and usually only the males have tusks.

IRI/Skylight Publishing, Inc.

THE HERO'S REWARD

(A Story about Dragons, Heroes, and Exponential Growth)

Long ago, in a land south of the Sahara called South Africa, there lived a very rich tribal chief. He had a beautiful daughter. One day, as the story goes, this beautiful daughter was carried off by an evil fire-breathing dragon. As the dragon was carrying the girl off to its cave, it encountered a handsome young man who was traveling through that part of the land. The young man promptly killed the fire-breathing dragon and rescued the beautiful girl.

Upon seeing his daughter returned to him, the chief asked the young man what reward he would like. "A sack of gold? My daughter's hand in marriage?" The young man's answer surprised the chief. Having noticed the chief's chessboard, he went over to it, cleared away the pieces, and then began to talk. "I would like as my reward to return to you once a day for sixty-four days—one day for each square of your chessboard—and pick up a certain amount of grain each day. The first day, I will get just one kernel; the second day I will get two; the third day four; the fourth day eight; and so on, doubling the number of kernels of grain for each day for each square on your chessboard." The chief, thinking this to be a most peculiar and meager reward, agreed immediately.

The next day, the young man came and got his one kernel of grain. This pattern continued so that by day fourteen he had collected 8,192 kernels. On day eighteen, the young man collected 131,072 kernels of grain! Now, let's say that there are exactly 131,072 kernels of grain in a box. How many boxes would the young man have collected by day twenty-eight? 1,024. This much grain would cover the entire floor of a classroom to the depth of one inch! By day thirty-five, the grain would fill an entire classroom, wall to wall, floor to ceiling.

At first, everyone in the village made fun of the young man each time he came for his grain. But as the number of carts grew, even the chief began to get worried. So he called in his advisors and asked just how much grain the young man would get by day sixty-four. The answer so astonished the chief that he immediately had his warriors set upon the young man and kill him!

This may seem harsh to you, but you should know what the chief's advisors told him: They said that by day sixty-four the chief would owe the young man all of the grain in the entire kingdom, *plus* all the grain the entire kingdom would produce for the next ten thousand years!

—Judy Stoehr

IRI/Skylight Publishing, Inc.

CHECKER BOARD

1	2	3	4	5	6	7	8
1	2	4		16	32		128
9	**10**	**11**	**12**	**13**	**14**	**15**	**16**
	512	1,024			8,192		32,768
17	**18**	**19**	**20**	**21**	**22**	**23**	**24**
	131,072						
25	**26**	**27**	**28**	**29**	**30**	**31**	**32**
33	**34**	**35**	**36**	**37**	**38**	**39**	**40**
41	**42**	**43**	**44**	**45**	**46**	**47**	**48**
49	**50**	**51**	**52**	**53**	**54**	**55**	**56**
57	**58**	**59**	**60**	**61**	**62**	**63**	**64**

Figure 3.19

IRI/Skylight Publishing, Inc.

Just Do It!

African elephants have very large ears. Their foreheads don't have big bumps on them. The back of an African elephant bends down in the middle, and both the males and females have tusks. (Bellanca & Fogarty, 1991)

Give each student a blank sheet of paper and instruct them to listen again as you reread the description of each elephant. They are to select and draw, based on prior knowledge and your descriptions, either an Asian elephant or an African elephant. When they are finished, instruct the students to share their drawings with their neighbors. Ask if anyone would like to share their drawings with the class.

Assessment: Portfolio

Have the students imagine that they are going to move to a south African nation. They may choose which one. Instruct them to write a letter to a friend about their upcoming move and include which nation they have chosen and why and whether they will live in the city or the country.

Assessment: Traditional

Have the students write about what their lives will be like in their new homes (include information such as weather, culture, school, transportation, housing, etc.).

Learn an African hand jive. Have the students stand and face their partners. Learn the hand positions. Each person should have their left palm facing upward and their right palm facing downward, palm to palm with their partners.

African Hand Jive

Version 1

Pattern 1: Tap partner's palms.
  Clap your hands.
  (Repeat above)

Pattern 2: Tap partner's palms two times.
  Clap your hands two times.

Once the students know this version of the hand jive, have them practice it to the beat of music such as "Africa" by Toto. (Do not move on to version 2 until students are comfortable with version 1.)

Just Do It!

Version 2

Pattern 1:(same as version 1)

Pattern 2:Tap partner's palms ONE time.
 Flip hands over and tap ONE time.
 (To flip, face left palm downward and right palm upward.)
 Clap your hands two times.

Have the students practice this new, harder version of the hand jive.

Version 3

Instruct the students to move from partner formations to one large circle. Place hands in same position as in pattern 1, versions 1 and 2; but, this time, instead of having hands directly in front, as with partner, move hands outward some-what to find the palm of the person on either side in the circle. Have the group practice the hand jive, either version 1 or 2, with the music. (For variety, or if you have a large group, have several students form an inner circle.)

Version 4

If the students are really good at the hand jive, have them try moving to the right (step to the right on the right foot, bring the left foot to it) at the same time. The inner circle can either move in the same direction as the outside circle, or they can move in the opposite direction.

Calculate relief allotments. Because so many South African children die or are crippled by famine and malnutrition each year, the Red Cross has set up relief stations to feed and care for the hungry and sick. Based on a one-month allotment of one hundred pounds of grain per family, instruct the students to calculate the daily allotment per person for a family of four (100 lbs. $\div$ 30 days = 3.33 $\div$ 4 = .83 lbs. of grains per person per day). Have the students make a chart of the approximate weight of the food they eat each day for a week, then compare it with both the African allotment and that of their class-mates.

Predict South Africa's future. Direct the students to imagine that they are journalists for a magazine and have been assigned to write an article predict-ing what South Africa will be like in twenty years. Have them write the article based on what they know about Africa's past and present.

Assessment: Performance
Make Masks. After learning about different tribal cultures, including art, dance, religion, etc., have the students make masks based on what they have learned. They may work alone or in pairs.

IRI/Skylight Publishing, Inc.

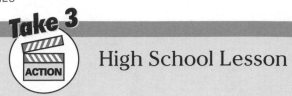

High School Lesson

MEDIEVAL EUROPE DURING THE BLACK DEATH
Subject Matter Web

Often, the activities and assessments developed for a theme are discipline based because it is the existing method for organization in the school. High schools and middle schools that have traditional departments find that webbing themes to various subject areas is the easiest structure to use. In fact, by selecting a theme that can be webbed out to various disciplines, the model takes on a multidisciplinary look. That is to say, once the theme is selected, each teacher representing multiple disciplines can then do a lot of the actual planning outside of the team meeting and planning time. Then, after the ideas for the various subject areas are individually designed, teachers can meet again to share their ideas and coordinate the elements that lend themselves to a cross-disciplinary effort. This makes the webbed model quite appealing to schools whose departmental structure reigns supreme, because these schools

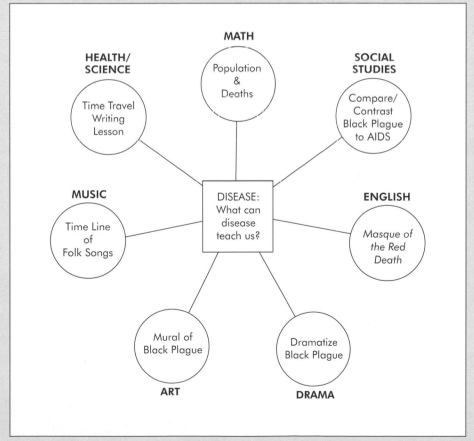

Figure 3.20

IRI/Skylight Publishing, Inc.

Just Do It!

often have difficulty providing chunks of team planning time. An example of the disciplined-based model is illustrated in figure 3.20. A complete and comprehensive high school unit follows.

The Black Death in Medieval Europe: What's in a Song?

Begin with the song "Scarborough Fair." Make an overhead transparency of the words of the song, then have everyone sing it with you or a recording. Following are just three of the many verses of this song.

Scarborough Fair
(English Folk Song)

Are you going to Scarborough Fair?
Parsley, sage, rosemary, and thyme.
Remember me to one who lives there.
She once was a true love of mine.

Tell her to make me a cambric shirt.
Parsley, sage, rosemary, and thyme.
Without a seam or needlework.
She once was a true love of mine.

Tell her to wash it in yonder well.
Parsley, sage, rosemary, and thyme.
Where never rain or water fell.
She once was a true love of mine.

Have the students discuss what a folk song is. (It is a song that has been passed down orally and reflects the history and culture of that time.)

Extension

Making a time line using contemporary folk songs, ask the students to think of any songs that were composed as a result of events in the last fifty years. As a class project, make a time line showing political, cultural, and historical events, and song titles. Ask the students what they think this song is about.

Ask the students if they remember the song "Ring around the Rosie." Does anyone know where it came from? (The Black Death, which entered Europe in 1347. "Pocket full of posies" refers to the herbs and spices used at that time to embalm bodies. "Ashes! Ashes! We all fall down" describes the burning of dead bodies.)

The herbs and spices used in medieval Europe to preserve dead bodies were parsley, sage, rosemary, and thyme. They were called "posies." During the plague, people developed the superstition that if they carried a small bag

IRI/Skylight Publishing, Inc.

Just Do It!

containing posies they would be saved. Of course, it didn't work. With that in mind, direct the students to look at "Scarborough Fair" again. Does the song take on a new meaning? It could be about someone who is dying. A cambric shirt without a seam or needlework is a death shroud.

Cooperative Learning

Direct the students to discuss in their groups what the third verse could be about. Then have a spokesperson from each group report to the class. (There is not one right answer.)

Learning about the Black Death

The Black Death was brought to Europe in 1347 by fleas riding on the backs of rats. The rats came on merchant ships. It was called the Black Death because of the dark blotches on its victims' skin. It is estimated that between one fourth and one half of the entire population of Europe died from the Black Death. Paris records indicate that about eight hundred people died per *day*. The Black Death is generally given credit for bringing Feudalism to an end, since by the law of averages, more serfs survived than lords. As a result, at the end of the plague serfs became landowners by default.

Putting the Number of Deaths into Perspective

Ask the students what the population of their town or city is. Have them figure out how long it would take to wipe out their town or city based on eight hundred deaths per day.

A Time-Travel Writing Lesson

Have the students imagine they are doctors and have just traveled back in time to the year 1347. Instruct each student to write three things they would hear, see, or smell. Then, randomly ask individuals to share their lists with the class.

Have each student write a paragraph comparing how their treatment of those dying from the plague would be different from treatment in the twentieth century and why. After everyone finishes, ask several students to share what they wrote and encourage a discussion among the entire class.

Assessment: Traditional
Picturing the Black Death
(Cooperative Group Activity)

Give each group a large sheet of butcher paper and colored markers; then, direct them to create a mural of medieval Europe during the Black Death. Put the finished murals up around the room.

IRI/Skylight Publishing, Inc.

Just Do It!

Learning That No One Is Invincible

Have the students read *Masque of the Red Death* by Edgar Allan Poe and ask the following questions:

1. Why do you think the lord thought he could keep death out by closing up the castle?
2. Who was the uninvited guest?
3. What do you think the moral of *Masque of the Red Death* is?

Relating the Past to the Present

Have the students compare the Black Death to AIDS. How are they different? How are they the same? Ask the students to relate what they learned from *Masque of the Red Death* to what they know about the spread of AIDS. Have the students compare modern embalming techniques to the primitive embalming of medieval Europe. How and why are they different?

 Assessment: Performance

Dramatizing the Black Death

Divide the class into groups of six to eight and instruct them to act out a three-minute scene of medieval Europe during the Black Death. Each scene should include sounds and movement, and every member of the group should be involved.

 Assessment: Portfolio

Learning from the Past

Have the students write in their journals what they learned in this lesson that could make an impact on their lives—both present and future.

Can We Talk?

CAN WE TALK?

Themes as organizing centers for developing curriculum and for igniting learning are, without a doubt, useful approaches to integrating the curricula. Within the planning process, perhaps the most critical step is exploring the theme for breadth and depth. To explore a theme, hold a "question session" in the staff room with the teacher team. Brainstorming with students also enriches the question bank and the teams' search for key questions to hook students with. Survey the following list to see the kinds of "hook" questions other teams have generated.

IRI/Skylight Publishing, Inc.

"HOOK" QUESTIONS OR STATEMENTS FOR THEMES

Theme	Question/Statement
Information Highway	Am I lost?
Water	Water, water everywhere . . .
Cultural Diversity	Who do you think you are?
Enterprise	Why work together?
Families	Family matters
Ecology	Man vs. nature
Milwaukee	A great place on a great lake?
Computers	Friend or foe?
Technology	Good, bad, ugly?
Responsibility	Who me?
Adolescence	What will my friends think?
Parenthood	Pants or pantyhose?
Crime	Gang up on crime!
Conflict	Fighting fair?
Time	How does time fly?
Choices	Will I or won't I?
Communication	Are you getting the message?
Travelers	Discoverers or intruders?
Travel	Which way are we going?
Goals	Where am I? Where am I going?
Circus	Is life a circus?
Survival	Instinct or extinct?
Well-Being	Who's in charge?
Relationships	Love 'em or leave 'em?
Leadership	Consensus vs. confusion?
Violence	Is might right?

After reviewing the "hooks," brainstorm about any topic with your team-mates and generate questions. See figure 3.21 to understand how the brain-storming process usually works.

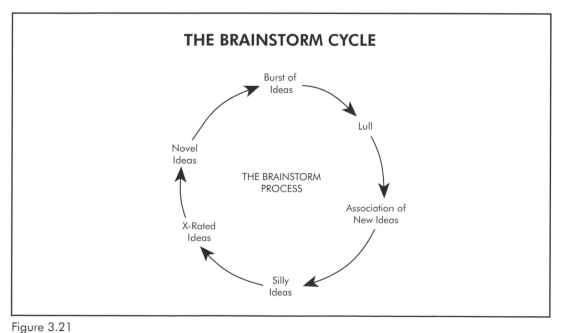

THE BRAINSTORM CYCLE

Figure 3.21

IRI/Skylight Publishing, Inc.

What's in It
for Me?

WHAT'S IN IT FOR ME?

Answer: They're all obsolete.

"This will cover all my projects for this year . . .
For science, it's an amoeba. For art, it's a
sculpture. Wind whistles through it, so I can use it
for music, and since it's made of flour, I can frost
it and use it for foods class!"

Reflection . . .

1. Reflecting on one of the two cartoons, write a few paragraphs about themes and the multiple intelligences.

   _____

   _____

   _____

   _____

   _____

   _____

   _____

   _____

2. Review the completed umbrella chart (see fig. 3.22). Then, use the umbrella organizer to help plan a thematic unit that targets all seven intelligences. Or, try using the matrix mixer (see fig. 3.23) to force a combination of models for integrating curricula with one of the seven intelligences.

Umbrella Organizer for Projects Using the Seven Intelligences

THEME OR CONCEPT
"Form or Function?"

Discipline	Verbal/ Linguistic	Logical/ Mathematical	Musical/ Rhythmic	Visual/ Spatial	Bodily/ Kinesthetic	Interpersonal/ Social	Intrapersonal/ Introspective	Assessment
SCIENCE	Discuss findings. Questions & answers.	Use resource materials.	Create a sound machine.	Study & sketch bird nest. Prepare a report – include visuals.	Create a 3-D replica. Group presentation.	Cooperative learning; Compare/ discuss sketches. List forms. Discuss.	Journals: What did I like? How can I use what I learned?	Group presentation: Written report, visuals, sound machine replica.
GOVERN-MENT	Invite a school board member to speak, answer questions.	Decide on the issues.	Create a campaign jingle, T.V. commercial.	Create a campaign poster.	Create & perform T.V. commercial. Have an election.	Cooperative learning: Work to get a candidate elected. Group processing.	Being a candidate. Journals: How did I feel? Would I want to be?	Group reflection: 1) What did you learn? 2) What should be changed? 3) Who should be on the board?
MUSIC	Review what an ostinato is.	Based on what they know, which part of the song could become an ostinato?	Sing the song. Add ostinato(s). Sing with "Kunsa in D." Create ostinatos.	Write the song & ostinatos.	Perform. Walk while singing.	Cooperative learning: List rounds. Group processing.	Assign parts. Journals: How did I feel about singing in front of others?	Performance (Choice)
LITERATURE	Review characteristics of forms of poetry. Write an advertising jingle. Read poem aloud.	Based on what they know, identify form.	Add rhythm or instruments to jingle.	Use visuals to help "sell" the product.	Groups act out poems. Perform finished jingle.	Cooperative learning: Read, identify form of poem. Group processing.	Read poem to self. Write three words or phrases to describe what you liked about lesson.	Ability to transfer learning to own creativity. (Journal)
PHYSICAL EDUCATION	Name dance forms. Identify points of video.	Identify dance structure. Give rationale.	Add music to the dance that group creates.	Show the dance portions of videos.	Create a dance. Perform dance.	Cooperative learning: Work together to create a dance. Group processing.	Performance. Draw a picture of how you feel when dancing.	Self-assessment (own dance). Assessment of other dances.
FOREIGN LANGUAGE	Learn sign language. Guest explains signs.	Ask: What makes sign language the same/ different from other languages?	Sing "You Are My Sunshine."	Venn diagram or semantic map.	Visitor field trip. Perform (sign & sgn).	Cooperative learning: Learn about sign language. Group processing.	Performance. Journals: What would I like to know more about, and why?	Performance: 1) Song 2) Communicate non-verbally

Figure 3.22

IRI/Skylight Publishing, Inc.

MATRIX MIXER

Intelligence / Model	Verbal/ Linguistic	Musical/ Rhythmic	Bodily/ Kinesthetic	Logical/ Math- matical	Visual/ Spatial	Interper- sonal/ Social	Intrapersonal/ Introspective	
1 Fragmented								
2 Connected		Ⓐ						
3 Nested								
4 Sequenced								
5 Shared							Ⓑ	
6 Webbed								
7 Threaded			●		● Ⓒ			
8 Integrated								
9 Immersed								
10 Networked								

Three examples:

Ⓐ Connected Model: Using musical intelligence

Ⓑ Shared Model: Using intrapersonal intelligence

Ⓒ Threaded Model: Using bodily and visual intelligences

Figure 3.23

IRI/Skylight Publishing, Inc.

SHOW ME!

CHAPTER 4

Threads

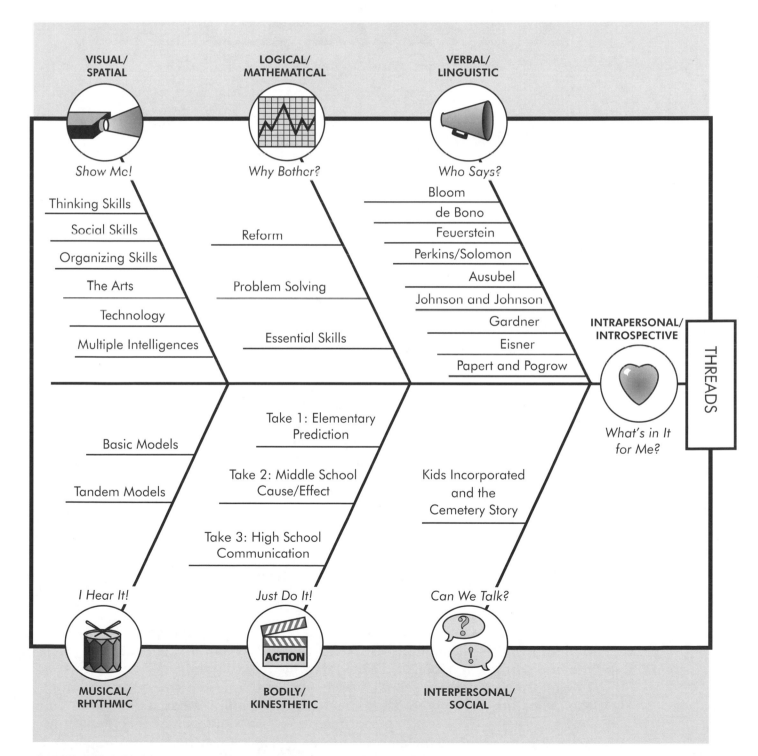

VISUAL/ SPATIAL

Show Me!

Thinking Skills

Social Skills

Organizing Skills

The Arts

Technology

Multiple Intelligences

Basic Models

Tandem Models

I Hear It!

MUSICAL/ RHYTHMIC

LOGICAL/ MATHEMATICAL

Why Bother?

Reform

Problem Solving

Essential Skills

Take 1: Elementary Prediction

Take 2: Middle School Cause/Effect

Take 3: High School Communication

Just Do It!

ACTION

BODILY/ KINESTHETIC

VERBAL/ LINGUISTIC

Who Says?

Bloom

de Bono

Feuerstein

Perkins/Solomon

Ausubel

Johnson and Johnson

Gardner

Eisner

Papert and Pogrow

Kids Incorporated and the Cemetery Story

Can We Talk?

INTERPERSONAL/ SOCIAL

INTRAPERSONAL/ INTROSPECTIVE

What's in It for Me?

THREADS

IRI/Skylight Publishing, Inc.

CHAPTER

4 THREADS

*It is not true that life is one damn thing after another—it's one
damn thing over and over.*

—Edna St. Vincent Millay

Why Bother?

WHY BOTHER?

In contrast to the thematic approach to curriculum integration, which focuses
on concepts that become designated themes, the threaded approach targets
specific skills to thread through subject matter content. In the threaded approach, the various disciplines are barely disturbed in terms of traditional
content and/or organization and sequence. Instead, predetermined skills in
thinking, cooperation, organization, technology, the arts, or multiple intelligences are infused into the academic content. This is a viable tool for beginning early curricular work in traditional schools. However, the threaded
approach is not only for individuals new to curriculum integration, but also for
all levels of schooling and school reform. This approach weaves relevant and
necessary skills into an academic format and speaks directly to the idea of
purposeful learning and learning for a lifetime.

REFORM FOR THE TWENTY-FIRST CENTURY

The concept of school restructuring seems to be a mission impossible. It can
be like building a tree house: The existing vertical structure is solidly in place,
and scraps are used to improvise a structure that keeps people out. Although
the tree house is functional, it is bound by the tree's limitations. The same is
true for the restructured school. The results are often obscure and are lost in
the magnitude of the preexisting structure. On the other hand, the mission
possible seems to be one of *reconceptualizing* our schools. Reconceptualizing
schooling is more like building a sand castle. The natural resources are plenti-

IRI/Skylight Publishing, Inc.

Why Bother?

ful and there is an ever-expanding horizontal design. The vision of the sand castle becomes inviting as it takes shape. Interested parties begin to dig in and become energized by the creativity involved. The results are almost always visible and oftentimes actually plausible.

The difference between restructuring schools and reconceptualizing schooling is critical. The vision of a sand castle is appealing: it engages our spirits as well as our skills. The reasons behind a school's successful reconceptualization are (1) they have a distinct and clear mission of schooling that guides every action of the educator-architect; (2) they have a mission made possible by the collaborative efforts of all involved; and (3) they are energized by their belief in what they are doing. Following is a description of this school and its typical activities. See what you think. Are these mission impossible? Do they burden teachers with unfounded mandates? Or are these missions *possible?* Do they renew the spirit and the skills of teachers?

The head of the P.E. division guides a group down the main hallway of the school and past the gym to the lower level, where there is a health club atmosphere. In a caged area in the center of the gym, there is a group of students using exercise equipment: bicycles, weight machines, a stair stepper, and a cross-country ski machine. Other students are running, jogging, and walking around the quarter-mile track that circles the center cage. In another area, an intern leads a small group in stretching and toning routines.

One young teacher leads a freshman through orientation proce-dures by walking her through a series of evaluations: fat con-tent, endurance, agility, flexibility, cardiovascular limits, and the usual height, weight, and body type assessments. Using this information, the student sets a ten-week goal to either lose weight, break her mile record, train for a marathon, or simply maintain a particular metabolism rate. Together, they develop a physical-fitness plan based on the student's particular trouble spots. In the meantime, students in the upstairs gym participate in a field-hockey drill as part of their two-day-a-week traditional P.E. program. Boys and girls together scramble up and down the court as they practice the rudiments of the game.

Based on the enthusiastic responses of both teachers and students to this problem-solving approach to health and fitness, the faculty launched the idea of threading life skills across all the curricular areas. Embracing problem solving as their pri-mary life-skill strategy, IDEAL (**I**dentify problem, **D**evelop alter-natives, **E**valuate alternatives, **A**pply alternatives, **L**ook over and evaluate), a simple generic model, is introduced to the entire faculty through a series of staff development offerings: mini-workshops during lunch-hour breaks, after-school sessions, and in-depth release time trainings for interested volunteers. With

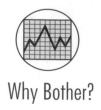

Why Bother?

in-district leadership of educators committed to staff development and support of key departmental figures and administrators, training tasks get done. Supporting the problem-solving goal, large laminated posters hang on the walls of every classroom. The IDEAL model permeates the climate and, more importantly, the instructional focus of the high school.

PROBLEM SOLVING BECOMES THE THREAD

In a rare and refreshing approach to traditionally sequenced math and biology classes, an energetic team of five math teachers decided to realign their math content to coincide with relevant applications in biology classes. Breaking radically from the standard scope and sequence that follows an algebra-geometry-trigonometry format, these creative math experts met with the school's biology team.

Through scheduling initiatives that clustered students and assigned them to math and science teams for four years, innovative curriculum designs were put in place and conversations across disciplines ignited. The conversations lead to commonsense connections between content areas (e.g., students were introduced to math concepts that applied to their work in the science lab). Although not all members of the two departments were ready for this sort of radical shift in content, the problem-solving approach was certainly at work in this pilot project. Team members decided to gather data for four years in order to evaluate the approach. They explain:

> "We're not happy with the math program the way it is. We're losing a lot of kids at the upper levels and their skills seem lost and isolated from practical applications."

> "While we understand that not everyone thinks this is a good idea, we're ready to go."

> "We know we're going to need solid data to convince others, but we think that by working with the same group of kids over the four years, we'll get to know them well enough to ensure success for all students in our cluster. Of course, it will have to show on their ACTs and SATs if we're to convince others, but we feel pretty confident that we've got a good, solid plan here."

Integration of life skills was also the target of a family living course directed by a team of two teachers. The team was well grounded in business education, home arts, social studies, and psychology. Budgets, babies, and the business of daily living were the concerns of this class. Following is an example of an activity that began their day.

138

"O.K., roll the dice. Let's see if these young marrieds are about to have a baby. Remember, if seven or eleven comes up, you'll be the lucky parents of a newborn baby girl or boy."

"Well, here goes, Marla. Keep your fingers crossed," yells David as he tosses the dice onto the tabletop.

"Congratulations! You're the proud parents of a baby boy! Now, don't forget, you'll need to complete the birth certificate, revise your budget, and plan for the baby's arrival home."

After the excitement dies down, small groups disperse to the various designations. One couple at the computer displays a spreadsheet that contains budget figures. Another group calculates the cost of inexpensive, nutritious meals for the week while another couple makes decisions about furnishing an apartment.

"How's it going? Are you able to purchase everything you'll need?" one teacher asks.

"Well, the money's going faster than we thought. There definitely won't be a television in our kitchen."

"What about the essentials, like a toaster, kitchen utensils, bedroom furniture, and linens?"

"Oh, yeah! We've got the basics covered. We're just trying to stretch it to include the 'wanna gets' too. But, it's not looking very promising."

Following the tour through this sea of problematic situations, the two teachers expound on the benefits and serendipitous effects on them as teachers.

"Teaming is the best vitamin my teaching has had in a long time. I'm so energized for this class, I can't believe it."

"I feel the same way. Working with a colleague this closely has provided an unbelievable boost to my spirit . . . and skills. It's really fun to be able to share the things the kids think of with someone who knows them as well as I do. I'll team every chance I get."

The faculty has also agreed to (1) develop student responsibility and self-esteem as integral parts of the mission; and (2) read across the curriculum (see fig. 4.1).

Why Bother?

Both threads have been introduced over time, and the teachers approve:

"*Jurassic Park*! Perfect! What a timely theme for us to use with the students. It bridges biology and literature and sets up a viable platform for theorizing and hypothesizing."

"And the kids are crazy with dinosaur fever because of the movie. It's relevant and interesting to them. It really is a good idea for both the problem-solving thread and the reading goals."

"In fact, we can even include the responsibility piece as we talk about the responsibilities that accompany man's scientific advances."

"It really is timely, too, because we can feed off the movie and have the kids analyze the similarities and differences between the book and the film."

"Not only that, but I'm excited about having teachers use science fiction as a problem-solving method."

Without a doubt, over the past three years, the high school has turned its vision of schooling into a mission *possible*. Students have been enabled to grow and mature with skills they will use not only for a test, but also for a lifetime.

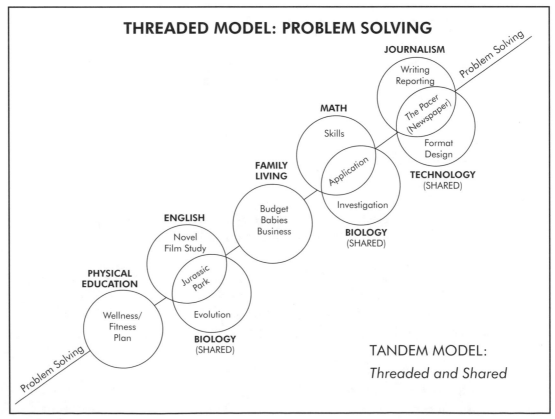

Figure 4.1

IRI/Skylight Publishing, Inc.

Following is a list of essential life skills that offer other plausible threads.

ESSENTIAL SKILLS AS THREADS

Data Gathering Skills
Acquire information from a variety of sources
Compile and organize information
Evaluate and interpret information

Problem-Solving/ Decision-Making Skills
Define the problem
List alternative solutions
Determine consequences of each strategy
Assess consequences of such actions in relationship to democratic principles
Act based on those decisions

Reasoning Skills
Compare things, ideas, events, and situations on basis of similarities and differences
Classify or group items in categories
Ask appropriate and searching questions
Draw conclusions or inferences from evidence
Arrive at general ideas

Communication Skills
Listen to gain information and to respond thoughtfully
Read to enjoy, learn, and improve communication skills
Participate actively in oral expression
Write effectively to achieve purpose

Interpersonal Skills
Assess one's own values and beliefs in light of their effect on relations with others
Use group generalizations without stereotyping
Acknowledge beliefs and feelings different from one's own or one's group
Work effectively alone and with others
Give and receive constructive criticism
Accept responsibility
Respect the rights and property of others

IRI/Skylight Publishing, Inc.

Who Says?

WHO SAYS?

To fully represent the voices from the tower and others in the field who advocate life skill threads, the areas must be designated and defined. For the purposes of this book, the following life skill areas are targeted: thinking skills, social skills, organizing skills, multiple intelligences, artistic skills, and technological skills.

BLOOM et al. (Thinking)

Familiar to many is Bloom's *Taxonomy of Educational Objectives* (1984) with its six levels of thinking and questioning. Moving from the lowest level to the highest, Bloom's classifications are knowledge, comprehension, application, analysis, synthesis, and evaluation. Fogarty and Bellanca (1989) and Costa (1991) use the concept of the three-story intellect to condense Bloom's taxonomy into three discernible phases of thinking. The following text and graphic illustrate an easy-to-grasp concept of thoughtful behavior.

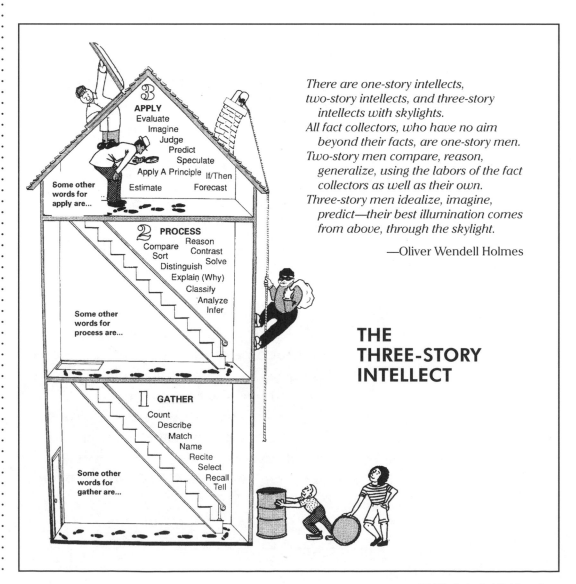

There are one-story intellects, two-story intellects, and three-story intellects with skylights.
All fact collectors, who have no aim beyond their facts, are one-story men.
Two-story men compare, reason, generalize, using the labors of the fact collectors as well as their own.
Three-story men idealize, imagine, predict—their best illumination comes from above, through the skylight.

—Oliver Wendell Holmes

THE THREE-STORY INTELLECT

de BONO et al. (Thinking)

Moving beyond the conceptual models, de Bono (1976), Marzano and Arredondo (1988), and Fogarty and Bellanca (1989) present practical strategies for classroom use.

FEUERSTEIN et al. (Thinking)

While Beyer (1989) and Fogarty and Bellanca (1986) advocate the explicit teaching of the microskills of thinking, Feuerstein (1980), Swartz and Perkins (1987), Costa (1985), Brown and Palinscar (1978), and Fogarty (1994) advocate the concept of metacognition, or reflective self-awareness, of thoughtful behavior.

JOHNSON AND JOHNSON et al. (Cooperative Learning)

Well known in the field for their prolific writings on developing social skills, the Johnsons (1986) believe that students must care as much about the other person as they care about themselves. That is their vision of the cooperative learning group at work.

Slavin's (1983) work in developing curriculum packages that create interdependence and individual accountability parallel the Johnsons' theoretical base. All four researchers are grounded in the work of Deutch (1949).

Kagan's (1992) social structures, and Bellanca and Fogarty's *Blueprints for Thinking in the Cooperative Classroom* (1991) provide a wealth of practical, easy-to-implement strategies for the K–college classroom or adult staff room.

Other citations in cooperative learning involve Sharan (1980), who developed a full classroom model for group investigations; Cohen (1986); and Schmuck and Schmuck (1983), well known for their work in small group process.

AUSUBEL et al. (Graphic Organizers)

Ausubel's theory (1978) of "meaningful reception learning" resulted in a technique called the "structured overview" in which students were presented a visual that organized information into hierarchical order. The "advanced organizer," as it was called, provided an overview or "big picture" of what students were about to read.

Lyman and McTighe (1988) cover cognitive maps in their discussion of theory-embedded tools.

Parks and Black's two-volume handbook of lessons, *Organizing Thinking* (1992; 1990), illustrates ways of integrating the teaching of thinking skills into instruction.

Fogarty and Bellanca (1989) present graphic organizers as part of a thinking classroom, and Bellanca (1992) presents twenty-four graphics with models for use with elementary, middle, and high school students.

Who Says?

IRI/Skylight Publishing, Inc.

GARDNER (Multiple Intelligences)

To read more about Gardner's theory of multiple intelligences, please refer to chapter one, which also discusses other authorities in the field.

GARDNER AND EISNER (The Arts)

Leading voices in the arts, Howard Gardner and Elliott Eisner (1983) both write extensively in the field of arts education. Gardner's work in the arts led him to reexamine the role of visual and performing arts as tools for authentic assessments of human potential. His theory of multiple intelligences impacts not only assessment, but also the heart of instructional and curriculum design. Eisner (1983) focuses his efforts on qualitative analysis of programs and personnel in the schools. Eisner's message of "educational connoisseurship" is as powerful now as ever, as schools look to portfolio development and performance assessment as tools to view the whole child.

PAPERT AND POGROW (Technology)

Coauthor and developer of Logo (a computer programming language for children), Seymour Papert (1993) believes the computer is a catalyst for deep and radical change within the educational system. Using computer-based media, Papert shows how children can master areas of knowledge that were previously inaccessible.

Pogrow's work with the HOTS program utilizes computers to teach students problem solving and higher-order thinking processes.

I Hear It!

I HEAR IT!

Threads
(round)

1. Learn - ing is the nee - dle. Life skills are the thread.

2. Weave them through a life - time Through my heart and head.

BASIC MODELS

Threaded Curriculum

The most basic model for threading life skills into standard subject matter content is epitomized in two examples of this kind of curriculum integration: *writing across the curriculum* and *reading in the content areas*. Keeping a math log of problem-solving strategies or reading a biology text and creating a

I Hear It?

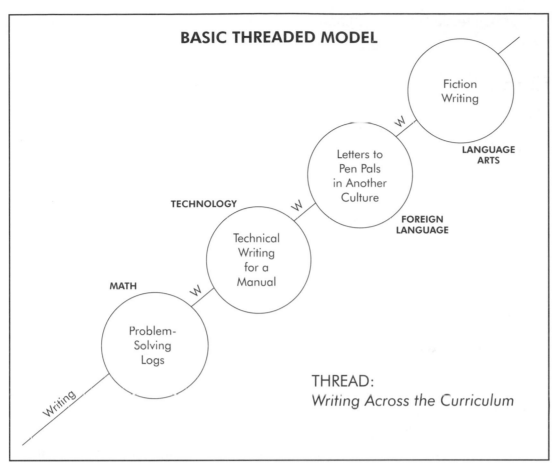

BASIC THREADED MODEL

Fiction Writing

LANGUAGE ARTS

Letters to Pen Pals in Another Culture

TECHNOLOGY

FOREIGN LANGUAGE

Technical Writing for a Manual

MATH

Problem-Solving Logs

Writing

THREAD:
Writing Across the Curriculum

Figure 4.2

Venn diagram to compare and contrast characteristics are typical activities that exemplify the threaded approach to curriculum integration.

The basic model looks like a string of pearls (see fig. 4.2). In this example, writing is threaded through the content in four disciplines. Students keep a problem-solving log in their math class, and in their technology class they are given opportunities to do technical writing to develop a manual. These same students may be expected to write letters and correspond with a student from another culture. At the same time, they are writing short stories in their English class.

The basic threaded model is simple to implement and requires minimal team time. In brief, forty-five-minute faculty meetings in which all departments are represented, decisions can easily be made about common threads to use for a designated period of time. Once the threads are selected, each teacher uses the thread appropriately within the natural course of events. As the content unfolds, prime opportunities occur for the inclusion of the targeted thread.

The threaded model works in self-contained, "compartmentalized" classrooms, where students study all of their subjects in one classroom, and in "departmentalized" classrooms, where students move to different rooms for different subjects. In both cases, teachers take every opportunity to thread life skills into the content. The tools of life—thinking, teaming, and organizing—are embedded into meaningful content. Without content there is nothing to organize or think about; there is no project to work on as a team. In summary,

I Hear It!

threading life skills into content is a viable, efficient, and already accepted "best practice."

Multiple Threads

Once the basic model is understood, the next step is to work with multiple threads (see fig. 4.4). Select threads in several life-skill areas. Introduce a comprehensive list of life skills to the faculty and choose those that everyone agrees are relevant, critical, and applicable across content.

Choose three life-skill areas.
Write in the microskills for each.

- Technology: _____
- Thinking Skills: _____
- Social Skills: _____
- Multiple Intelligences: _____
- Graphic Organizers: _____
- The Arts: _____

Life Skills

To thread life skills through content in all disciplines, use the lists provided in this section of the six designated life-skill areas: thinking, socializing, organizing, multiple intelligences, technology, and the arts. In addition to the lists of life skills, a basic threaded example for each one is represented in text and in graphic form. Again, the illustrations provide easy-to-share, easy-to-implement ideas for introducing or maintaining life-skill threads for meaningful, purposeful curriculum integration. Take a moment to survey the six basic models for a clearer picture of the threading process.

THINKING SKILLS

Creative Skills (Generative, Productive)
1. Brainstorming
2. Visualizing
3. Personifying
4. Inventing
5. Associating relationships
6. Inferring
7. Generalizing
8. Predicting
9. Hypothesizing
10. Making analogies
11. Dealing with ambiguity and paradox
12. Problem solving

Critical Skills (Analytical, Evaluative)
1. Attributing
2. Comparing
3. Classifying
4. Sequencing
5. Prioritizing
6. Drawing conclusions
7. Determining cause/effect
8. Analyzing for bias
9. Analyzing for assumptions
10. Solving for analogies
11. Evaluating
12. Decision making

Adapted from Robin Fogarty and James Bellanca, *Teach Them Thinking*. (Palatine, IL: IRI/Skylight Publishing, 1986), p. 2.

Figure 4.3

IRI/Skylight Publishing, Inc.

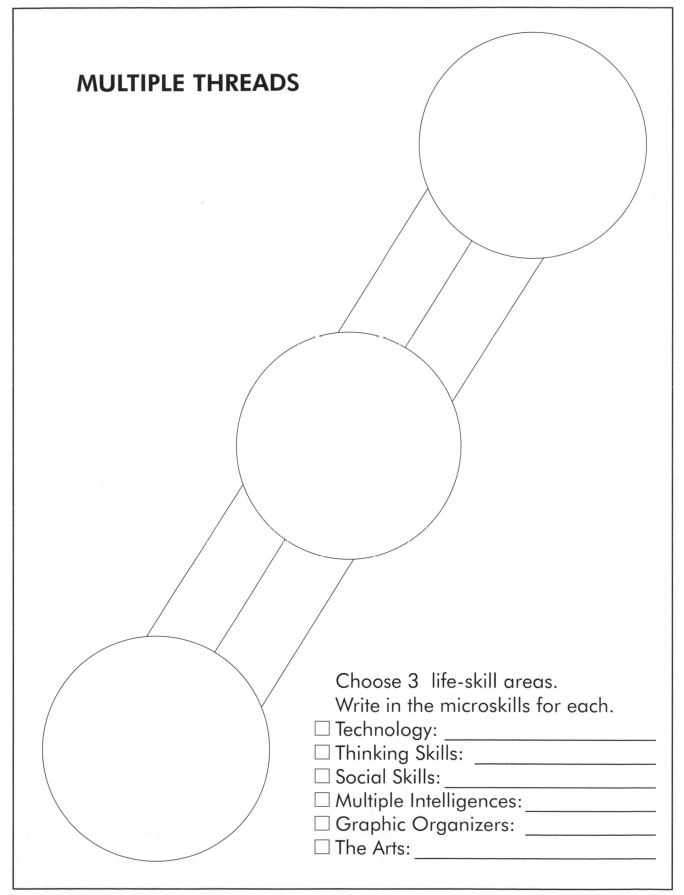

MULTIPLE THREADS

Choose 3 life-skill areas.
Write in the microskills for each.
☐ Technology: _____
☐ Thinking Skills: _____
☐ Social Skills: _____
☐ Multiple Intelligences: _____
☐ Graphic Organizers: _____
☐ The Arts: _____

Figure 4.4

IRI/Skylight Publishing, Inc.

I Hear It!

Thinking Skills

By reviewing a list of higher-order thinking skills (see fig. 4.3), faculty members can decide what skills to focus on and for how long. For example, if members of the English department choose the thinking skill of prediction, teachers can brainstorm how to explain the skill to students and how to have them apply it (see fig. 4.5). It is important to remember that the students must understand the terminology used for referring to specific thinking skills, social skills, or multiple intelligences. If we expect students to think about their own thinking and to "learn how to learn" through metacognition, they must be aware of the skills they are using so they can consciously draw upon those skills later.

Social Skills

The time line for focusing on each social skill will vary by grade level. An essential skill like "attentive listening" can be emphasized for longer periods of time or introduced early in the year and reinforced or revisited later. Teachers may emphasize a basic social skill such as "including everyone in a group" for only a few weeks at the beginning of the school year, whereas they might save more sophisticated conflict resolution skills until later in the year to make sure that all the students are first exposed to the social skills of

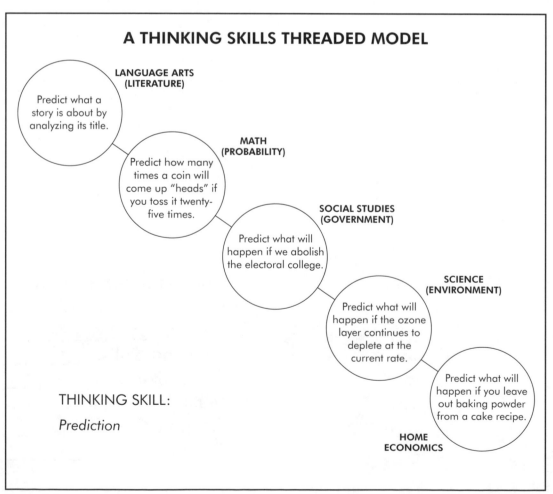

A THINKING SKILLS THREADED MODEL

LANGUAGE ARTS (LITERATURE)
Predict what a story is about by analyzing its title.

MATH (PROBABILITY)
Predict how many times a coin will come up "heads" if you toss it twenty-five times.

SOCIAL STUDIES (GOVERNMENT)
Predict what will happen if we abolish the electoral college.

SCIENCE (ENVIRONMENT)
Predict what will happen if the ozone layer continues to deplete at the current rate.

HOME ECONOMICS
Predict what will happen if you leave out baking powder from a cake recipe.

THINKING SKILL:

Prediction

Figure 4.5

IRI/Skylight Publishing, Inc.

SOCIAL SKILLS

TEAM-BUILDING SKILLS

- ☑ Choose new partners
- ☑ Sit knee to knee
- ☑ Make eye contact
- ☑ Use each other's names
- ☑ Share materials
- ☑ Follow role assignments
- ☑ Include others
- ☑ Develop guidelines
- ☑ Identify with team

LEADERSHIP SKILLS

- ☑ Check for understanding
- ☑ Offer help
- ☑ Ask group for help
- ☑ Encourage each other
- ☑ Energize the group
- ☑ Accept role and responsibility
- ☑ Follow guidelines
- ☑ Affirm
- ☑ Stay on task

COMMUNICATION SKILLS

- ☑ Use quiet voices
- ☑ Take turns
- ☑ Listen to the speaker
- ☑ Wait for speaker to finish
- ☑ Clarify
- ☑ Paraphrase
- ☑ Sense tone
- ☑ Give examples
- ☑ Elaborate

CONFLICT RESOLUTION SKILLS

- ☑ Disagree with idea only
- ☑ Respect others' opinions
- ☑ Think for yourself
- ☑ Explore different points of view
- ☑ Negotiate and/or compromise
- ☑ Reach consensus
- ☑ Offer alternatives
- ☑ Probe for differences
- ☑ Keep an open mind

(Adapted from Bellanca and Fogarty, 1991, Ch. 3)

Figure 4.6

IRI/Skylight Publishing, Inc.

I Hear It!

communication and team building. Before learning conflict resolution skills, students need to understand basic social skills. It is important to spend time actually teaching a social skill by modeling it so students know what it looks and sounds like.

A teacher may decide to focus on the social skill of disagreeing with an idea and not the person presenting it (see fig. 4.7). The teacher can have the students discuss or debate controversial issues, while reminding them that it is OK to disagree with the ideas expressed by a person without attacking the person expressing them. Following is a chart of what it looks and sounds like to disagree with an idea instead of a person:

DISAGREE WITH IDEA

Looks Like	*Sounds Like*
1. Shaking hands at end of debate or argument.	1. I disagree with one point you made.
2. Nodding when a reasonable point is made.	2. May I give another point of view?
3. Eye contact.	3. Would you clarify that point?

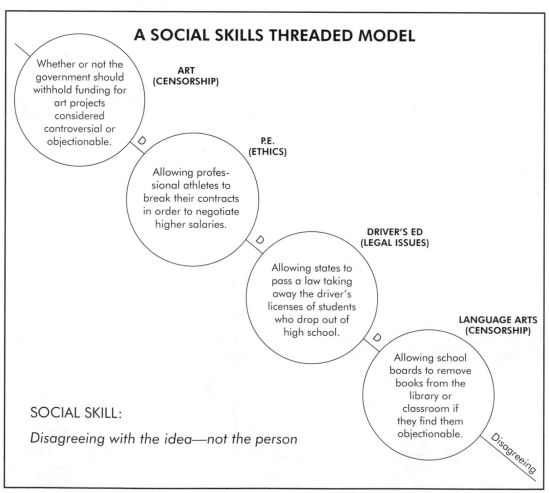

Figure 4.7

IRI/Skylight Publishing, Inc.

Organizing Skills

Discuss the issue of how students learn best. Some students learn best in a visual mode. Therefore, an array of graphic organizers can be introduced over time for application in the classroom. A group of teachers reviewed a list of organizers (see figs. 4.8 and 4.9) and decided that the fishbone analysis would be useful for students. The analysis chart using the fishbone actually charts like an outline, which many of their students were having trouble with. In a fishbone outline, a certain topic is focused on and major elements and details are filled in. This is a nice parallel to outlining (see fig. 4.10).

Multiple Intelligences

The teachers selected multiple intelligences to thread in this example for grades seven and eight. The multiple threads provide many opportunities for a meaningful integration of life skills into existing content (see fig. 4.11): For cooperative learning groups, teachers used the interpersonal intelligence to target the leadership skill of encouraging others; the visual/spatial intelligence was used in various ways in each subject area; and the bodily/kinesthetic intelligence was applied for hands-on, experiential learning in each class.

In a simple technology example, one school team decided to target introductory skills during the first five weeks of school. Specifically, the English department threaded into a critical reading unit the skills needed for reading technical manuals; biology teachers required lab reports to be typed; business teachers targeted the typing of reports; and the art teacher taught students how to draw basic graphics and design covers for their technology portfolios. In this threaded model, each teacher proceeded with a predetermined unit (see fig. 4.13).

In the arts model, two threads were used with a specific purpose in mind: helping the students create their portfolios. The teachers decided to use the visual arts skill of drawing and videotaping in each discipline to motivate the students to compile creative portfolios. The threads are illustrated in figure 4.15 and include traditional activities such as drawing and labeling a cell in biology or viewing a movie of a novel being read in English. Some less traditional activities also appear, including "drawing" a solution to a math problem or videotaping a demonstration of cell division.

In Conclusion

The threaded model may be the easiest and most effective way to introduce faculty members to a relatively painless, and risk-free model of curricular integration at the elementary, middle, and high school levels. The threaded model allows each teacher to preserve existing content while threading a thinking skill, social skill, organizational skill, multiple intelligence, technology skill, or the arts through the curriculum and across all subject areas. The skill can be threaded for a few days, a month, a semester, or a year, depending on how much emphasis the faculty wants to place on the threaded piece. If a faculty wants to implement the threaded model of curriculum integration, the following sequence chart (see fig 4.16) may help them map this course of action.

I Hear It!

IRI/Skylight Publishing, Inc.

GRAPHIC ORGANIZERS I

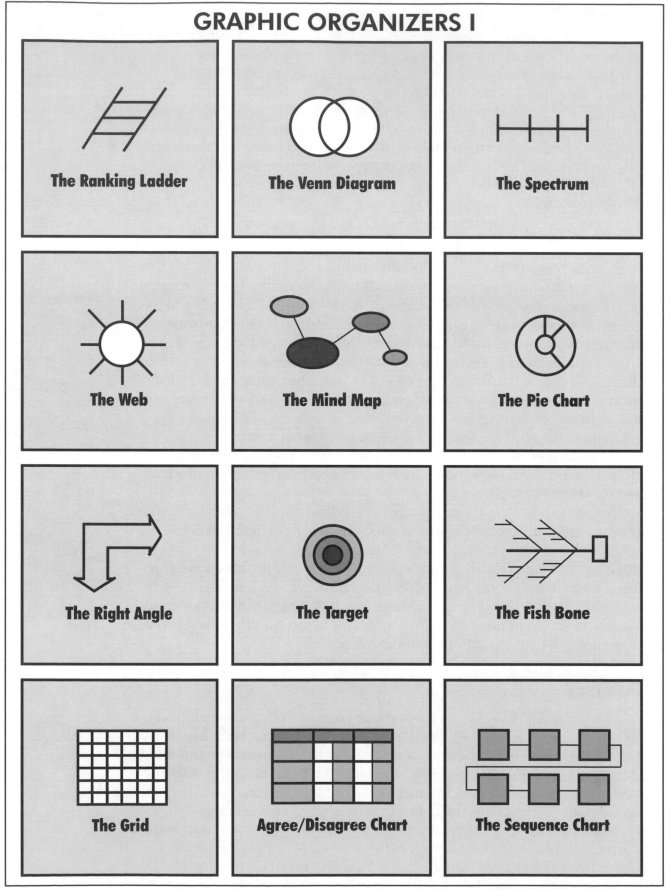

The Ranking Ladder

The Venn Diagram

The Spectrum

The Web

The Mind Map

The Pie Chart

The Right Angle

The Target

The Fish Bone

The Grid

Agree/Disagree Chart

The Sequence Chart

(From Bellanca, 1990)   Figure 4.8

IRI/Skylight Publishing, Inc.

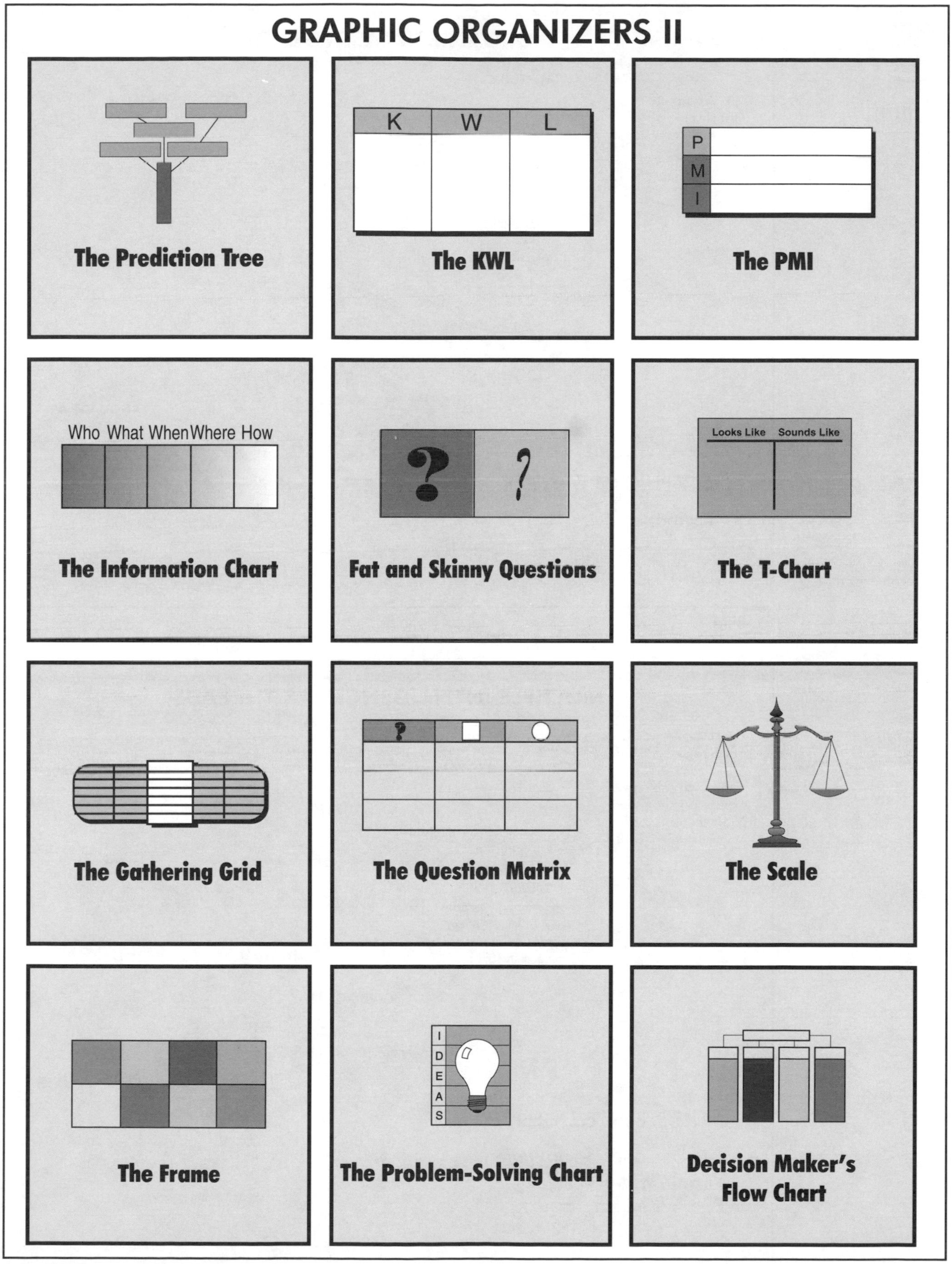

GRAPHIC ORGANIZERS II

The Prediction Tree

The KWL

K	W	L

The PMI

P	
M	
I	

Who What When Where How

The Information Chart

Fat and Skinny Questions

Looks Like | Sounds Like

The T-Chart

The Gathering Grid

The Question Matrix

The Scale

The Frame

IDEAS

The Problem-Solving Chart

Decision Maker's Flow Chart

Figure 4.9   (From Bellanca, 1992)

IRI/Skylight Publishing, Inc.

I Hear It!

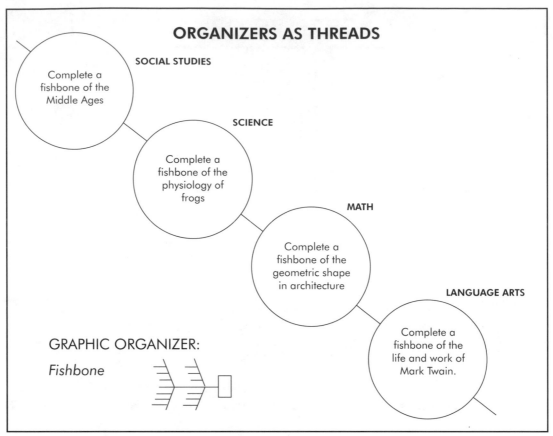

Figure 4.10

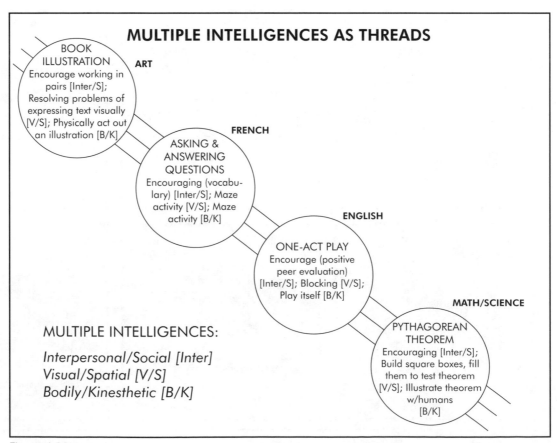

Figure 4.11

IRI/Skylight Publishing, Inc.

I Hear It!

TECHNOLOGY SKILLS

Basic Programs/Applications

Word Processing

Spreadsheets

Databases

Graphics/Drawing

Page Layout

Animation

Multimedia

Support Skills

Using a manual

Knowledge of hardware

Keyboarding

Using a modem and FAX

Using E-mail and Internet

Programming

Basic troubleshooting

Figure 4.12

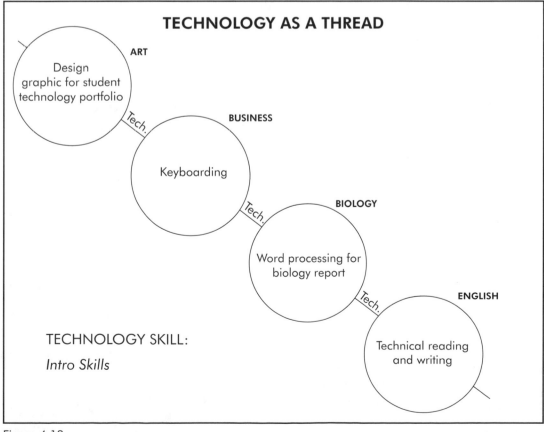

TECHNOLOGY AS A THREAD

ART

Design graphic for student technology portfolio

Tech.

BUSINESS

Keyboarding

Tech.

BIOLOGY

Word processing for biology report

Tech.

ENGLISH

Technical reading and writing

TECHNOLOGY SKILL:

Intro Skills

Figure 4.13

IRI/Skylight Publishing, Inc.

I Hear It!

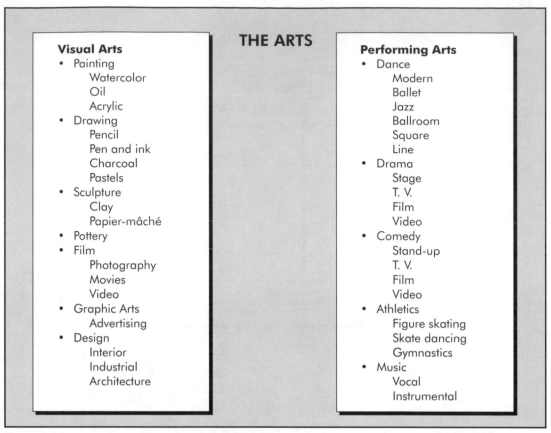

THE ARTS

Visual Arts
- Painting
    Watercolor
    Oil
    Acrylic
- Drawing
    Pencil
    Pen and ink
    Charcoal
    Pastels
- Sculpture
    Clay
    Papier-mâché
- Pottery
- Film
    Photography
    Movies
    Video
- Graphic Arts
    Advertising
- Design
    Interior
    Industrial
    Architecture

Performing Arts
- Dance
    Modern
    Ballet
    Jazz
    Ballroom
    Square
    Line
- Drama
    Stage
    T. V.
    Film
    Video
- Comedy
    Stand-up
    T. V.
    Film
    Video
- Athletics
    Figure skating
    Skate dancing
    Gymnastics
- Music
    Vocal
    Instrumental

Figure 4.14

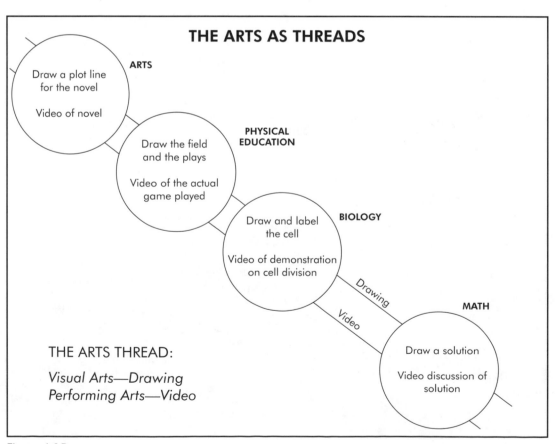

THE ARTS AS THREADS

ARTS

Draw a plot line for the novel

Video of novel

PHYSICAL EDUCATION

Draw the field and the plays

Video of the actual game played

BIOLOGY

Draw and label the cell

Video of demonstration on cell division

Drawing

Video

MATH

Draw a solution

Video discussion of solution

THE ARTS THREAD:

Visual Arts—Drawing
Performing Arts—Video

Figure 4.15

IRI/Skylight Publishing, Inc.

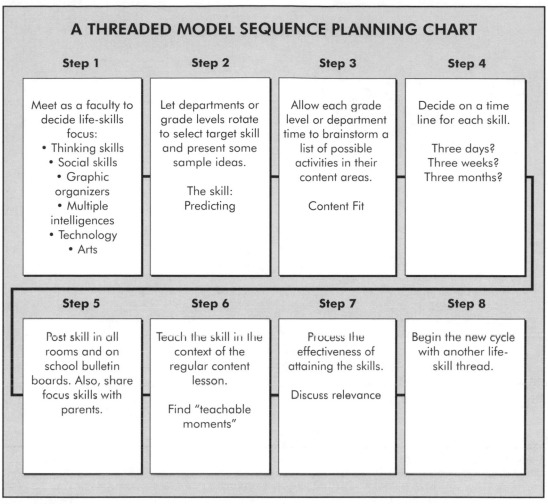

A THREADED MODEL SEQUENCE PLANNING CHART

Step 1

Meet as a faculty to decide life-skills focus:
• Thinking skills
• Social skills
• Graphic organizers
• Multiple intelligences
• Technology
• Arts

Step 2

Let departments or grade levels rotate to select target skill and present some sample ideas.

The skill: Predicting

Step 3

Allow each grade level or department time to brainstorm a list of possible activities in their content areas.

Content Fit

Step 4

Decide on a time line for each skill.

Three days?
Three weeks?
Three months?

Step 5

Post skill in all rooms and on school bulletin boards. Also, share focus skills with parents.

Step 6

Teach the skill in the context of the regular content lesson.

Find "teachable moments"

Step 7

Process the effectiveness of attaining the skills.

Discuss relevance

Step 8

Begin the new cycle with another life-skill thread.

Figure 4.16

I Hear It!

INTRODUCTION TO TANDEMS—THREADED

Tandems (Rap)

Working as a team and planning side by side
Synergy in motion capturing the pride.
Relevance in learning, and in our teaching, too.
Innovative plans that work for me and you!

Use the tandems rap to introduce the tandem models idea, which is to combine other integration schemes with the threaded model. One simple tandem for threading is to *thread* and *nest* at the same time (see fig. 4.17). One life skill can easily be threaded—in this case the bodily/kinesthetic intelligence for hands-on learning—while a number of other life skills are nested into the lesson simultaneously. Thus, students can act out the parts of speech, while the teacher targets the social skill of accepting ideas and the thinking skill of brainstorming. Small groups of students can also plan to act out the parts of speech.

Tandem combinations are as varied as the creative connections teachers make with their content. A few typical examples are the following: *threaded*

I Hear It!

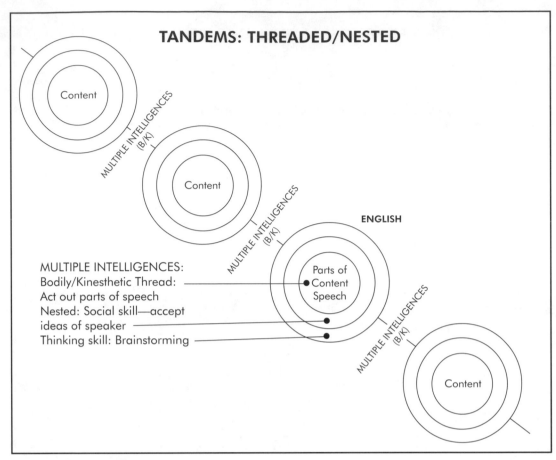

Figure 4.17

and connected; threaded and nested; threaded and sequenced; and threaded and shared.

In figures 4.18 and 4.19 are two further examples of tandems. They illustrate how natural the connections become as teachers familiarize themselves with the tools of integration. Figure 4.18 shows a connected model used in an English class in which a theme emerges. In figure 4.19, three models of integration are used in tandem. Problem solving is the thread used, but there are several other natural connections that can be made across the content. All of the classes resequenced their lessons to coincide with one another.

The webbed/threaded model is shown in figure 4.20. A technology theme, which branches out to the seven intelligences, is used in this example. The activities shown in the illustration are relevant subject-specific applications of the theme with the life-skill thread of cooperation.

A rare look at integrating with tandem models of personal connection making is presented in figure 4.21. In this example, an immersed learner (a geologist) is threading problem solving through his work, and the threaded/networked learners (chemist, editor, and graphic artist) are working together to solve problems on a book project.

IRI/Skylight Publishing, Inc.

I Hear It!

TANDEMS: THREADED AND CONNECTED

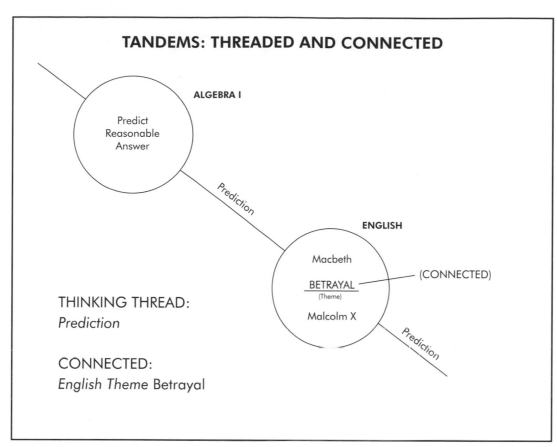

ALGEBRA I

Predict Reasonable Answer

Prediction

ENGLISH

Macbeth

BETRAYAL
(Theme)

Malcolm X

(CONNECTED)

Prediction

THINKING THREAD:
Prediction

CONNECTED:
English Theme Betrayal

Figure 4.18

TANDEMS: THREADED, SHARED, AND SEQUENCED

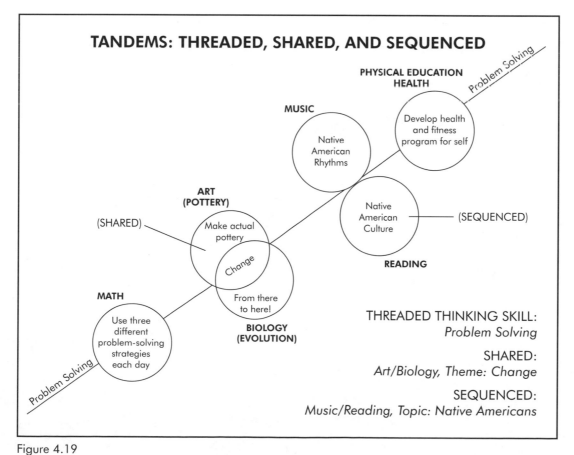

Problem Solving

PHYSICAL EDUCATION
HEALTH

Develop health and fitness program for self

MUSIC

Native American Rhythms

ART
(POTTERY)

(SHARED)

Make actual pottery

Change

From there to here!

Native American Culture

(SEQUENCED)

READING

MATH

Use three different problem-solving strategies each day

BIOLOGY
(EVOLUTION)

Problem Solving

THREADED THINKING SKILL:
Problem Solving

SHARED:
Art/Biology, Theme: Change

SEQUENCED:
Music/Reading, Topic: Native Americans

Figure 4.19

IRI/Skylight Publishing, Inc.

I Hear It!

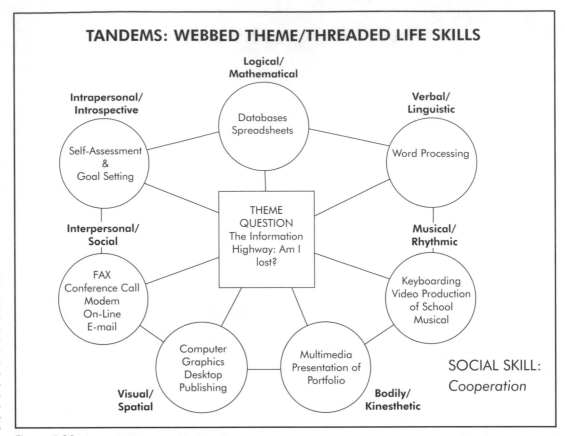

Figure 4.20

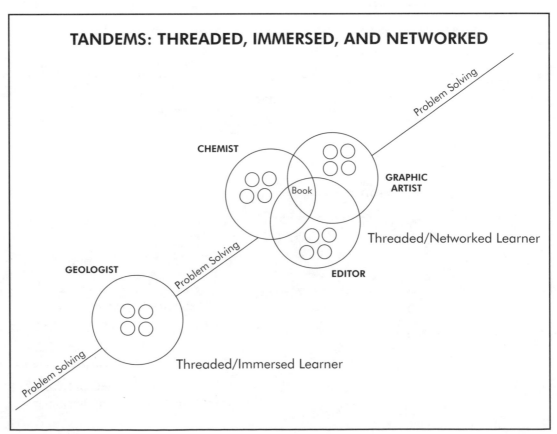

Figure 4.21

JUST DO IT!

Take 1

Elementary Lessons

THREADED MODEL: PREDICTION

Threaded Skill: Predicting
Threaded Intelligences: Logical/Mathematical and Verbal/Linguistic

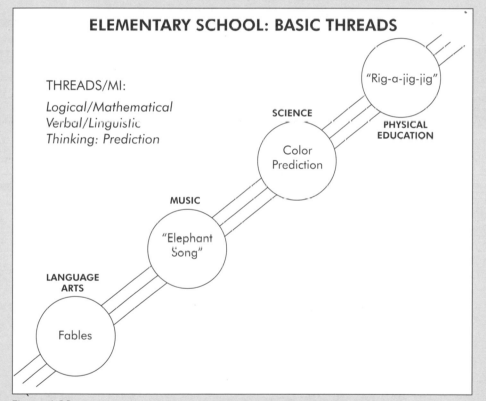

ELEMENTARY SCHOOL: BASIC THREADS

THREADS/MI:

Logical/Mathematical
Verbal/Linguistic
Thinking: Prediction

"Rig-a-jig-jig"

SCIENCE

PHYSICAL EDUCATION

Color Prediction

MUSIC

"Elephant Song"

LANGUAGE ARTS

Fables

Figure 4.22

Language Arts

Lesson: Learning about Fables
Materials: fables, including "The Crow and the Pitcher" from *Aesop's Fables.*

Explain that a fable is a short tale that teaches a lesson or moral. Then, read "The Crow and the Pitcher" (or other fable) aloud to the class. Ask them what the following means: "Never give up. There's always a way." Ask the students how they can use this lesson in their own lives.

IRI/Skylight Publishing, Inc.

Just Do It!

Read another fable to the class, but stop just before you read the moral. Ask them what they think the moral of this fable will be and why. Then, read the moral aloud. Read one last fable to the class and be sure to stop just before reading the moral.

Assessment: Portfolio

Have the students write what they think the moral will be. Have them share their answers and explain their reasoning. Read the moral aloud.

Assessment: Traditional

Be sure to discuss the meaning of the moral each time. Also, discuss how the moral can be applied to the students' lives.

Assessment: Performance

Have the students act out the fable.

Music

Lesson: "Elephant Song"
Materials: Yarn
A copy of the "Elephant Song" (no recording)

In a large open space in the room, use yarn to create a "spider's web" on the floor. (Suggestion: Make an outside circle with the yarn first, then weave it in and out throughout the space in the circle.) Instruct the students to stand around the outside of the web. To play the game, follow these directions:

1. Sing the song as you walk like an elephant on the outside circle of the web.
2. When the song ends, stop and look at the person standing nearest you.
3. Call that person by name, and invite him or her to join you. Now there are two elephants.
4. Tell the students that the next time the song stops they will each invite another person. Ask how many elephants there will be then. (4)

Assessment: Traditional

Before the song restarts each time, ask the students how many elephants there will be at the end.

Assessment: Performance

Once everyone is an "elephant," tell them they can walk anywhere on the web as they sing the song, as long as they don't run into anyone. Ask the following questions: (1) What does each person need to do in order to not run into anyone? and (2) Can you plan your route before you start? How?

Assessment: Portfolio

Have the students discuss how they felt during the first part of the game if they did not get invited to join.

IRI/Skylight Publishing, Inc.

The Elephant
(play song)

One e-le-phant went out to play

on a spi-der's web one day. He had such e-

nor-mous fun that he asked a-no-ther e-le-phant to come.

Science

Lesson: Color Prediction

Materials: Petri dishes — Jars
Food coloring — Waxed paper
Overhead projector — Popsicle sticks
Eye droppers — Color-prediction forms

Put water in three petri dishes. Add red food coloring to one dish, blue to the second, and yellow to the third. Set the petri dishes side by side on a lighted projector. Ask the students to identify the three colors. Then, ask them what they think will happen if you mix the red and blue. Now, set the red petri dish on top of the blue. Ask them if this is the color they predicted. Ask them what they think will happen if you mix the blue and yellow. Set the yellow petri dish on top of the blue. Ask them if this is what they predicted.

Now, divide the class into teams of two. Give each team several eyedroppers and jars of colored water (include both primary and secondary colors). Give each team a large sheet of waxed paper, two drinking straws, and a color-prediction form, which should have three columns labeled "Colors," "I Think," and "Actual."

Assessment: Performance

Have the teams select two colors to mix. Instruct the students to record the colors on their forms under the "Colors" column. Before they actually mix the colors, have them predict what the new color will be; then, have them write that color under "I think." Direct the students to use the eyedropper to put the colored water on the waxed paper. Have them stir the drops of water with a Popsicle stick.

Just Do It!

Assessment: Traditional

Once the students have mixed the colors, direct them to write the resulting color under "Actual." Discuss whether or not the actual color was what they predicted, and why or why not.

Assessment: Portfolio

Have the students decide on other colors they would like to mix. Determine how they can use what they have learned in other activities.

Physical Education

Lesson: Learning "Rig-a-jig-jig"
Materials: A copy of "Rig-a-jig-jig" (no recording)

Instruct the students to stand in a large circle. Teach the song and sing it. Walk around the inside of the circle to the beat during the lines "As I was walking down the street, down the street, down the street. A friend of mine I chanced to meet, heigh-ho, heigh-ho, heigh-ho." Make sure that on the last "heigh-ho" you are in front of someone in the circle. Stop and face that person.

Take your partner's hands, and on the words "rig-a-jig-jig" move them back and forth to the rhythm of the words. On "away we go, away we go, away we go," swing your arms from one side to the other, on the beat. On "heigh-ho, heigh-ho, heigh-ho," wring the dishrag with your partner. When the song is finished, invite your new "friend" to join you in the circle.

Rig-a-Jig-Jig
(folk song)

164

Lesson: Exponential growth

Each time you sing the song, the number in the middle will double.

 Assessment: Traditional
Before beginning the song each time, have the students predict the number that will be in the circle by the end.

 Assessment: Portfolio
Ask the students if they think it will get easier or harder to stop in front of someone each time the song is sung. (Harder.) Why? (More open spaces.) What will they need to do as they walk in order to stop in front of someone?

 Assessment: Performance
Play the game.

Just Do It!

Middle School Lesson

THREADED MODEL: CAUSE AND EFFECT

Threaded Skill: Cause and Effect
Threaded Intelligences: Musical/Rhythmic, Interpersonal/Social, and Intrapersonal/Introspective

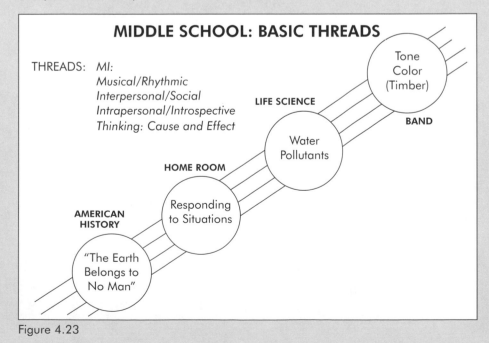

MIDDLE SCHOOL: BASIC THREADS

THREADS: *MI:*
Musical/Rhythmic
Interpersonal/Social
Intrapersonal/Introspective
Thinking: Cause and Effect

Tone Color (Timber)

BAND

LIFE SCIENCE

Water Pollutants

HOME ROOM

Responding to Situations

AMERICAN HISTORY

"The Earth Belongs to No Man"

Figure 4.23

Just Do It!

History

Lesson: American History

Materials: "The Earth Belongs to No Man," a letter from Chief Sealth to President Franklin Pierce in 1855 (on next page).

Discuss what cause and effect is; then, direct the students to read "The Earth Belongs to No Man" on their own. Ask the students what the letter is about and if Chief Sealth talks about cause and effect. Have them explain their answers.

Assessment: Portfolio

Direct the students to look at the last paragraph of the letter. Have them select one part of the paragraph (e.g., "All things are connected like the blood which unites one family.") and write a cause-and-effect paragraph of how it relates to them.

Assessment: Traditional

Discuss the emotional impact of music in movies and television shows. Then, divide the class into cooperative groups and direct each group to do the following:

1. *Discuss the letter.*
2. *Brainstorm what kind of music would be appropriate as a background to the letter as it is read aloud.*
3. *Create a musical background using voices and environmental sounds.*
4. *Select a narrator within the group.*

Assessment: Performance

"Perform" for the class.

Homeroom

Lesson: Identifying the ways we currently respond to situations

Materials: Paper
Pencils
Pens

Divide the group into teams of three, and have them decide who will be "character 1," "character 2," and the "observer," who takes notes about how each character reacts, in the following role-playing game.

Character 1 is missing his or her new jacket and thinks character 2 took it. Character 2 is not always the most honest, but in this instance did *not* take the jacket.

Give the teams one minute to play their roles. Then, have the observers name some of the behaviors they discussed. Ask the students who played the characters to share how they felt.

IRI/Skylight Publishing, Inc.

The Earth Belongs to No Man

(letter written by Chief Sealth to President Franklin Pierce in 1855)

There is no quiet place in the white man's cities. No place to hear the unfurling of leaves in spring or the rustle of insects' wings. But perhaps it is because I am a savage and do not understand. The clatter only seems to insult the ears. And what is there to life if a man cannot hear the lonely cry of the whippoorwill or the arguments of the frogs around a pond at night. I am a red man and I do not understand.

The Indian prefers the soft sound of the wind darting over the face of a pond, and the smell of the wind itself, cleansed by a midday rain, or scented with the pinion pine.

Even the white man, whose God walks and talks with him as a friend, cannot be exempt from the common destiny. We may be brothers after all, we shall see. One thing we know, which the white man may one day discover—our God is the same God. You may think now that you own Him as you wish to own land; but you cannot. He is the God of man and His compassion is equal for the red man and the white.

The Earth is precious to Him, and to harm the Earth is to heap contempt on its creator. The whites too shall pass, perhaps sooner than all the other tribes. Continue to contaminate your bed and you will one night suffocate in your own waste. This we know. The Earth does not belong to man: man belongs to the Earth. This we know. All things are connected like the blood which unites one family. All things are connected. Whatever befalls the Earth befalls the sons of the Earth. Man did not weave the web of life; he is merely a strand in it. Whatever he does to the web he does to himself.

IRI/Skylight Publishing, Inc.

Just Do It!

Assessment: Portfolio

In their journals, have the students compare the feelings and reactions they have had in a previous situation to the feelings and reactions experienced by the characters in the situation just enacted.

Finding New Ways to Respond to Situations

Assessment: Traditional

Ask the students how they could change some of their behaviors and reactions in order to lessen conflict.

Assessment: Performance

After the students offer suggestions, instruct them to role play again, keeping the same roles. Use some of the suggestions made by the students earlier, and have the observers describe the changes they witnessed. Ask the characters to describe how they felt this time compared to before.

Applying What We've Learned

Instruct the students to get into their cooperative groups. Have them talk about similar situations in which they can use what they have just experienced. Then, direct each group to create a rap about what they have learned. Have the students perform their raps for the rest of the class.

Life Science

Lesson: Identifying water pollutants
Materials: Paper
                      Pencil

Ask the students to name as many major causes of water pollution as they can (sewage, fertilizers, metals, chemicals, oil, etc.). Ask the students how many pollutants they think occur in the area and what effect they have on the environment. Answers should include the following:

1. They make water unsafe for drinking, washing, and recreation.
2. They kill living things.
3. They take oxygen out of the water, which kills fish.

Responding to an Oil Spill

Divide the students into their cooperative groups, and tell them to pretend they work for the Environmental Protection Agency. Explain to them that they are in a fishing village, where there has just been a major oil spill caused by a large tanker.

IRI/Skylight Publishing, Inc.

 Assessment: Traditional
Have the students name and discuss what immediate effects there would be from the oil spill. (One group member should act as secretary for this activity.)

Assessment: Performance
Have the students name long-term effects of the spill and their causes.

Creating a Public Service Announcement

Tell the groups that they are to create, based on what they have observed, a public service announcement for young children about pollution. They should make up a song, rap, or jingle, using simple language that young children can understand. Have each group perform their rap for the class.

Journal Writing

Assessment: Portfolio
Have the students write what they would do if they actually lived in the fishing village where the oil spill occurred. Have them include how they would feel about this kind of event.

Band

Lesson: Reviewing what we know about the tone color of instruments
Materials: Students' instruments

It is the quality of sound that distinguishes one instrument from another—not pitch. It is affected by size, shape, and materials used in making the instrument, as well as the method of producing sounds. Sound is produced by these types of instruments:
  a. Woodwind: Player blows past a reed(s) or across the edge of a hole.
  b. Brass: Player forces air through the instrument using a cupped metal mouthpiece.
  c. String: Player bows, plucks, or strums the strings, producing a vibration.
  d. Percussion: Player strikes or shakes.

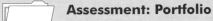 **Assessment: Traditional**
To check for understanding, give the students a written quiz covering the information above.

Creating Tone Color

Demonstrate how blowing too softly or too forcefully will change the tone color of an instrument. Direct each student to practice a variety of ways of playing his or her instrument in order to find the most pleasing tone color.

Just Do It!

Assessment: Performance
Have the students work in their sections to develop a tone color that is consistent.

Relating to an Instrument

Assessment: Portfolio
Direct each student to draw the instrument they think they are most like. Then, have them write why they are like that instrument.

Take 3

High School Lesson

THREADED MODEL: COMMUNICATION

Threaded Skill: Social (Communication)
Threaded Intelligences: Bodily/Kinesthetic and Visual/Spatial

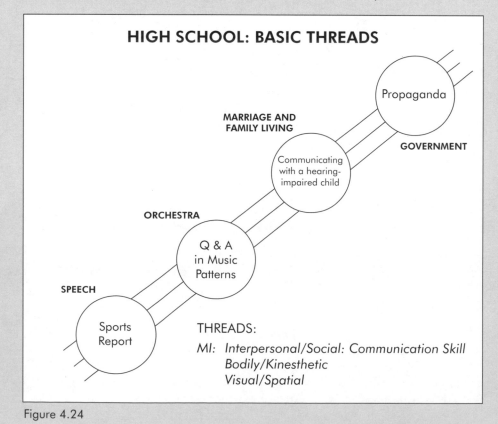

Figure 4.24

IRI/Skylight Publishing, Inc.

Just Do It!

Speech

Lesson: Interpreting a sports report
Materials: Sports sections of local newspapers or videos of sportscasts
Large chart paper
Colored markers

Direct the students to either read the sports section of a local paper or watch a sportscast. Have them name different words used to indicate that one team has beaten another. On a large chart, make a semantic map of the words they name. Ask the students why the writers and reporters use exaggerated terms such as "slaughtered," "annihilated," and others.

Assessment: Portfolio
Have the students answer the following questions in their journals: Do words like these communicate something different than if the reporter had simply said "the Monarchs beat the Bruins"? How do they affect you? Do you ever use exaggerated terms in your own descriptions? Why?

Have each group select one sports article.

Cooperative Learning

Direct the groups to pretend they don't know anything about the sport being reported.

Assessment: Performance
Have each group act out their article based on its actual words.

Assessment: Traditional
Have each group make a visual to accompany their dramatization, which shows the difference between what is implied through prior knowledge and what is understood through literal interpretation.

Orchestra

Lesson: Ear Training and Composition
Materials: Staff paper
Pencils
Pens
Colored markers and pencils
Instruments

Sing the following pattern (question) for the students, and ask them to finish it (answer).

Just Do It!

They should sing the following:

Then play your same pattern, and have them play the answer on their instruments. Play the following pattern:

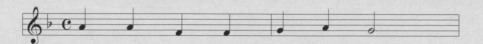

Ask the students if this pattern sounds finished and why not. (It doesn't end on "do," or home tone.)

Play the pattern again and direct the students to play a pattern that "finishes" it. Then, have individual students play their answers. After each performance, ask the class if it worked, and why or why not. If it didn't work, talk about why; then, have the student create another "answer" on his or her instrument.

Cooperative Learning

Divide the class into teams of two. Instruct the teams to create some musical questions and answers. (Have the students take turns being the leader.) Let them practice using either melodic patterns they know, or let them create their own. Instruct them to create an original musical question or answer.

 Assessment: Traditional
Instruct the students to notate the answer they come up with.

 Assessment: Portfolio
Have the students add some sort of artwork around the notation that gives some meaning to their "conversation."

 Assessment: Performance
Have the students perform their pieces for the class.

Marriage and Family Living

Lesson: Communicating with a hearing-impaired child
Materials: A copy of *Speak to Me!* by Marcia Calhoun Forecki
Large chart paper
Colored markers

After the students have read *Speak to Me!*, invite a hearing-impaired guest (or a person with a hearing-impaired child) from the community to visit. Ask the

IRI/Skylight Publishing, Inc.

guest to share some of his or her experiences with the class. Ask the guest to teach the class a few signs that are necessary for communication in a family with a deaf member. Encourage the students to ask questions.

Cooperative Learning

Put the students into their "family" groups. Direct each group to select a "change" that affects families, such as birth, death, relocation, divorce, or separation. Tell the groups to pretend that at least one "family" member is a young hearing-impaired child.

Assessment: Traditional
Direct the groups to figure out how they will communicate with the child. The communication must include both action and visual representations.

Assessment: Performance
Have the groups role play for the rest of the class and share their visual(s).

Assessment: Portfolio
Have the students write in their journals what they think it would be like to be deaf.

Government

Lesson: Propaganda's bad reputation
Materials: Posters
                Music from World War I and World War II
                Poster board
                Colored markers
                A record, compact disc, or tape player

Direct the students to try to find posters and/or music from World War I or World War II. (Have them check the local library, their grandparents, veterans, etc.) Ask the students the following questions about their materials:
   1. What is the message of the poster or song?
   2. What emotion do you think it is trying to raise?

Tell the students that this kind of material is considered to be propaganda. Ask them the following:
   1. Is it good or bad propaganda?
   2. Is it effective? Why?

Learning about Propaganda

Since the purpose of propaganda is to influence people to believe certain ideas or to take certain actions, it is not necessarily bad. For instance, Smokey the

Just Do It!

Bear's message, "Only you can prevent forest fires," and the slogan "Just say no" are propaganda. Propaganda earned its bad reputation with rulers such as Adolf Hitler, who wrote, "The great masses of the people will more easily fall victims to a great lie than a small one."

Cooperative Learning

Assessment: Traditional

Ask the groups to list propaganda issued by governments (including ours) since the two world wars (e.g., elections, the Gulf War, health care reform, etc.). Ask the students the following questions:

1. *What is the slogan?*
2. *Are there pictures or symbols?*
3. *Is it effective?*

Creating Propaganda

Assessment: Performance

Have each student find a partner and select a current event about which they can develop propaganda either for or against. Have them create a slogan and a poster. Have them present the propaganda to the class in a convincing manner, using music if desired.

Assessment: Portfolio

Have the students think about and discuss which of the above made the most impact on them and why. Ask them if they felt the impact was positive or negative.

Can We Talk?

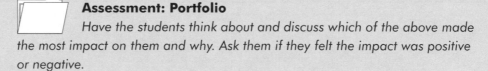

CAN WE TALK?

Read about Kids Incorporated and their cemetery study and discuss the threaded tandems that naturally evolved in the unit. Refer to figure 4.25 if confused.

KIDS INCORPORATED AND THE CEMETERY STUDY

Kids Incorporated is an alternative school within a school. It comprises two teachers, fifty-four children (aged eight to twelve), siblings, and parent volunteers. The teachers' vision is to create a school setting that embodies the natural elements of family, which nurture authentic learning and authentic outcomes.

To foster cooperation and a sense of collegiality and team spirit for students of all ages, an extensive outdoor education week was built into the fall schedule of events. After raising money all summer and part of the fall, the

IRI/Skylight Publishing, Inc.

teachers scheduled a mid-October trip to a camp. Parents were polled for talent and willingness to participate in small-group sessions, and an itinerary was put together that included several learning opportunities.

Integration of curriculum is a natural outgrowth of the learning experiences designed for Kids Incorporated. Their cemetery study illustrates how key goals such as cooperation and critical thinking are threaded through each camp activity. Working in small groups, the students chose from a list of tasks in their cemetery packet. The suggested activities included the following:

1. Creating five art etchings or rubbings that include borders, symbols, letters, and numerals.

2. Finding two epitaphs and writing two more.

3. Answering historical questions by viewing various tombstones and gathering pertinent data.

4. Drawing a map of the entire cemetery or a particular part of it.

5. Gathering mathematical information and generating statistical data for generalizations about the Civil War.

6. Comparing the weathering of the tombstones to the conditions of the earth surrounding them and drawing some conclusions.

The learning experiences orchestrated during the course of the week set the stage for activities and interactions for the rest of the year. More importantly, unbreakable bonds were made among all of the students.

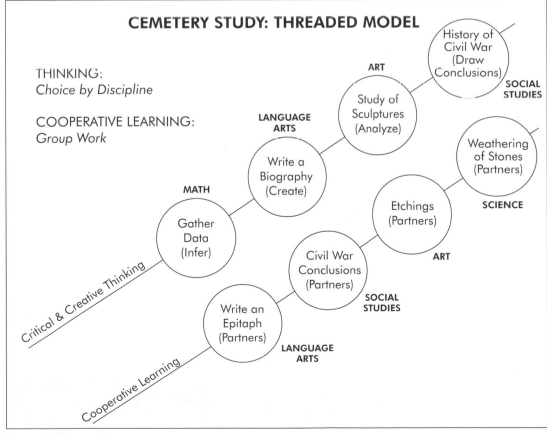

Figure 4.25

IRI/Skylight Publishing, Inc.

What's in It for Me?

WHAT'S IN IT FOR ME?

Reflection . . .

Take a moment to think back to an instructional unit recently completed in your classroom. Graphically show a threaded tandem that you can identify from that unit.

JOURNAL

Think about life skills that were implicitly threaded through the unit:

_____

_____

Did you resequence two subjects to coincide? Share a concept? Connect ideas?

_____

_____

Were themes used?

Selected: _____ (webbed)

Emergent: _____ (connected, shared, integrated)

Try to draw your threaded tandem in the space provided.

IRI/Skylight Publishing, Inc.

Authors' Note

In the process of integrating content by developing significant themes and threading life skills through subject matter, the lines begin to blur between disciplines. While some blurring of disciplines is desirable in order to create holistic, project-oriented learning, too much blurring causes concern about valid assessments, grades, and traditional discipline-based evaluations. In many cases, schools that use authentic learning and multiple intelligences to move toward an integrated curriculum continue to use traditional assessment measures to determine grades, grade-point averages, and rankings. However, these measures don't always match active, holistic learning models.

THE TRI-ASSESSMENT MODEL

The tri-assessment model (see fig. 1) provides a reasonable compromise for teachers who are moving toward more authentic assessments, but are reluctant to totally abandon more traditional measures. By *combining* **portfolio** and **performance** assessments with **traditional** assessments, a truer, more holistic look at students is permitted. Each assessment targets a focus as well as specific features that are practical and relevant to the total picture. Each assessment also utilizes multiple intelligences to assess a wider range of human potential.

IRI/Skylight Publishing, Inc.

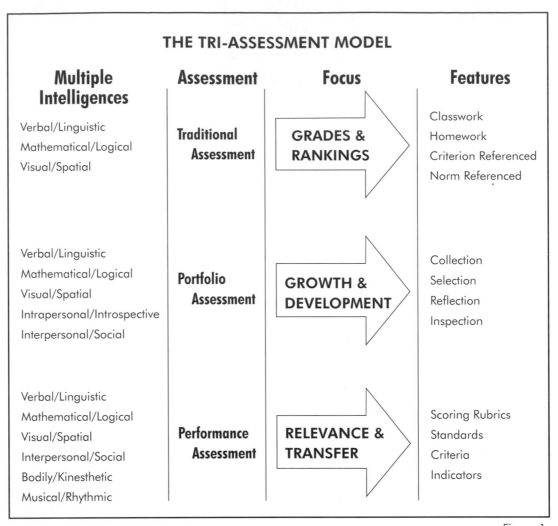

THE TRI-ASSESSMENT MODEL

Multiple Intelligences	Assessment	Focus	Features
Verbal/Linguistic Mathematical/Logical Visual/Spatial	Traditional Assessment	GRADES & RANKINGS	Classwork Homework Criterion Referenced Norm Referenced
Verbal/Linguistic Mathematical/Logical Visual/Spatial Intrapersonal/Introspective Interpersonal/Social	Portfolio Assessment	GROWTH & DEVELOPMENT	Collection Selection Reflection Inspection
Verbal/Linguistic Mathematical/Logical Visual/Spatial Interpersonal/Social Bodily/Kinesthetic Musical/Rhythmic	Performance Assessment	RELEVANCE & TRANSFER	Scoring Rubrics Standards Criteria Indicators

Figure 1

Traditional assessment often focuses on grades, grade-point averages, and rankings. Included in traditional assessments are classwork, homework, criterion-referenced and standardized measures. Typically, traditional assessments tap primarily the verbal/linguistic and the logical/mathematical intelligences, although the visual/spatial intelligence might also be included.

Portfolio assessment, on the other hand, tends to focus on the growth and development of student potential. Phases of the portfolio development process include collecting and selecting items, reflecting on the significance of the items as indicators of growth, and inspecting the portfolio for signs of progress. Often, portfolio development calls into play the intrapersonal and interpersonal intelligences as well as the verbal, logical, and visual intelligences used in the traditional measures.

Performance assessment focuses on the direct observance of a student's performance. Procedures for using performance assessment effectively include developing scoring rubrics and using predetermined standards, criteria, and indicators. With this assessment, the bodily intelligence becomes a vehicle for showing what a student knows and can do. The visual, verbal, logical, musical, and interpersonal intelligences are also critical components.

IRI/Skylight Publishing, Inc.

A WORD ABOUT RUBRICS

Traditional measures as well as portfolio and performance assessments rely on preestablished standards and criteria; therefore, it follows that these criteria dictate how progress is shown. A scoring rubric is a typical tool used to fairly evaluate student growth (see fig. 2). This rubric suggests criteria and indicators to judge the themes and threads established by teacher teams. Using this model, other scoring rubrics can easily be constructed to fit appropriate student contexts.

RUBRIC FOR INTEGRATED LEARNING

Criteria for Themes/Threads: _____

Standard: _____ Relevant, holistic, thought-provoking instruction _____

Criteria	Not Yet!	Well on the Way!	This Is It!
Relevancy (Real Life)	Inert Knowledge	Relates to Theme	Real-World Application
Rigor (HOT) Higher Order Thinking	"Pour and Store"	Challenge	Struggle
Richness (Multi-dimensional)	Artificial Superficial Contrived	Single Authentic Dimension	Breadth and Depth

(Extrapolated from Doll, 1993.   ASCD/IMSA Consortium for Interdiscipline, Atlanta, 1994)

Figure 2

IRI/Skylight Publishing, Inc.

USING THE TRI-ASSESSMENT MODEL

Following is a lesson for the elementary level. In it, the various kinds of assessments are labeled.

SPEECH FUGUE: ELEMENTARY

Teach part three of the "Speech Fugue," instructing the students to speak in low voices. Next, teach part one, the "Me, too" line, in a high voice. Identify two small groups, and have one group do part one while the other group does part three. Then, add part two, in a "normal" voice.

Instruct the part three group to add two claps after they speak the word "inside." Instruct the part one group to add two finger snaps after "too" each time they say it.

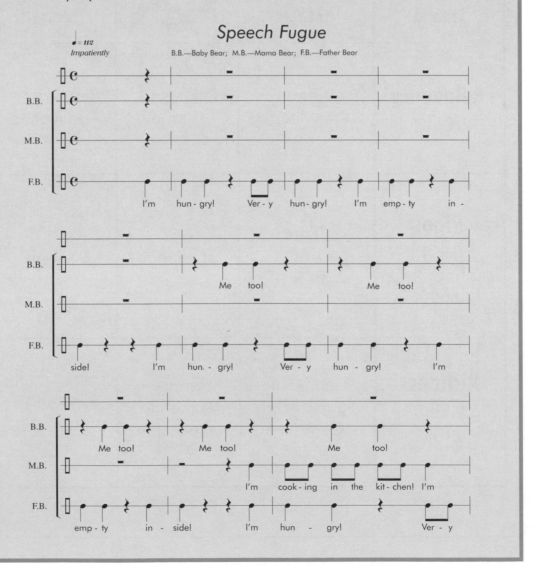

Speech Fugue

IRI/Skylight Publishing, Inc.

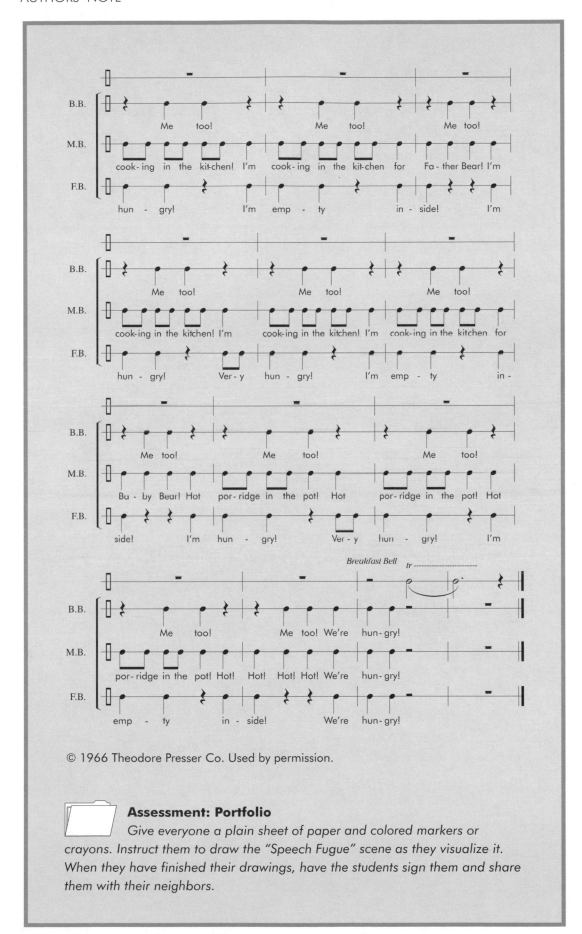

Assessment: Portfolio

Give everyone a plain sheet of paper and colored markers or crayons. Instruct them to draw the "Speech Fugue" scene as they visualize it. When they have finished their drawings, have the students sign them and share them with their neighbors.

IRI/Skylight Publishing, Inc.

Assessment: Traditional
Divide the class into groups of six to eight students. Instruct each group to figure out how to act out the "Speech Fugue" while they say it. (Suggestion: Each part can have two to three people.)

Assessment: Performance
Have each group perform its dramatization for the class.

IRI/Skylight Publishing, Inc.

Miscellaneous Tools

I. SIGN LANGUAGE

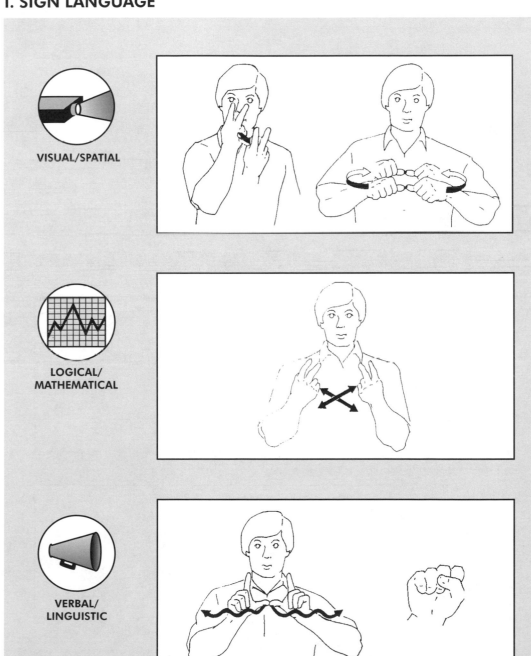

IRI/Skylight Publishing, Inc.

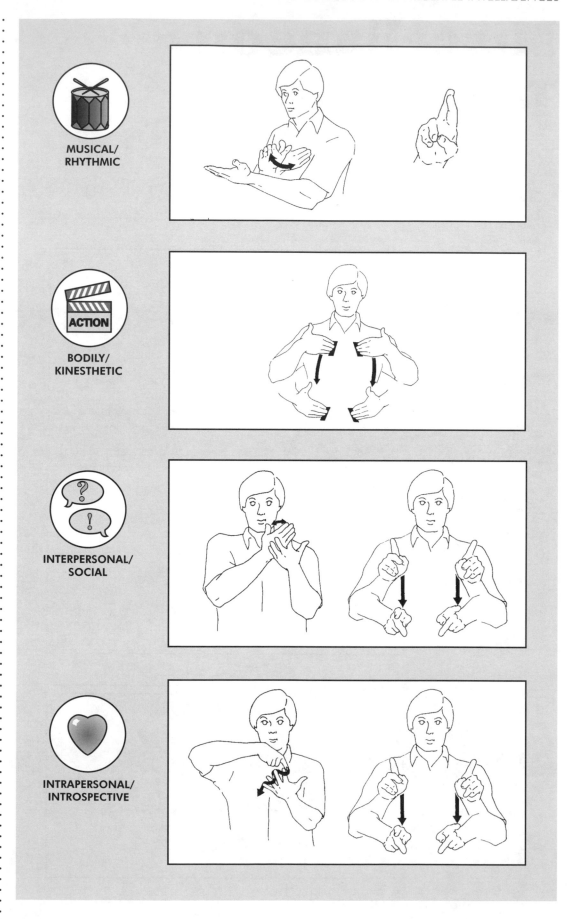

MUSICAL/
RHYTHMIC

BODILY/
KINESTHETIC

INTERPERSONAL/
SOCIAL

INTRAPERSONAL/
INTROSPECTIVE

IRI/Skylight Publishing, Inc.

II. PEOPLE SEARCH: INTEGRATED CURRICULA

1. Find someone who has SHARED something with another department or grade level.

    _____

2. Find someone with WEB-footed pets.

    _____

3. Find someone who has recently had the NESTing instinct or experienced the "empty NEST syndrome."

    _____

4. Find someone who can THREAD a needle without a magnifying glass.

    _____

5. Find someone who can INTEGRATE leftovers into a gourmet meal.

    _____

6. Find someone who has CONNECTED with another heritage.

    _____

7. Find someone who regularly watches two different NET-WORK news programs.

    _____

8. Find someone who has a "SEQUENCED" gown or outfit.

    _____

9. Find someone whose brain is FRAGMENTED due to economic stress, carpools for children, work overload, or automobile difficulties.

    _____

10. Find someone who is IMMERSED in a second language.

    _____

IRI/Skylight Publishing, Inc.

III. THE UMBRELLA ORGANIZER

						Discipline
						Verbal/ Linguistic
						Logical/ Mathematical
						Musical/ Rhythmic
						Visual/ Spatial
						Bodily/ Kinesthetic
						Interpersonal/ Social
						Intrapersonal/ Introspective
						Assessment

Umbrella Organizer for Projects Using the Seven Intelligences

THEME OR CONCEPT

IRI/Skylight Publishing, Inc.

IV. MULTIPLE INTELLIGENCES/LEARNING STYLES: A COMPARISON

Attributes	Multiple Intelligences	Learning Styles
Theory Base	Neuro/Biological/ Psychological/ Anthropological	Psychological
Domain	Cognitive	Affective
Origin	Evolutionary/ Developmental	Personality/Tendency
Nomenclature	Frames of Mind, Ways of Knowing, Intelligences	Styles, Mindstyles, Modalities
Components	Seven Intelligences 1. Verbal/Linguistic 2. Logical/Mathematical 3. Musical/Rhythmic 4. Bodily/Kinesthetic 5. Visual/Spatial 6. Interpersonal 7. Intrapersonal	Various Combinations • Concrete/Sequential Abstract/Random • Concrete/Abstract Active/Reflective • Thinking/Feeling Intuitive/Sensing
Worth	Culturally Valued	Individual Awareness
Teaching Tool	Curriculum Planning Instructional Methodology	
Learning Tool	Conceptualizing/Performing (Receptive/Expressive)	
Assessment Tool	Authentic Assessment	
Researchers	Based on an interpretation of Howard Gardner's work at Harvard University Graduate School of Education	Based on an interpretation of the work of Meyers/Briggs, Gregorc, McCarthy, Butler, Dunn & Dunn

IRI/Skylight Publishing, Inc.

V. FAT AND SKINNY QUESTIONS

FAT QUESTIONS

Fat questions require lots of discussion and explanation with interesting examples. Fat questions take time to think through and answer in depth with fat responses.

SKINNY QUESTIONS

Skinny questions require a simple, one-word answer or a nod or shake of the head. They take up no space or time.

THEME: "ORIGINS"

FAT	SKINNY	QUESTIONS
	X	Where did it start?
X		How do you explain its beginning?
X		How is every ending a beginning?
	X	Do you know your origins?
X		Why are origins important?
	X	What is evolution?

IRI/Skylight Publishing, Inc.

The Naturalist Intelligence

Howard Gardner refers to a "naturalist" intelligence in the November 1995 issue of *Phi Delta Kappan* in the article "Reflections on Multiple Intelligences: Myths and Messages." Gardner says, "It seems to me that the individiual who is able readily to recognize flora and fauna, to make consequential distinctions in the natural world, and to use this ability productively (in hunting, in farming, in biological science) is exercising an important intelligence and one that is not adequately encompassed in the current list." Based on this speculation, the naturalist intelligence is included in this appendix.

To further describe the naturalist intelligence, the label naturalist/physical world (N/PW) is used in the suggested exercises. The exercises included are part of the section in the "Teams" chapter entitled "Just Do It." On page 71, the naturalist intelligence can be substituted for the candidate intelligence in the "Jagged Profile" exercise.

Naturalist/Physical World

Read the list of associations and add words of your own.

NATURAL/PHYSICAL WORLD

Field Trips	Planting
Bird Watching	Uncovering
Nature Walks	Digging
Forecasting	Comparing
Collecting	Classifying
Star Gazing	Displaying
Fishing	Sorting
Observing	Selecting
Exploring	Relating
Categorizing	Discovering

IRI/Skylight Publishing, Inc.

Lead Activity—Observation or Inference

Frame 1

Cover the three frames and reveal only frame 1. Observe obvious facts.

Observations: (1) there are two sets of tracks; (2) one set is larger than the other; (3) they appear to be converging.

Then, make some inferences about frame 1.

Inferences: (1) one is a bear, one is a duck; (2) the tracks were left at the same time; (3) they are tracks in the snow.

Frame 1	Frame 2	Frame 3
Observations 1. 2. 3.	Observations 1. 2. 3.	Observations 1. 2. 3.
Inferences 1. 2. 3.	Inferences 1. 2. 3.	Inferences 1. 2. 3.

Frame 2

Reveal frame 2 and repeat the sequence. List observations first, then inferences.

Observations: (1) the tracks converge; (2) the tracks are in a random pattern; (3) the tracks are mixed up.

Inferences: (1) the animals were fighting; (2) they were dancing; (3) they were mating; (4) they were marking the same spot at different times.

Frame 3

Reveal frame 3 and repeat the sequence.

Observations: (1) there is one set of tracks; (2) the larger tracks remain; (3) the smaller tracks have disappeared

Inferences: (1) one animal ate the other (survival of the fittest); (2) one carried the other (friendship theory); (3) or one flew away (escapist theory).

IRI/Skylight Publishing, Inc.

LEAD ACTIVITY: OBSERVATION OR INFERENCE

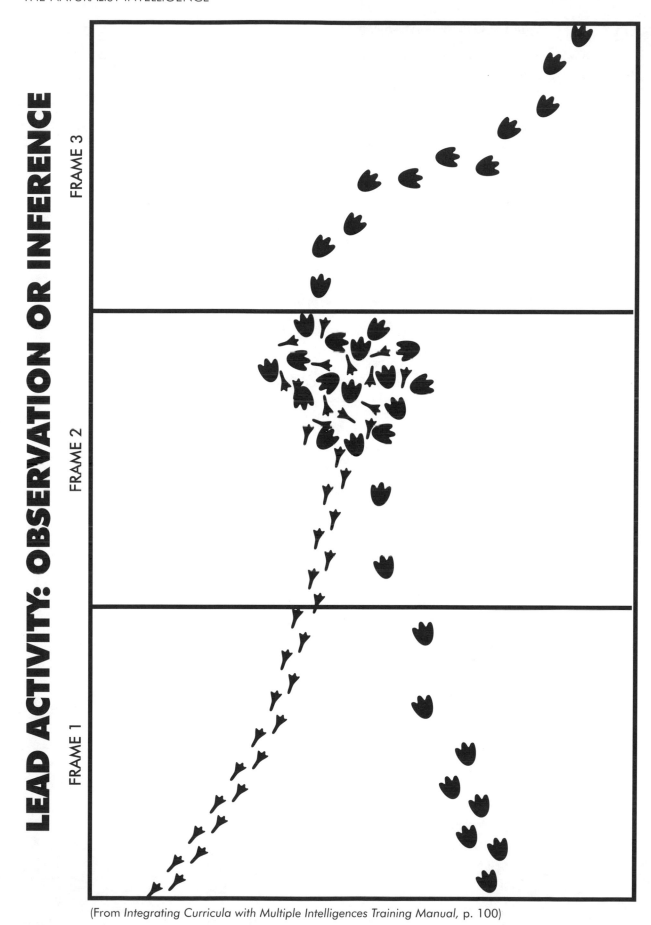

FRAME 1 FRAME 2 FRAME 3

(From *Integrating Curricula with Multiple Intelligences Training Manual*, p. 100)

IRI/Skylight Publishing, Inc.

Optional Activity—Classifying

Regroup the following list of words into categories that make sense. Use as many classifications as you need and justify your final groupings.

OPTIONAL ACTIVITY: CLASSIFYING

Apple	Maple
Buffalo	Ocelot
Carnivores	Omnivores
Coniferous	Oppossum
Deciduous	Oxen
Dog	Pine
Elk	Spruce
Elm	Tiger
Herbivores	Trees
Human	Yew
Lion	

Quotes

Read the quotes below and identify with one or the other.

Let us a little permit
Nature to have her
way; she understands
her own business
better than we do.
          —*Michel de Montaigne*

Nature, heartless,
witless nature.
          —*A.E. Housman*

IRI/Skylight Publishing, Inc.

"Good news, honey! We've just been declared a wilderness area!"

Mark your graph for the eighth intelligence, the naturalist. Tear off the remainder of the bar.

IRI/Skylight Publishing, Inc.

WAYS TO EXPERIENCE LEARNING

V/L	V/S	L/M	M/R	Inter./S	Intra./I	B/K	N/PW
reporting	story-boarding	reasoning	singing	discussing	journaling	dancing	relating
writing essays	painting	collecting	listening	responding	intuiting	sculpting	discovering
creating	cartooning	recording	playing	dialoguing	reflecting	performing	uncovering
reciting	observing	analyzing	composing	reporting	logging	preparing	observing
listing	drawing	graphing	audio-taping	surveying	meditating	constructing	digging
telling/retelling	illustrating	comparing/contrasting	improvising	questioning	studying	acting	planting
listening	diagraming	classifying	attending concerts	paraphrasing	rehearsing	role-playing	comparing
labeling	depicting	ranking	selecting music	clarifying	self-assessing	dramatizing	displaying
joking	showing	evaluating	critiquing music	affirming	expressing	pantomiming	sorting

(From *Integrating Curricula with Multiple Intelligences Training Manual*, p. 153)

IRI/Skylight Publishing, Inc.

TYPES OF ACTIVITIES

V/L	V/S	M/L	M/R	Inter./S	Intra./I	B/K	N/PW
Symbols	Mosaics	Mazes	Performance	Group Projects	Journals	Role-Playing	Field Trips (Farm/Zoo)
Printouts	Paintings	Puzzles	Songs	Group Tasks	Meditations	Dramatizing	Field Studies
Debates	Drawings	Outlines	Musicals	Observation	Self-Assess- ments	Skits	Bird Watching
Poetry	Sketches	Matrices	Instruments	Charts	Intuiting	Body Lan- guage	Observing
Jokes	Illustrations	Sequences	Rhythms	Social Interac- tions	Logs	Facial Expres- sions	Nests
Speeches	Cartoons	Patterns	Compositions	Dialogs	Records	Experiments	Planting
Reading	Sculptures	Logic	Harmonies	Conversations	Reflections	Dancing	Photographing
Storytelling	Models	Analogies	Chords	Debates	Quotations	Gestures	Nature Walks
Listening	Constructions	Timelines	Trios/Duos	Arguments	"I Statements"	Pantomiming	Forecasting Weather
Audiotapes	Maps	Equations	Quartets	Consensus	Creative Expression	Field Trips	Star Gazing
Essays	Storyboards	Formulas	Beat	Communicat- ion	Goals	Lab Work	Fishing
Reports	Videotapes	Theorems	Melodies	Collages	Affirmations	Interviews	Exploring Caves
Crosswords	Photographs	Calculations	Raps	Murals	Insight	Sports	Categorizing Rocks
Fiction	Symbols	Computations	Jingles	Mosaics	Poetry	Games	Ecology Studies
Nonfiction	Visual Aids	Syllogisms	Choral Read- ings	Round Robins	Interpreta- tions		Catching Butterflies
Newspapers	Posters	Codes	Scores	Sports			Shell Collect- ing
Magazines	Murals	Games	Acappella- Choirs	Games			Identifying Plants
Internet	Doodles	Probabilities		Challenges			
Research	Statues	Fractions					
Books	Collages						
Biographies	Mobiles						
Bibliographies							

(From *Integrating Curricula with Multiple Intelligences Training Manual*, p. 152)

IRI/Skylight Publishing, Inc.

BIBLIOGRAPHY

Aesop. (1976). *The Aesop for children.* Mattituck, NY: Amereon.

Anderson, R. H. (1993, January). The return of the nongraded classroom. *Principal*, pp.
9–12.

Anderson, R. H., & Pavan, B. N. (1993). *Nongradedness: Helping it to happen.* Lancaster, PA: Technomic.

Armstrong, T. (1993). *Seven kinds of smart: Identifying and developing your many intelligences.* New York: A Plume Book.

Ashton-Warner, S. (1963). *Teacher.* New York: Simon & Schuster.

Ausubel, D. (1978). *Ed. psych: A cognitive view* (2nd ed.). New York: Holt, Rinehart & Winston.

Barell, J. (1991). *Teaching for thoughtfulness.* New York and London: Longman.

Barth, R. S. (1990). *Improving schools from within: Teachers, parents and principals can make a difference.* San Francisco: Jossey-Bass.

Beane, J. A. (1993, September). Problems and possibilities for an integrative curriculum. *Middle School Journal*, pp. 18–23.

Bellanca, J. (1992a). *The cooperative classroom.* Palatine, IL: IRI/Skylight Publishing.

Bellanca, J. (1992b). *The cooperative think tank II.* Palatine, IL: IRI/Skylight Publishing.

Bellanca, J. (1990). The cooperative think tank. Graphic organizers to teach thinking in the cooperative classroom. Palatine, IL: IRI/Skylight Publishing.

Bellanca, J., & Fogarty, R. (1991). *Blueprints for thinking in the cooperative classroom,* (2nd. ed.) Palatine, IL: IRI/Skylight Publishing.

Bellanca, J., & Fogarty, R. (1986). *Catch them thinking: A handbook of classroom strategies.* Palatine, IL: IRI/Skylight Publishing.

Beyer, B. (1987). *Practical strategies for the teaching of thinking.* Boston: Allyn and Bacon.

Black, S., & Black, H. (1990). *Organizing Thinking—Book II.* Pacific Grove, CA: Critical Thinking Press & Software.

Bloom, A. (1987). *The closing of the American mind.* New York: Simon and Schuster.

Bloom, B. S. (1984). *Taxonomy of educational objectives: The classification of educational goals, handbook I: Cognitive domain.* New York: Longman.

Bornstein, H., Saulnier, K. L., & Hamilton, L. B. (Eds.). (1983). *The comprehensive signed English dictionary.* Washington, DC: Gallaudet University Press.

Bowick, J. D. (1983, November 14). Crowded back-to-basics bandwagon is off, veering crazily. *Los Angeles Times.*

Brandt, R. (1988, April). On teaching thinking: A conversation with Arthur Costa. *Educational Leadership,* pp. 10–13.

Brandt, R. (1987/1988, December/January). On discipline-based art education: A conversation with Elliot Eisner. *Educational Leadership*, pp. 6–9.

Briggs, K. C., & Myers, I. B. (1993). *Myers-Briggs type indicator.* Palo Alto, CA: Consulting Psychologists Press.

Brown, A., & Palincsar, A. (1982). *Inducing strategic learning from texts by means of informed, self-control training* (Technical Report No. 262). Cambridge, MA: Bolt, Beranek and Newman.

Bruchac, J. (1992). *Native American animal stories.* Golden, CO: Fulcrum.

Bruner, J. (1975). *Toward a theory of instruction.* Cambridge, MA: Belknap Press.

Burke, K. A. (1993). *The mindful school: How to assess authentic learning.* Palatine, IL: IRI/Skylight Publishing.

Burke, K. A. (1993). *What to do with the kid who . . . : Developing cooperation, self-discipline, and responsibility in the classroom.* Palatine, IL: IRI/Skylight Publishing.

Burke, K. A. (Ed.). (1992). *Authentic assessment: A collection.* Palatine, IL: IRI/Skylight Publishing.

Burris, D. (1985). *Future view: A look ahead.* WI: Burris Research Associates.

Butler, K. A. (1987). *Learning and teaching style in theory and practice.* Columbia, CT: The Learner's Dimension.

Caine, R. N., & Caine, G. (1991). *Making connections: Teaching and the human brain.* Alexandria, VA: Association for Supervision and Curriculum Development.

Caine, R. N., & Caine, G. (1990, October). Understanding a brain-based approach to learning and thinking. *Educational Leadership*, pp. 66–67.

Campbell, B. (1994). *The multiple intelligences handbook.* Stanwood, WA: Campbell & Associates.

IRI/Skylight Publishing, Inc.

Campbell, L. (1992). *Teaching and learning through multiple intelligences.* Seattle: New Horizons for Learning.

Carbol, B. (Project Leader). (1990). *The intermediate program: Learning in British Columbia.* Ministry of Education, Educational Programs, Victoria, Province of British Columbia.

Carnegie, D. (1981). *How to win friends and influence people.* New York: Simon and Schuster.

Chapman, C. (1993). *If the shoe fits . . . :How to develop multiple intelligences in the classroom.* Palatine, IL: IRI/Skylight Publishing.

Cohen, E. G. (1986). *Designing groupwork: Strategies for the heterogeneous classroom.* New York: Teachers College Press.

Costa, A. L. (1991). *The school as a home for the mind.* Palatine, IL: IRI/Skylight Publishing.

Costa, A. (1991). The search for intelligent life. In A. Costa (Ed.), *Developing minds: A resource book for teaching thinking*, Vol. 1, pp. 100–106. Alexandria, VA: Association for Supervision and Curriculum Development.

Costa, A., Bellanca, J., & Fogarty, R. (Eds.). (1992). *If minds matter: A foreword to the future, Vol. 1.* Palatine, IL: IRI/Skylight Publishing.

Costa, A., Bellanca, J., & Fogarty, R. (Eds.). (1992). *If minds matter: A foreword to the future, Vol. 2.* Palatine, IL: IRI/Skylight Publishing.

Costa, A. L., & Garmston, R. (1988). *The art of cognitive coaching: Supervision for intelligent teaching.* Paper presented at the Annual Conference of the Association for Supervision and Curriculum Development in Chicago.

Costello, E. (1983). *Signing—How to speak with your hands.* New York: Bantam.

de Bono, E. (1992). *Serious creativity: Using the power of lateral thinking to create new ideas.* New York: HarperCollins.

de Bono, E. (1976). *Teaching thinking.* New York: Penguin.

Deutch, M. (1949). *The resolution of conflict.* New Haven, CT: Yale University Press.

Dewey, J. (1938). *Education and experience.* New York: Macmillan.

Diagram Group. (1976). *Musical instruments of the world: An illustrated encyclopedia.* New York: Paddington Press.

Doll, W. (1993). Curriculum possibilities in a "post-future." *Journal of Curriculum and Supervision, 8* (4), 270–292.

Dunn, R., & Griggs, S. A. (1989, January). Learning styles: Key to improving schools and student achievement. *Curriculum Report 18* (3).

Eisner, E. (1991, February). What really counts in schools. *Educational Leadership*, pp. 10–11, 14–17.

Eisner, E. (1979). *The educational imagination: On the design and evaluation of school programs.* New York: Macmillan.

Eisner, E., & Vallance, E. (1974). *Conflicting conceptions of curriculum.* Chicago: National Society for the Study of Education.

Elvin, L. (1977). *The place of common sense in educational thought.* London: Unwin Educational Books.

IRI/Skylight Publishing, Inc.

Emerson, R. W. (1982). *Selected essays.* New York: Penguin.

Faces of Africa: Art and man. (1991, November). *Scholastic, 22*(2).

Feller, M., & Feller, R. (1985). *Paper masks and puppets.* Seattle, WA: The Arts Factory.

Feuerstein, R. (1980). *Instrumental Enrichment.* Baltimore: University Park Press.

Fitzgerald, F. S. (1925). *The great Gatsby.* New York: Scribner.

Fogarty, R. (1994). *The mindful school: How to teach for metacognitive reflection.* Palatine, IL: IRI/Skylight Publishing.

Fogarty, R. (1993). *The mindful school: How to integrate the curricula: Training manual.* Palatine, IL: IRI/Skylight Publishing.

Fogarty, R. (1991). *The mindful school: How to integrate the curricula.* Palatine, IL: IRI/Skylight Publishing.

Fogarty, R. (1991, October). Ten ways to integrate curriculum. *Educational Leadership,* pp. 61–65.

Fogarty, R. (1990). *Designs for cooperative interactions.* Palatine, IL: IRI/ Skylight Publishing.

Fogarty, R. (1990). *Keep them thinking: Level II.* Palatine, IL: IRI/Skylight Publishing.

Fogarty, R. (1989). *From training to transfer: The role of creativity in the adult learner.* Doctoral Dissertation. Loyola University of Chicago.

Fogarty, R., & Bellanca, J. (1989). *Patterns for thinking: Patterns for transfer.* Palatine, IL: IRI/Skylight Publishing.

Fogarty, R., & Bellanca, J. (1986). *Teach them thinking.* Palatine, IL: IRI/ Skylight Publishing.

Fogarty, R., & Opeka, K. (1988). *Start them thinking: A handbook of classroom strategies for the early years.* Palatine, IL: IRI/Skylight Publishing.

Fogarty, R., Perkins, D., & Barell, J. (1992). *The mindful school: How to teach for transfer.* Palatine, IL: IRI/Skylight Publishing.

Forecki, M. C. (1985). *Speak to me!* Washington, DC: Gallaudet University Press.

Fullan, M. (1991). *The new meaning of educational change.* New York: Teachers College, Columbia University.

Gallant, R. (1984). *101 questions and answers about the universe.* New York: Macmillan.

Gallaudet University Press. (1993). *Gallaudet survival guide to signing.* Washington, DC: Author.

Gardner, H. (1993). *Multiple intelligences: The theory in practice.* New York: HarperCollins.

Gardner, H. (1989). *To open minds.* New York: Basic Books.

Gardner, H. (1983). *Frames of mind: The theory of multiple intelligences.* New York: Basic Books.

Gardner, H. (1982). *Art, mind, and brain.* New York: Basic Books.

Gibbs, J. (1987). *Tribes.* Santa Rosa, CA: Center Source Publications.

Glasser, W. (1986). *Control theory in the classroom.* New York: Harper.

Glenn, S. (1989, November). Chart 1.3. *Developing capable people.* Provo, UT: Sunrise Books, Tapes, and Video.

Goodlad, J. I. (1984). *A place called school: Prospects for the future.* New York: McGraw Hill.

Goodlad, J. I., & Anderson, R. H. (1987). *The nongraded elementary school* (rev. ed.). New York: Teachers College, Columbia University.

Gregorc, A. F., & Butler, K. A. (1984). Learning is a matter of style. *VocEd,* pp. 27–29.

Grun, B. (1991). *The timetables of history.* New York: Simon & Schuster.

Guilbault, D. (Producer), & Paul, G. (Director). (1993). *Common miracles: The new American revolution in learning* [videotape]. Oak Forest, IL: MPI Home Video.

Hague, M. (1985). *Aesop's fables.* New York: Holt, Rinehart & Winston.

Hamilton, V. (1988). *In the beginning: Creation stories from around the world.* New York: Harcourt Brace Jovanovich.

Hirsch, E. D., Jr. (1987). *Cultural literacy.* Boston: Houghton Mifflin.

Hirst, P. H. (1964). *Knowledge and curriculum.* London: Routledge and Kegan Paul.

Holmes, O. W. (1916). *The poet at the breakfast table.* Boston: Houghton Mifflin.

Hord, S., & Loucks, S. (1980). *A concerns-based model for delivery of inservice.* Austin: CBAM Project, Research and Development Center for Teacher Education, The University of Texas at Austin.

Howard, D. L. (1994). *From need to knowledge: Solving information problems.* Doctoral Dissertation, University of Hawaii, Honolulu.

Hunter, M. (1971). *Teach for transfer.* El Segundo, CA: TIP Publications.

Hyde, A., & Bizar, M. (1989). *Thinking in context.* White Plains, NY: Longman.

Jacobs, H. H. (1991, Winter). Curriculum integration, critical thinking, and common sense. *Cogitare,* p. 2.

Jacobs, H. H. (Ed.). (1990). *Interdisciplinary curriculum: Design and implementation.* Alexandria, VA: Association for Supervision and Curriculum Development.

Jacobs, H. H., & Borland, J. H. (1986, Fall). The interdisciplinary concept model: Theory and practice. *Gifted Child Quarterly,* pp. 159–163.

Jacobs-Hayes, H. (1991, September). The integrated curriculum: What it is, why your students need it. *Instructor,* pp. 22–23.

Johnson, D., & Johnson, R. (1979, Winter). Conflict in the classroom: Controversy and learning. *Review of Educational Research,* pp. 51–69.

Johnson, D., Johnson, R., & Johnson-Holubec, E. (1986). *Circles of learning.* Medina, MN: Interaction Book Co.

Jones, B. F., Palincsar, A., Ogle, D. S., & Carr, E. G. (1987). *Strategic teaching and learning: Cognitive instruction in the content areas.* Alexandria, VA: Association for Supervision and Curriculum Development.

Jones, B. F., Tinzmann, M., Friedman, L., & Walker, B. (1987). *Teaching thinking skills: English/language arts.* Washington, DC: National Educational Association.

Joyce, B. R. (1986). *Improving America's schools.* White Plains, NY: Longman.

Joyce, B. R., & Showers, B. (1980, February). Improving inservice training: The message of research. *Educational Leadership,* pp. 379–385.

Joyce, B. R., & Showers, B. (1983). *Power and staff development through research and training.* Alexandria, VA: Association for Supervision and Curriculum Development.

Kagan, S. (1992). *Cooperative learning.* San Juan Capistrano, CA: Resources for Teachers, Inc.

Kagan, S. (1977). Social motives and behaviors of Mexican American and Anglo American children. In J. L. Martinez (Ed.), *Chicano psychology.* New York: Academic Press.

Kimmel, E. (1988). *Anasi and the moss-covered rock.* New York: Holiday House.

Kipling, R. (1972). *Just so stories.* Skokie, IL: Rand McNally.

Kovalik, S. (1993). *ITI: The model: Integrated thematic instruction.* Oak Creek, AZ: Books for Educators.

Krupp, J. A. (1982). *The adult learner: A unique entity.* Manchester, CT: Author, 40 McDivitt Dr.

Krupp, J. A. (1981). *Adult development: Implications for staff development.* Manchester, CT: Author, 40 McDivitt Dr.

Lawton, D. (1975). *Class, culture and curriculum.* Boston: Routledge and Kegan Paul.

Lazear, D. (1994). *Multiple intelligence approaches to assessment.* Tucson, AZ: Zephyr.

Lazear, D. (1994). *Seven pathways of learning: Teaching students and parents about multiple intelligences.* Tucson, AZ: Zephyr.

Lazear, D. (1991). *Seven ways of knowing.* Palatine, IL: IRI/Skylight Publishing.

Lazear, D. (1991). *Seven ways of teaching.* Palatine, IL: IRI/Skylight Publishing.

Link, M., & Blood, C. L. (1976). *The goat in the rug.* New York: Parents' Magazine Press.

Little, J. W. (1981). *School success and staff development in urban desegregated schools: A summary of completed research.* Boulder, CO: Center for Action Research.

Lobel, A. (1980). *Fables.* New York: Harper.

Lortie, D. C. (1975). *School teacher: A sociological study.* Chicago: University of Chicago Press.

Loucks-Horsley, S., Phlegar, J., & Stiegelbauer, S. (1992). New visions for staff development. In A. Costa, J. Bellanca, & R. Fogarty (Eds.), *If minds matter: A foreword to the future, Vol. 1* (pp. 149–162). Palatine, IL: IRI/Skylight Publishing.

Lounsbury, J. H. (Ed.). (1992). *Connecting curriculum through interdisciplinary instruction.* Columbus, OH: National Middle School Association.

Luria, A. R. (1976). *Cognitive development: Its cultural and social foundations.* Cambridge, MA: Harvard University Press.

Lyman, F., & McTighe, J. (1988, April). Cueing thinking in the classroom:

IRI/Skylight Publishing, Inc.

The promise of theory-embedded tools. *Educational Leadership*, pp. 18–24.

Macauley, D. (1977). *Castle.* Boston: Houghton Mifflin.

Macauley, D. (1973). *Cathedral.* Boston: Houghton Mifflin.

Many faces of the world. (1979, October). Supplement to *Learning Magazine*. Palo Alto, CA: Education Today.

Marcus, S. (1992, February). *Are four good groups enough?* Doctoral Dissertation, Walden University, Minneapolis.

Marzano, R. J., & Arredondo, D. E. (1986, May). Restructuring schools through the teaching of thinking skills. *Educational Leadership*, pp. 20–26.

Marzano, R. J., Pickering, D., & Brandt, R. (1990, February). Integrating instructional programs through dimensions of learning. *Educational Leadership,* pp. 17–24.

Maute, J. (1989, March). Cross curricular connections. *Middle School Journal,* pp. 20–22.

McCarthy, B. (1980). *The 4MAT system.* Barrington, IL: Excel.

Merenbloom, E. Y. (1991). *The team process: A handbook for teachers.* Columbus, OH: National Middle School Association.

Ministry of Education. (1991, September). *Integration: A framework for discussion,* Draft #2, Ministry of Education, Curriculum Development Branch, Victoria, BC.

National Commission on Excellence in Education. (1983). *A nation at risk: The imperative for educational reform: A report to the nation and the Secretary of Education; United States Department of Education.* Washington, DC: National Commission on Excellence in Education.

National Endowment for the Arts, National Endowment of Arts in Education, and U.S. Department of Education. (1994). *Arts education research agenda for the future.* Washington, DC: Office of Educational Research and Improvement and Office of Research.

Nordoff, P., & Robbins, C. (1966). *Speech fugue in* The three bears. Bryn Mawr, PA: Theodore Presser.

O'Connor, A., & Callahan-Young, S. (1994). *Seven windows to a child's world: 100 ideas for the multiple intelligences classroom.* Palatine, IL: IRI/Skylight Publishing.

Osborn, A. F. (1963). *Applied imagination.* New York: Scribner.

Papert, S. (1993). *The children's machine: Rethinking school in the age of the computer.* New York: Basic Books.

Parks, S., & Black, H. (1992). *Organizing Thinking—Book I.* Pacific Grove, CA: Critical Thinking Press & Software.

Parnes, S. J. (1975). *Aha! Insights into creative behavior.* Buffalo, NY: D.O.K. Publishing.

Pavan, B. N. (1973, March). Good news: Research on the nongraded elementary school. *Elementary School Journal*, pp. 233–242.

Perkins, D. N. (1992). *Smart schools: From training memories to educating minds.* New York: Free Press.

IRI/Skylight Publishing, Inc.

Perkins, D. N. (1988). *Thinking frames.* Paper presented at ASCD Conference on Approaches to Teaching Thinking, Alexandria, VA.

Perkins, D. N., & Salomon, G. (1989, January–February). Are cognitive skills content bound? *Educational Leadership.*

Perkins, D. N., & Salomon, G. (1988, September). Teaching for transfer. *Educational Leadership.*

Peter, L. S. (1977). *Peter's quotations: Ideas for our time.* New York: Morrow.

Peters, T., & Waterman, R., Jr. (1982). *In search of excellence.* New York: Warner Communications.

Piaget, J. (1972). *The epistemology of interdisciplinary relationships.* Paris: Organization for Economic Cooperation and Development.

Pogrow, S., & Buchanan, B. (1987, March). The HOTS program: The role of computers in developing thinking skills. *TechTrends*, pp. 10–13.

Polya, G. (1945). *How to solve it: A new aspect of mathematical method.* Princeton, NJ: Princeton University Press.

Posner, M. I., & Keele, S. W. (1973). Skill learning. In R. M. W. Travers (Ed.), *Second handbook of research on teaching* (pp. 805–831). Chicago: Rand McNally College Publishing.

Prewitt, B. W., & Butler, K. A. (1993). *Learning styles and performance assessment.* Columbia, CT: The Learner's Dimension.

Prutzman, P., & Others. (1978). *The friendly classroom for a small planet: A handbook on creative approaches to living and problem solving for children.* New York: Avery Publishing Group.

Ravitch, D. (1985). Why educators resist a basic required curriculum. In B. Gross and R. Gross (Eds.), *The great school debate*. New York: Simon and Schuster.

Resnick, L. B., & Klopfer, L. (1989). Toward the thinking curriculum: Current cognitive research. *1989 ASCD yearbook.* Alexandria, VA: Association for Supervision and Curriculum Development.

Richards, M. C. (1980). *The public school and the education of the whole person.* Philadelphia: Pilgrim Press.

Richmond, G. H. (1973). *The micro-society school: A real world in miniature.* New York: Harper.

Ross, C. M., & Stangl, K. M. (1994). *The music teacher's book of lists.* West Nyack, NY: Parker Publishing.

Sandoz, M. (1986). *The horsecatcher.* Lincoln, NE: University of Nebraska Press.

Sarason, S. (1990). *The predictable failure of educational reform.* San Francisco: Jossey-Bass.

Scearce, C. (1993). *100 ways to build teams.* Palatine, IL: IRI/Skylight Publishing.

Schlechty, P. C. (1990). *Schools for the twenty-first century: Leadership imperatives for educational reform.* San Francisco: Jossey-Bass.

Schmuck, R. A., & Schmuck, P. A. (1988). *Group processes in the classroom.* Dubuque, IA: W. C. Brown.

Schuman, J. M. (1981). *Art from many hands: Multicultural art projects.* Worcester, MA: Davis Publications.

IRI/Skylight Publishing, Inc.

Sergiovanni, T. (1987, May). Will we ever have a *true* profession? Supervision in context. *Educational Leadership*, pp. 44–49.

Sharan, S. (1980). Cooperative learning in small groups: Recent methods and effects on achievement, attitudes, and ethnic relations. *Review of Educational Research*, 50, 241–271.

Shoemaker, B. (1991, June). Education 2000: Integrated curriculum. *Phi Delta Kappan*, pp. 793–797.

Shoemaker, B. (1989, October). Integrative education: A curriculum for the twenty-first century. *OSSC Bulletin*.

Shoyer, E. H. (1982). *Signs of the times.* Washington, DC: Gallaudet University Press.

Slavin, R. E. (1983). *Cooperative learning.* New York: Longman.

Sternberg, R. J. (1986). *Intelligence applied: Understanding and increasing your intellectual skills.* Boston: Harcourt Brace Jovanovich.

Sternberg, R. J. (1984, September). How can we teach intelligence? *Educational Leadership,* pp. 38–48.

Stiggins, R. J. (1985, October). Improving assessment where it means the most: In the classroom. *Educational Leadership*, pp. 69–74.

Swartz, R., & Perkins, D. (1987). *Teaching thinking skills: Theory and practice.* New York: Freeman.

Timberlake, L. (1986). *Famine in Africa.* New York: Gloucester Press.

Tyler, R. W. (1986, December–1987, January). The five most significant curriculum events in the twentieth century. *Educational Leadership*, pp. 36–38.

Vacca, R. (1989). *The content area reading.* Glenview, IL: Scott Foresman.

Vars, G. F. (1991, October). Integrated curriculum in historical perspective. *Educational Leadership*, pp. 14–15.

Vars, G. F. (1987). *Interdisciplinary teaching in the middle grades: Why and how.* Columbus, OH: National Middle School Association.

Vygotsky, L. S. (1986). *Thought and language* (Rev. ed.). Cambridge, MA: MIT Press.

Wallace, R. (1966). *World of Leonardo (1452–1519).* New York: Time, Inc.

Walther, T. (1981). *Make mine music!* Boston: Little Brown.

Warren, L. (1972). *The dance of Africa.* Englewood Cliffs, NJ: Prentice-Hall.

Williams, R. B. (1993). *More than 50 ways to build team consensus.* Palatine, IL: IRI/Skylight Publishing.

Willis, S. (1991, November). Teach to the brain. *ASCD Update*, pp. 14–17.

Wittrock, M. C. (1967). Replacement and nonreplacement strategies in children's problem solving. *Journal of Educational Psychology, 58*(2), 69–74.

IRI/Skylight Publishing, Inc.

MUSIC RESOURCES

Judy Stoehr has available through Warner Bros. Publications a series of theme-based early childhood musicals. They are all original productions, recorded with vocal tracks for rehearsal and instrumental tracks for performance.

Suggestions are included for costumes, settings, props, staging, choreography, and more. Teacher tips, learning activities, and extensions turn these musicals into tools for integrating children's learning through the arts.

Puxatawnee Phil: The Tale of the Groundhog

Phil would rather sleep in than get up and see his shadow. Titles include: *Get Up, Hide and Seek, You Never Know,* and *The Puxatawnee Polka.*

The World Is Growing Smaller

A musical to help children better understand other cultures and countries through games, songs, and dance. Titles include: *The Piñata, Pass to the Left, Springtime in Japan,* and *The World Is Growing.*

You Can Do It!

Children will learn to make new friends and to believe in themselves in this musical. Titles include: *Two Heads Are Better Than One, I Gotta Like Me,* and *Lookin' for My Best Friend.*

The Clean-Up Kids

A "gang" of "clean-up kids" presents songs about different kinds of simple ecology and environmental issues. Titles include: *The Clean-Up Kids, Pollution, The R's of Ecology, R-E-C-Y-C-L-E, Saving Planet Earth,* and *Clean Up Your Part of the World.*

IRI/Skylight Publishing, Inc.

INDEX

IRI/Skylight Publishing, Inc.

IRI/Skylight Publishing, Inc.

IRI/Skylight Publishing, Inc.

IRI/Skylight Publishing, Inc.

IRI/Skylight Publishing, Inc.

IRI/Skylight Publishing, Inc.

SkyLight
Training and Publishing Inc.

We Prepare Your Teachers Today
for the Classrooms of Tomorrow

Learn from Our Books and from Our Authors!

Ignite Learning in Your School or District.

SkyLight's team of classroom-experienced consultants can help you foster systemic change for increased student achievement.

Professional development is a process, not an event. SkyLight's seasoned practitioners drive the creation of our on-site professional development programs, graduate courses, research-based publications, interactive video courses, teacher-friendly training materials, and online resources—call SkyLight Training and Publishing Inc. today.

SkyLight specializes in three professional development areas.

Specialty #  **1**

Best Practices

We **model** the best practices that result in improved student performance and guided applications.

Specialty #  **2**

Making the Innovations Last

We help set up **support** systems that make innovations part of everyday practice in the long-term systemic improvement of your school or district.

Specialty #  **3**

How to Assess the Results

We prepare your school leaders to encourage and **assess** teacher growth, **measure** student achievement, and **evaluate** program success.

Contact the SkyLight team and begin a process toward long-term results.

SkyLight
Training and Publishing Inc.

2626 S. Clearbrook Dr., Arlington Heights, IL 60005
800-348-4474 • 847-290-6600 • FAX 847-290-6609
http://www.iriskylight.com

There are
one-story intellects,
two-story intellects, and three-story
intellects with skylights. All fact collectors, who
have no aim beyond their facts, are one-story men. Two-story men
compare, reason, generalize, using the labors of the fact collectors as
well as their own. Three-story men idealize, imagine,
predict—their best illumination comes from
above, through the skylight.
—*Oliver Wendell*
Holmes

SkyLight
Training and Publishing Inc.